BEHIND

THE

SCENES

OF
THE NEW TESTAMENT

PAUL BARNETT

FOREWORD BY MICHAEL GREEN

INTERVARSITY PRESS
DOWNERS GROVE, ILLINOIS 60515

InterVarsity Press
P.O. Box 1400, Downers Grove, Illinois 60515, U.S.A.

© *1990 Paul W. Barnett*

InterVarsity Press is the book-publishing division of InterVarsity Christian Fellowship, a student movement active on campus at hundreds of universities, colleges and schools of nursing in the United States of America, and a member movement of the International Fellowship of Evangelical Students. For information about local and regional activities, write Public Relations Dept., InterVarsity Christian Fellowship, 6400 Schroeder Rd., P.O. Box 7895, Madison, WI 53707-7895.

ISBN 0-8308-1329-2

Printed in the United States of America ∞

Library of Congress Cataloging-in-Publication Data

Barnett, Paul (Paul William)
  [Bethlehem to Patmos]
  Behind the scenes of the New Testament/by Paul Barnett.
     p.   cm.
  Previously published under title: Bethlehem to Patmos.
  Includes bibliographical references.
  ISBN 0-8308-1329-2
     1. Bible. N.T.—History of contemporary events. 2. Bible. N.T.—
  History of Biblical events. 3. Christianity—Early church, ca.
  30-600. I. Title.
  BS2410.B275   1990
  225.9'5—dc20   90-45492
                                                                  CIP

---

13   12   11   10   9   8   7   6   5   4   3   2   1
99   98   97   96   95   94   93   92   91   90

For E. A. Judge,
Historian

MAPS

TABLES

Foreword

In an age which blandly assumes that religions are all much the same, the claims of Christianity are particularly shocking and unacceptable. For in addition to claiming that it makes God known in a unique and sufficient way, Christians believe that the death and resurrection of Jesus are of crucial significance for the destiny of the world and the individual. On the cross of Calvary, in the person of his Son Jesus, God took responsibility for the total wickedness of the world — such is the claim. Moreover, death itself could not contain him. On the third day Jesus rose again to reaffirm his claim to be the Way to God, to be the Truth of God and to embody the Life of God.

Such claims are scandalous and arrogant — unless the 'Beyond' really has come into our midst. It is plain that much hangs on the truthfulness of the New Testament story. If it can be shown that Jesus never existed, that he was not crucified, or that he never rose from the tomb, then Christianity can safely be discounted. It would simply not be true. Historical examination is, therefore, very important.

Such is the investigation which has stimulated this most interesting book. Dr Paul Barnett is a lecturer in a secular Australian university. He is a historian and a New Testament scholar who knows a lot about the Jewish and Graeco-Roman world of the first two centuries. With that combination of skills he lectures regularly to a mixture of Christian and non-Christian students on the evidence there is to illuminate the New Testament. He writes in a very readable style, and the popularity of his previous book, *Is The New Testament History?* is an indication both that there is a wide readership for such material among thinking people, and that he has a special gift for helping people to assess for themselves the truth claims in the New Testament.

To be sure, he writes as a believer. But he writes as

a scholar too. He allows the New Testament material to speak for itself against the background of the Graeco-Roman world of the first century. He seeks to be scrupulously fair, and when the evidence does not justify a firm conclusion he does not seek to push it further than it warrants. There is no need to have any prior knowledge of the subject in order to understand this book. Those who do have that knowledge will realise that Paul Barnett has it too, and is on almost every page making probability judgements based on careful scholarship. They will not always agree with him. But nobody, after reading this book, will be able to deny that the New Testament material fits with great credibility into the world of the first century as it is known from secular and Jewish sources. The links he shows between the Gospels and Acts and secular history are very extensive and very convincing.

Of course, no historical enquiry can prove the claims of the New Testament. You can demonstrate historically that Jesus died on a cross: you cannot prove that he bore away the sins of the world. You can demonstrate that the tomb was empty on the first Easter day; you cannot prove that God raised Jesus from the dead. Dr Barnett does not make the mistake of trying to prove theological claims by historical evidence. He does show, most convincingly, that the historical framework of the New Testament is extremely reliable. You will have to make up your own mind on *who* Jesus was. Paul Barnett shows you *that* Jesus was. The book will be of inestimable help both to genuine seekers, who want to know if intelligent modern people can credit the New Testament story, and to Christian students who are looking to an expert for 'a reason for the hope that is within them'. It deserves a wide audience. I am confident it will get one.

Paul Barnett is a wonderful teacher, a warm personality, and a balanced scholar, as those who know him in the flesh are well aware. I count it a deep privilege to have him as a friend. But those who have not known him personally can make up for it to a large extent by reading this book. It shows you an honest, able, friendly man sifting the truth. There is no higher calling.

Michael Green

Introduction

Bethlehem is a small village five miles south of Jerusalem, Patmos a barren island in the Aegean Sea sixty miles to the west of Asia Minor. Yet both Bethlehem and Patmos are visited by thousands of tourists each year simply because of their place in the New Testament. Bethlehem is the birthplace of Jesus of Nazareth, where the New Testament story begins; Patmos is the island from which, almost exactly one hundred years later, John wrote the Revelation, the last book of the New Testament.

The New Testament records the greatest events in history — the birth, life, death and resurrection of the Son of God, Jesus Christ. It throbs and pulsates with the astonishing conviction that in the birth of Jesus at Bethlehem, God, the Eternal One, has personally entered the stream of human history.

The New Testament, a collection of twenty-seven mostly short writings, testifies to this amazing and awesome fact: that the Word became flesh and dwelt among us (John 1:14). This is both a theological and an historical statement. It is theological because it concerns the divine, Creator-Word who is eternally present with God and it is historical because that Word came into the world, to live among men. The theological element declares what this means for us, the historical relates what happened.

Although written from the standpoint of faith, by one who accepts the theological interpretation of the New Testament, this book is concerned with the historical, with what happened and when and where it happened. Regrettably many Christians regard the historical elements as boring and unimportant; yet, if they are not verifiable, the theological content is easily dispensed with as irrelevant. However, these writings are crammed full of historical

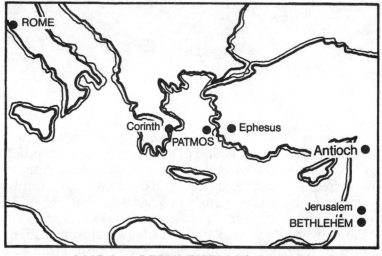

MAP 1 — BETHLEHEM TO PATMOS

information, a fact which reinforces the challenge of their amazing theological statements about the identity and mission of Jesus.

But, some will ask, why not pick up the New Testament and simply read it? Don't we encounter the New Testament's story as we read the gospels and Acts? Why is it necessary to write a separate history?

One reason is that it is hard to follow the story-line of the New Testament simply by opening the gospel of Matthew and beginning to read. At the very outset we are faced with the problems of incompleteness — thirty years of Jesus' life are passed over in silence — and repetition — after Matthew's there are three other gospels about the life of Jesus.

As we read on, we find that the story of the early church in the Acts of the Apostles is also incomplete and needs to be complemented by information from Paul's letters. Further, the narrative of the Acts stops short with Paul in Rome in the early sixties, thirty years before John wrote from Patmos to the seven churches of Roman Asia.

However, our recognition that there are information gaps does not necessarily mean that we can fill them. I will not plug them up with guesses. Nor is this reconstruction of the story, or anyone else's, on the same level as scripture. God addresses us through the writings of the apostles, with their inextricable blend of theology and history. This book aims merely to provide some sense of sequence, to provide the reader with historical bearings, so that the biblical texts will be more easy to follow.

A second reason for writing is that the New Testament as it stands tells the reader very little of the political and social context of Jesus and the apostles. You the reader and I the writer have our political and social contexts; so too did Jesus and the first Christians. It is now widely recognised that study of their historical context should accompany study of the early Christian writings.

The third reason for writing is to challenge the widespread assumption that the New Testament is not concerned with history. As a result Christianity is thought to lack objectivity. Many think that you either have a mystical attitude called "faith" and "believe in Jesus", or you don't, and that's all there is to it. For many Christians, even, Jesus is a kind of timeless redeemer, the time and place of whose entry into history are of no consequence. Many non-Christians quickly pick up this a-historical attitude, and dismiss the New Testament message as mythological and so of no importance.

The media often report some new discovery or publication which, it is claimed, finally proves that Jesus was, after all, nothing but a magician, a freedom fighter or a devout mystic. Television or newspaper features appear, quoting the opinions of scholars to the effect that Jesus was not really the supernatural figure Christians had believed him to be. These matters are seldom presented in a balanced way by allowing scholars who hold orthodox beliefs an opportunity to respond. Only the sensationalist opinions tend to be reported. The cumulative effect has been that many people think that the New Testament has been effectively discredited.

I believe many readers will be surprised at the wealth of solid historical information to be found within the New Testament and the degree to which the New Testament story can be reconstructed. The data is, of course, uneven in its distribution. At some points we are able to plot the movements of Jesus and Paul with pinpoint accuracy as to both time and place. At other times, however, a whole decade is passed over in silence. That, however, is the nature of all evidence from antiquity, not merely of the New Testament.

This book makes no claim to be the last word on the subject of a New Testament story; others will tell it differently. My aim is to show that there is a story to be told, based on solid data, and to tell it as simply as I can.

To assist the reader may I suggest an analogy, based on the course of a river. Imagine you are on a high mountain and you are looking down on a river. You are able to see its beginnings but its course is hidden for some distance by hills and high trees. Then it comes fully into view for a short distance only to divide into two branches. One branch continues into the distance, sometimes in view, sometimes hidden. The other branch, after being partially concealed for a space, itself divides and its two branches continue separately.

The original river is the story of Jesus which flows on directly to become the story of the earliest community of Christians in Jerusalem. This soon divides into two racial branches, one Gentile, led by Paul, and the other Jewish, led by James. In time, the Jewish branch also divides into two sub-branches — one Palestinian, led by James, the other non-Palestinian, led by Peter and John.

As you read on into this book you will be able to trace the course of the river and the main branches into which it divides, as it flows from Bethlehem where it began to Patmos where the New Testament ends.

Bethlehem and Patmos are symbolic of a historic process within the New Testament story which begins with the Jews in Bethlehem of Judaea, and concludes with Graeco-Roman Gentiles in Patmos.

Patmos, however, is itself the beginning of the next phase of the story of the Christian church down to our own times. It was from Patmos that John wrote to Christians in a province which would soon become the major centre of Christianity and where the Roman authorities would launch repeated attacks on the new faith. Patmos symbolizes the challenge the One born in Bethlehem would soon become to world rulers at that time, and down to our own age. From Patmos John issues a call to Christians of every epoch not to bow the knee to merely human leaders who portray themselves as "gods" and "saviours" and who demand to be worshipped and followed blindly, but to worship God and to follow the Lamb.

1
Bethlehem: The Beginning

Some people refer disparagingly to the "myth of Bethlehem" and the "myth of Christmas". Raymond Brown, for example, in a major book *The Birth of the Messiah* rejects many of the details in the nativity stories as "unhistorical". He doubts Luke's account of the journey from Nazareth to Bethlehem and Matthew's description of the flight to Egypt, the massacre of the infants and the return to Israel. So, how "historically" true are these familiar stories?

In order to speak with confidence of "the beginning of the New Testament story" we must first examine the biblical passages in their historical context. We may say that the narrative is like a stage play while the historical context is the theatre in which it is enacted. The versions of the story as told by Matthew and Luke have been well known for almost two thousand years. The historical context, provided chiefly by the Jewish historian Josephus, is, regrettably, almost unknown to Christians. Although this context does not supply more details for the story, by tying those we have into the history of the times it makes the story more intelligible and believable.

Two versions: Matthew and Luke
Significant differences exist between Matthew's and Luke's accounts.

Each author has his own distinctive theological emphases which may be discerned from the opening chapters of each gospel. Matthew starts with a genealogy to establish the important point that Jesus is the Messiah, descended from King David (from whom, as it was widely believed, the

Anointed One would come). He begins by referring to "Jesus *Christ*, the Son of David"; he concludes by numbering the generations "from Abraham . . . to the Christ". Clearly Matthew wants us to understand that Jesus is the Christ, the Messiah or Anointed One.

Matthew's genealogy, however, subtly changes when it comes finally to Joseph. Unlike every other person Joseph is listed not as "the father of" anybody, but as "the *husband* of Mary". It was from Mary, not Joseph, that Jesus was born (Matthew 1:16). After Joseph discovered that his betrothed, Mary, was pregnant — before their marriage it was supernaturally revealed to him that the pregnancy was not caused by another man, but by the direct intervention of God the Holy Spirit. The son to be born would be "Emmanuel" (="God with us"), in fulfilment of the prophet Isaiah's promise (7:14). His name was to be "Jesus" because he would save his people from their sins. (Jesus means "Yahweh is salvation") Joseph married Mary, but had no sexual intercourse with her until after the child was born in Bethlehem, the expected home of the Messiah. Guided by a star, *magoi* (astrologers) from the East subsequently came to pay homage to the boy as King of the Jews.

Matthew narrates that Joseph and Mary took the child to Egypt to escape the jealous wrath of Herod, King of the Jews. The family's return to Israel after Herod's death was, according to Matthew, to fulfil the prophecy "out of Egypt I have called my Son" (Hosea 11:1). Matthew teaches us that Jesus the Son of God relived Israel's escape from Egypt.

The gospel known as Matthew's is written with attention drawn to Joseph. It was to Joseph that the angel of the Lord spoke. It was Joseph who had the problem with Mary's pregnancy but who obediently married her. Joseph named the child, took the mother and child to and from Egypt. Mary remains silent throughout this account.

Luke for his part portrays the birth of Jesus as the fulfilment of God's ancient promise to save his chosen people. God's angel, Gabriel, went first to tell the aged priest Zechariah that he and his wife Elizabeth were to have a son, despite their advanced years. The child's name was to be John and he would make ready for the Lord "a people prepared". In the sixth month of Elizabeth's pregnancy Gabriel told her cousin Mary, a young virgin betrothed to a man named Joseph, that she was to have a son who would be the Son of the Most High, who would reign on the throne of his forefather David, forever. This son would be born through the agency of the Holy Spirit.

Whereas in Matthew's account the spotlight is on Joseph, with Mary in the shadow, in Luke, Joseph is in the shadow, with all attention focused on Mary. According to Luke it is Mary who has the dilemma. How can she bear the son of whom Gabriel spoke since she is not yet married? Despite the improbability of the angel's words Mary "believed . . . what was spoken to her from the Lord" (Luke 1:45). In her song Mary acknowledges, on the one hand, her lowliness and, on the other, the might and mercy of God. God would keep his promise to her and also, at the end, uplift his down-trodden people while destroying his enemies. Mary is thus both a model believer and also a representative of "God's Poor", his People. In believing the promise and bearing her son Mary would be the first of the people of God ultimately to be uplifted.

It is quite clear, therefore, that Matthew and Luke emphasize different theological points at the beginnings of their respective gospels.

There are also differences in *historical* detail and in their silences. Luke places the birth of Jesus in the context of a census for which Joseph and Mary must travel to Bethlehem. Matthew simply states that Mary gave birth to a son.

Geographical differences exist between the two accounts. According to Luke, Joseph and Mary came from Nazareth in Galilee to Bethlehem in Judaea, from which they returned to Nazareth, after presenting the child in the temple in Jerusalem. Matthew, however, implies that Joseph and Mary came from Judaea and that they settled in Galilee after the death of Herod, fearing his successor Archelaus, the new ruler of Judaea.

Different *people* figure in the accounts of Matthew and Luke. Matthew alone mentions the *magoi*, Archelaus and the direct intervention of Herod and the chief priests and scribes. Only in Luke are found references to the angel

Gabriel, Zechariah, Elizabeth, the unborn John, the shepherds, the aged Simeon and the prophetess Anna.

It is clear, therefore, that in addition to their distinctive theological emphases, major differences — in historical, geographical and personal perspective — exist between the gospels of Matthew and Luke. The genealogies are also dissimilar in both detail and form. Matthew begins with Abraham and ends with the child Christ; Luke begins with Jesus the adult and works back to Adam, the son of God.

These divergences are so great and the style of the gospels so unlike one another that it is difficult to see how either Matthew or Luke could have depended on the other's manuscript. It is much more likely that they wrote independently of each other, as indeed most scholars believe.

Yet despite the differences — both of theological emphasis and of historical detail — there is an underlying agreement about the essential structure of these versions of the first part of the New Testament story.

Both Matthew and Luke agree that Joseph was descended from King David, that he belonged to the royal line from which the Anointed One would come.[1]

Each writer carefully indicates in his own way that Joseph was not the biological father of Mary's son. In his genealogy Matthew states that Joseph was not Jesus' father but "Mary's husband" and it was from her that the Messiah came (Matthew 1:16). Luke, in his genealogy, states that Jesus was the son, "as was supposed", of Joseph (Luke 3:23).

Matthew and Luke are agreed that Mary's pregnancy was due, not to Joseph, but to God, through the Holy Spirit and that the pregnancy occurred during this betrothal period before the marriage. Matthew states and Luke implies that Joseph married Mary before the birth of the child. The evangelist John's description of the children of God as not "born of blood nor of the will of the flesh nor of the will of man" (1:13) is an apt description of the process by which Jesus was born. It may well have originated in John's knowledge of the virgin conception of Jesus.

Bethlehem was the place of the birth of Jesus in both gospels, something John also confirms, though in an oblique way (John 7:42).

Matthew is explicit that Herod was king at the time of Jesus' birth (Matthew 2:1). This is strongly implied in Luke, who indicates that the conception occurred within Herod's reign (Luke 1:5, 36).

Both authors mention that the birth was accompanied by spectacular illumination in the heavens. While this may seem to be a pious embellishment there is external evidence of extensive astronomical phenomena in the general period of Jesus' birth. According to astronomical calculations Jupiter and Saturn would have appeared close together on three occasions in 7 BC, the probable year of Jesus' birth.[2] Such phenomena would certainly have been noticed by the star gazers of Mesopotamia.

The agreement of our authors in such important details is impressive. If one writer was depending upon the other we would have but one source. But the differences make it much more likely that we have two quite separate traditions. Where two such different sources agree on details a strong case can be made for their underlying historical basis.

The problem of the virgin conception.

The mode of Jesus' birth was a stumbling block among the Jewish people, though for moral not scientific reasons. In the coming centuries this was a recurring theme in Jewish literature. One first century rabbi wrote of Jesus as a "man born of a woman, who would rise up and seek to make himself God."[3] From about the second century, Jesus was called "ben Pandira" as being born out out of wedlock to "Miriam" (= Mary) and her lover Pandira.[4] ("Pandira" meant "Panther" and was problably a nickname for the man the Jews claimed was Jesus' father.) But this is a tradition which arose in the next century or later.

From the present point in history we can only refer to the independent statements of Matthew and Luke that Jesus was conceived apart from a human father. As we have noted, this is indirectly confirmed by John 1:12, 13 where the theological idea of the birth of children to God, directly without human parentage, may have arisen from the historical fact of the birth of Jesus apart from a human father.

It is, however, unlikely that Christianity would have taken root among so moral a people as the Jews unless it was clear that Mary's irregular pregnancy was due to divine intervention.

Paul's knowledge of the virgin conception of Jesus is implied in his words that the Son of God was "born of a woman" (Galatians 4:4). It is difficult to see why Paul would have made this otherwise gratuitous statement unless it was to affirm the supernatural character of Jesus' conception, which was *without a man*. Paul, a leading younger Pharisee, would scarcely have embraced Christianity if he had thought Jesus was conceived out of wedlock.

Moreover, the early Christians must have been acutely aware that the supernatural conception of Jesus appeared to deny his descent from King David. The virgin conception removes Joseph's biological role in the procreative process, which means that, physically speaking, Jesus could not be "son of David". Matthew and Luke must have known this. It would have been easier for them to omit altogether the virgin conception in order to secure Jesus' messiahship. That they include it, despite the difficulties they knew it would create, is strong testimony to their belief in its reality.

How, then, were they able to think of Jesus as "son of David" since Joseph was not Jesus' biological father? This is a serious question, the answer to which must be that Joseph was the legal father, if not the biological father. Joseph doubtless acted as the legal father at both the naming and registering of his son (Matthew 1:20-21; Luke 2:1-5). Moreover the Jewish law of levirate marriage reminds us that biological paternity was not a prerequisite to legal fatherhood. According to Deuteronomy 25:5-10, if a man died without a son his brother was to marry the man's wife. The first son born to that union was to bear the name of the deceased brother. In Jewish law this boy was truly son of the deceased, although the biological offspring of someone else.

The levirate marriage helps us see why Matthew and Luke suggest no incompatibility between Jesus' virgin conception and his descent from David, through Joseph.

Herod's slaughter of the boys

Matthew's gospel says that Herod killed all the male babies in Bethlehem after the *magoi* failed to tell him the whereabouts of the boy-king they had come to worship (Matthew 2:1-10). Now Herod the Great is not only part of the contextual backdrop. He becomes part of the dramatic story, although some people believe this part of the gospel story is unhistorical, a pious detail added later. Who then was Herod?

Herod was not a Jew by birth but a native of Idumaea, a country to the immediate south of Judaea. His wily father Antipater started to become involved in Judaean politics in about 70 BC when Herod was about three years old. The Hasmonaean dynasty was losing its grip on the reins of power and two Hasmonaean princes were actually engaged in civil war at the time. Seven years later, in 63 BC, the inexorable eastward spread of Roman power finally reached Palestine with Pompey and his army.

By then Antipater, and his young sons Herod and Phasael, were ready to exploit both Hasmonaean weakness and the Romans' need for sympathetic local leadership. By 40 BC the Roman Senate had nominated the thirty-three-year-old Herod "King of the Jews".

Herod, like his father, cleverly won the support of successive great men of Roman politics, first Mark Antony then Caesar Augustus. In 40 BC, Mark Antony was dominant in the eastern part of the Roman Empire, to which Judaea belonged, and supported Herod in his struggle against Antigonus the Hasmonaean. The struggle ended in 37 BC with Herod the undisputed ruler of Judaea. When Antony was defeated in 31 BC at the battle of Actium Herod adroitly switched his loyalty to the victorious Augustus. As he had been Antony's client ruler from 40–31 BC, so Herod became Augustus' client ruler. From 31 BC until his death in 4 BC, Herod was said to be Augustus' favourite client-king. Only in Herod's latter years was there any deterioration in this relationship.

During the period 31–4 BC, Herod progressively enlarged his kingdom. By 20 BC he ruled an area bounded by Syria in the North and Egypt in the South, by the Mediterranean in the West and the Nabataean kingdom in the East, a realm comparable in size with that of David or Solomon.

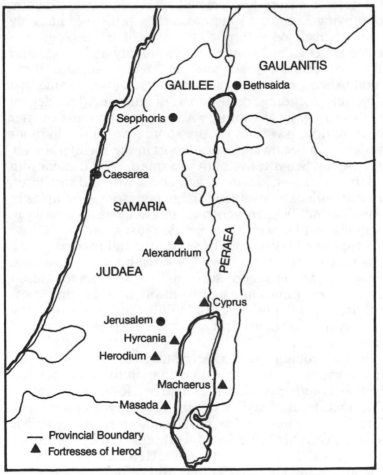

MAP 2 — KINGDOM OF HEROD THE GREAT

According to Josephus, Herod was a man of immense physical strength and daunting military prowess. He was also a prodigious builder and benefactor. Josephus' list of Herod's buildings and benefactions extends over many pages.[5] Ten impregnable fortresses were constructed, the most famous being Masada and Machaerus. In Jerusalem,

Herod built a king's palace, a hippodrome, a gymnasium and started the massive temple, which was not completed in his lifetime. The so-called temple mount or podium on which the temple shrine was erected was a massive structure occupying 35 acres. Its architectural significance has only been appreciated — through the work of archaeologists — since Israel gained control of the old city of Jerusalem in 1967. At Strato's Tower on the Mediterranean, Herod established a great artificial harbour, creating for the first time safe anchorage on the coast of Palestine. The elegant city of Caesarea Maritima, with a population of a quarter of a million, was built on the shore next to the harbour which soon became the busiest port in the Mediterranean. A new city, Sebaste, was built in Samaria. Not content with adorning his own kingdom with new towns and structures, Herod built extensively in foreign countries — temples in Rhodes and Tyre, an aqueduct in Laodicea, gymnasia in Tripolis and Damascus, to mention just a few.

Moreover, his generous benefactions endowed recurring Olympic Games not only in Caesarea but also in Athens, Sparta, Pergamum and Antioch. The Jews under Herod enjoyed enormous prosperity through trade and agriculture, but, after this orgy of building, it is not surprising that, by the time of his death, they were crying out for relief from taxation.

Herod probably rivalled Augustus as the greatest builder in the known world of that time. In both his buildings and benefactions he revealed himself to be a lover of Hellenism. The architectural style used in his many buildings was Greek and Roman, not Jewish. His endowment of Olympiads also reflects his affection for things Greek. Josephus commented that people thought Herod "was on more friendly terms with Greeks than with Jews".[6]

In Roman eyes Herod was an excellent client-king. He showed due reverence to his masters, Augustus in particular, by naming many buildings after them. His Jerusalem palace was called Caesareum, Strato's Tower Caesarea, the Samaritan city Sebaste, one of Augustus' honorific titles. Above all, Herod kept the peace within his borders.

Near the end of his reign, however, Herod did incur the

displeasure of Augustus, by invading the neighbouring kingdom of the Nabataeans. Herod made two attempts to regain the favour of Augustus and both brought him into conflict with the Pharisees who were the "grass roots" religious leaders of the Jews.

In 7 BC, soon after the Nabataean incident, Herod issued an order that all people of his kingdom should make an oath of loyalty to both him *and* Augustus. Six thousand Pharisees refused to comply for religious reasons and narrowly escaped severe punishment. His second desperate attempt to woo Augustus was foolhardy. He ordered a giant golden eagle, an important symbol for Rome, to be erected on the great gate of the Jerusalem temple. Incensed at this blatant disregard for the laws of God forbidding idolatry, the two leading rabbis, Matthias and Judas, incited their disciples to remove this blasphemous effigy. Herod had the rabbis and their offending disciples burnt alive.

This is the king at the end of whose long reign Jesus was born, the king who becomes a character in Matthew's gospel story with the report of his killing of the boys in Bethlehem. Is it a pious embellishment? There are two known aspects of Herod's character which are relevant to the action described in Matthew 2:16-18.

First, by the time his reign came to an end Herod was a depressed old man of seventy plagued with illness and the incessant disputes within his large family — he had, in all, ten wives and nineteen children!

As the King's death perceptibly approached, the bitter machinations within the family increased. Josephus, who used a reliable eye-witness report, commented,

His illness steadily grew worse, aggravated as were the attacks of disease by age and despondency. For he was now nearly seventy years old, and his tragic experiences with his children had so broken his spirit, that even in good health he no longer enjoyed any of the pleasures of life.[7]

He described Herod's illness as,

fever, though not a raging fever, an intolerable itching of the whole skin, continuous pains in the intestines, tumours in the feet... inflammation of the abdomen and gangrene of the privy parts engendering worms, in addition to asthma . . . . [8]

Second, Herod displayed throughout his rule, but increasingly towards the end, a deeply suspicious temperament and a ruthless determination to remove any opposition. The ordinary people were convinced that the religion of their fathers was rapidly disappearing under the king's influence. Herod forbade public assembly and established a vast network of spies. The king himself would go out in disguise to spy on the people. Many, taken openly or secretly to Herod's fortresses, were never seen again. Throughout his rule Herod also suppressed the Jewish aristocracy and ignored their seat of power, the Sanhedrin, preferring to be surrounded by his own advisers.

Herod's suspicion bordered on paranoia. He killed his own wife, the Hasmonaean princess Mariamne, and, at a later date, her adult sons Alexander and Aristobulus. At the end of his life he executed another son, Antipater the son of Doris. Augustus made the grim joke that it was safer to be Herod's pig than Herod's son.[9] The king's pig was safe, due to Herod's studied outward observance of Judaism; his sons were not. When he realised his death was near Herod ordered the arrest of the leading citizens of all the villages. These were to be killed at the news of the king's death. Tears would then be shed, even if not for him! Mercifully the village notables were released unharmed from the Hippodrome where they had been imprisoned.

Civil wars erupted throughout Herod's kingdom when his violent and repressive rule finally ended. Josephus commented that Herod had "an evil nature, relentless in punishment and unsparing in action against the objects of his hatred."[10]

A decade or so after his death an anonymous author wrote inferring that Herod was

an arrogant king...a reckless and godless man...who will exterminate their chief men...and bury their bodies in unknown places...he will slay the old and the young and show no mercy...terrible fear of him will come over all the land.[11]

What Matthew briefly narrates appears, then, to be

entirely consistent with all that we know of Herod, especially in his last days. The strong balance of probability is that Matthew's report of Herod's slaughter of the boys is historically based. If so, there is no good reason to doubt the truth of the flight to Egypt and the subsequent return, after Herod's death.

The visit of the *magoi*

What are we to make of the "wise men" (*magoi*) from the East (Matthew 2:1) who came to Jerusalem to worship the king of the Jews?

There are three elements in Matthew's account which encourage us to take it seriously. First, the word used is *magoi* which was originally used of astrologers from Persia and Assyria,[12] though it is also used in the Acts of the Apostles for sorcerers, charlatans and magicians.[13] We have some outside knowledge of *magoi*; they existed.

Second, their interest in the star which they saw in the East (Matthew 2:2,7,9) is consistent with the practice of astronomy and astrology in Mesopotamia at the time.

Third, there was a large Jewish community living in the Mesopotamia region. This originated with the earlier deportation of Jews by the conquering Assyrians and Babylonians. It is quite possible that through these Mesopotamian Jews the local Gentiles became familiar with Numbers 24:17, a much studied prophecy which promised that, "...a star shall come forth out of Jacob, a sceptre shall rise out of Israel".

Centuries before Christ, the Septuagint, the Greek version of the Hebrew Old Testament, had translated Numbers 24:17 as, "...a star shall come forth out of Jacob, a man shall arise out of Israel". This prophecy of a world ruler who would come from Israel was so famous that we find traces of it in the writings of the Roman historian Tacitus.[14] It is not unlikely that this prophetic oracle was known to the *magoi* from the East, especially in view of their interest in the stars.

It may be assumed that they did not know that the world ruler was to be of obscure background. Their visit was probably primarily a diplomatic gesture and their gifts designed to create a favourable impression upon the court of the new monarch. But they may well have also intended to express some form of worship towards the new ruler. Acts of reverence (*proskynesis*) towards kings were not unusual in the eastern world at that time. There is, therefore, no good reason to deny a historical basis to the story as it stands in Matthew's gospel which, despite the common belief that there were three *magoi*, does not give their number.

The census in Bethlehem

There is, however, a major dating problem in connection with the reason Luke gives for the journey of Joseph and Mary to Bethlehem, where Jesus was born. According to Luke it was to comply with Caesar Augustus' decree that everybody should return to their ancestral cities to be registered or enrolled. In Joseph's case this was Bethlehem, since he was a descendant of King David.

Luke refers, in 1:5 and 1:36, to the conception of Jesus as being in "the time of Herod, King of Judaea" whose reign ended in 4 BC and, in 2:2, to the birth of Jesus as occurring while "Quirinius was governor of Syria" which, according to Josephus, was ten years later. Josephus fully describes the banishment of Herod's son Archelaus, the subsequent annexation of Judaea as a Roman province and the census of the population by Quirinius the Legate of Syria.[15]

This suggests that Luke is about ten years "out" in his dating of Jesus' birth. The majority of scholars are convinced that Luke has made a glaring error. Some believe that he has deliberately manipulated the date to portray Joseph and Mary as godly, peaceable people who in AD 6 did not join in the Jewish revolution over the payment of taxes to the hated Gentiles.

Luke 2:2 is probably the major historical problem in the New Testament.

Before we decide that Luke's material is unreliable several observations should be made.

First, the problem is confined to one very short sentence of just eight Greek words. While the most likely translation is "This was the first enrolment, when Quirinius was governor of Syria", a number of scholars have argued for "this enrolment was before [that of] Quirinius governor of Syria". The latter translation, if acceptable, would be in reference to an earlier, less well-known census than Quirinius' famous enrolment of AD 6.

Possibly such an enrolment coincided with the oath of loyalty which all the people made to Herod and Augustus in 7 BC. As it happens, that would provide a date for Jesus' birth which could accommodate both Herod's order to kill the boys under two years of age (Matthew 2:16) and the triple conjunction of Jupiter and Saturn which also occurred in that year.

Second, Luke's supposed error must be weighed against the precision with which he writes in the very next chapter. In Luke 3:1-2 he carefully locates the beginning of John the Baptizer's ministry in the fifteenth year of Tiberius Caesar, Pilate being governor of Judaea, Herod (Antipas), Philip and Lysanias being tetrarchs respectively of Galilee, Iturea/Trachonitis and Abiline and the high priests being Caiaphas and Annas. This extensive and accurate information shows that Luke was fully aware of the complex division of Herod's kingdom, including that one part of it was by then under Roman rule. So, having fixed the *conception* of Jesus in Herod's lifetime (Luke 1:5,36) he is scarcely likely to have described the birth as occurring more than ten years later! Moreover, Quirinius' census applied only to the people of Judaea; Galilee had not been annexed, and Joseph and Mary as Galileans were not subject to the Roman census. It is improbable that an author who knew about the administrative division of Palestine would have anachronistically portrayed Joseph and Mary, citizens of the Tetrarchy of Galilee, being enrolled in the Roman province of Judaea.

We are two thousand years away from that era; Luke was less than a century removed from the events of which he wrote. It may be better to keep an open mind on this question, awaiting the availability of new information.

If there is a part of the New Testament which is hard to

swallow, people say, it is the very first sequence — the stories about the conception and birth of Jesus. Surely we must regard the miraculous pregnancy, the visit of the *magoi* and Herod's murder of the Bethlehem babies as mythical and not historically based.

Ironically it may be that those within the church have inadvertently fostered the idea that the elements of the Christmas story are mythical. Religious artists have painted romantic nativity scenes and church musicians have composed carols of powerful sentiment. The truth-basis, in all its starkness and pain, is easily buried beneath such aesthetic presentations. There is nothing romantic, in reality, about a pre-marital pregnancy, a hastily arranged marriage quickly followed by the birth of the child near farm animals! Something of that pain remains in the gospel narratives, though it is seldom expressed in Christmas celebrations in church. What is easily communicated to those outside the church is that the stories are myth, beautiful myth, but myth nevertheless. If baby Jesus seems to be less real to people at large than red-frocked Santa who makes his annual appearance as Christmas approaches then perhaps Christians have themselves to blame.

So we find that, despite their verbal independence, Matthew and Luke agree in the following essential details,

1   that Jesus was born *in Bethlehem*
2   after *Mary* his mother became pregnant
3   through direct *divine* intervention
4   *before her marriage to Joseph*
5   who was a *descendant of David*
6   Joseph was *not* the boy's *biological father.*

There are also, we find, other details in their stories which fit neatly into the known historical context of that period. Herod's murder of the children, the visit of the *magoi* from the East and the census of Quirinius are either explicitly or implicitly consistent with the historical setting. By locating the birth of Jesus in this geographical and political context Matthew and Luke say to us, their readers, that Jesus is a historical, not a mythological, figure.

Further reading to Chapter One:
P.W. Barnett, *Is the New Testament History?* Hodder and Stoughton, Sydney, 1986.

R.E. Brown, *The Birth of the Messiah*, Doubleday, New York, 1977.

R.T. France, "Scripture Traditions and History in the Infancy Narrative of Matthew" in *Gospel Perspectives* II, Ed. R.T. France and David Wenham, JSOT Press, Sheffield, 1981, pp. 239-267.

J.G. Machen, *The Virgin Birth of Christ*, Baker, Grand Rapids, 1967.

P.L. Maier, *First Christmas*, Mowbrays, London, 1971.

J. Marsh, *Jesus in His Lifetime*, Sidgwick and Jackson, London, 1981.

M.R. Mulholland, "The Infancy Narratives in Matthew Luke — of History, Theology and Literature" in *Biblical Archaeology Review* vii/2, 1981, 46-59.

E. Stauffer, *Jesus and His Story*, Knopf, New York, 1974.

Notes

[1] See also Acts 2:30, 13:23; Romans 1:3; Hebrews 7:14; 2 Timothy 2:8.

[2] See e.g. *Time* Magazine, 27 December, 1976, p. 27.

[3] Rabbi Eliezer quoted in J. Klausner, *Jesus of Nazareth*, Collier-Macmillan, London, 1929, p. 34.

[4] Babylonian Talmud *Sabbath* 104b and *Sanhedrin* 67d.

[5] Seven pages in the Loeb Edition of *BJ* 1:401-408.

[6] *AJ* xix, 329.

[7] *BJ* 1, 647.

[8] *BJ* 1, 656.

[9] Macrobius, *Saturnalia*, 2:4:11.

[10] *AJ* xix, 328.

[11] *Assumption of Moses*, 6:2 ff.

[12] Herodotus *Histories*, 1:101,132, Daniel 2:2.

[13] Acts 8:9; 13:6,8.

[14] Tacitus, *Histories*, 5:13.

[15] *AJ* xviii, 2.

2

Nazareth: The Hidden Years
(c. 3 BC-AD 29)

The years between Jesus' birth and his emergence as a
public figure are passed over in almost complete silence by
the New Testament writers. The single exception is the story
of Jesus' first visit to Jerusalem in his twelfth year (Luke
2:41-52). We know of nothing else that Jesus specifically did
or said throughout these "hidden years".

Thus the "river" of New Testament story may be seen
leaving Nazareth in about 3 BC and coming again into view
in about AD 28. In between those points it is hidden from
view except for that brief flash when in about AD 5 Jesus
first went to Jerusalem and was left behind in the temple.
Nevertheless, while the "river" is out of sight, the terrain
through which it passes is clearly visible.

From other contemporary historical records, as a result
of archaeological research, and the study of Galilean
geography, we can set Jesus and his family in context. We
know about the nature of his education, the religious ethos
underlying it, the district in which he lived and the major
political events of his times.

Over the centuries many Christians found it difficult
to accept the silence of the New Testament gospels
concerning the formative years of Jesus and numerous
stories were created to fill the gaps. Some of them have come
down to us in the so-called Apocryphal gospels, as, for
example, this extract from the "Gospel of Thomas".

And when Jesus was five years old, there fell a great rain
upon the earth, and the boy Jesus walked up and down
through it. And there was a terrible rain, and He collected

it into a fishpond, and ordered it by His word to become clear. And immediately it became so. Again He took of the clay which was of that fishpond, and made of it to the number of twelve sparrows. (Latin Form IV)

Scholars universally recognise these stories for what they are — patently contrived tales, far removed from the historical Jesus.

The gospels indicate that Jesus was a keen, sympathetic and sensitive observer of people and the life around him. Through the vivid imagery of his parables we can see the world through his eyes. When he asks, "Is a lamp brought in to be put under a bed?" we catch a glimpse of his Nazareth home at night. There are references to birds, snakes, foxes and wolves; comments about overburdened oxen; stories of swineherds and sowers of seed, pigs and weeds in the wheat fields, lost sheep, good and bad shepherds, that reflect his country childhood. There are descriptions of quarrelling children and elegantly dressed courtiers. The Parable of the Pounds is really an historical allegory based on Archelaus' visit to Rome in 4 BC — more than thirty years earlier — to take possession of his father Herod's kingdom. It reveals Jesus' awareness of politics and of recent history. When at last he opens his mouth to speak, the vivid imagery he uses conveys something of the impact on him of the things he saw in those intervening years.

Before proceeding to investigate the world of Jesus' boyhood and youth, the terrain, as it were, through which his life passed, two points must be emphasised. First, that for Jesus to be truly human, as he was, he had to live in a completely human context. Second, Luke's account of the boy Jesus in the temple establishes that even at twelve years of age and within this human context he was conscious that he was the Son of God (Luke 2:41-52). What we will portray is the ordinary environment in which he lived and matured. Jesus was three or four years of age when Joseph and Mary returned to Nazareth, preferring the Galilee of Antipas to the Judaea of Archelaus. In time other children were added to the family — sisters whose names are not given and four brothers: James, Joseph, Judas and Simon (Mark 6:3). Jesus was the eldest of at least seven children.

In addition to this immediate family there were also residing in Nazareth members of Jesus' extended family which may have included uncles, aunts, cousins and possibly grandparents (see Mark 6:4): Luke mentions that the group which travelled to Jerusalem for the Passover included relatives and friends (Luke 2:44). Mark specifically states that Jesus' "relatives" at Nazareth did not "honour" him (Mark 6:4). We know from the Nativity stories that Mary's kinswoman (cousin?) Elizabeth lived in the hill country of Judaea, where Mary visited her. (Luke 1:39)

Their common language would have been Aramaic, the dialect of Palestinian Jews since Persian times, which Galileans, and presumably Jesus, spoke with a distinctive accent (Matthew 26:73; Acts 2:7). This would have been the language used in Joseph's household and by the other families in Nazareth. Archaeologists have not discovered many remains of ancient houses at Nazareth. They have however, excavated a number of houses in Galilean villages such as Capernaum.[1] The house of Joseph and Mary probably consisted of a central courtyard surrounded by a number of rooms one of which would have been for Joseph's workshop.

Joseph was a "carpenter" (Greek: *tekton*), a tradesman who worked in any hard material — wood, metal or stone. We assume he was occupied in a range of building and repair work in and around Nazareth, from the making of chairs and tables to the building of houses. As was customary, Jesus took up his father's trade (Mark 6:3) and doubtless learnt from him to measure, cut and join all kinds of building materials. Some teachings of Jesus about God may have been originally cast in parable-form in which Joseph was the father-teacher and Jesus the son and apprentice.

When, in John 5:19-20, Jesus comments,

the Son can do nothing of his own accord, but only what he sees the Father doing. For the Father loves the Son, and shows him all that he is himself doing. . .

he may be reflecting on his relationship to his master-tradesman father, Joseph, who because of his *love* for his son showed him how to master the builder's trade. Jesus' words in Matthew 11:27 can probably be understood in a similar light. "All things have been delivered to me by my Father and no one knows the Son except the Father and no one knows the Father except the Son."

Are his words about the man who gives good gifts to his son (Matthew 5:9-11) also an oblique recognition of a kind father?

Joseph was still alive in AD 5 or 6 when Jesus first visited Jerusalem aged twelve (Luke 2:41-52). That he is not mentioned either at the wedding in Cana (John 2:1-11) or when Jesus returned during his ministry to Nazareth (Mark 6:1-6), suggests that he was not then alive. The adult Jesus is, however, referred to as "the son of Joseph" (John 1:45, 6:42) which may suggest that Joseph had died in the recent past. It is possible that Jesus delayed his entry into public life until James, the next brother, was sufficiently mature to take over the responsibilities left by Joseph's absence.

The few references to Mary during the ministry of Jesus suggest that she was a woman of some standing and initiative. At the marriage in Cana, about four miles to the north of Nazareth, Mary "was there," whereas Jesus was "also invited". At least in that early stage of his ministry she took social precedence over him. It was Mary who spoke first to Jesus about the failure of the wine and then authoritatively to the servants (John 2:1,3,6). Her journey from Nazareth to Capernaum to retrieve the son who was said to be "beside himself" is a further indication of her initiative as well as of her concern for Jesus. (Mark 3:21, 31)

It is well known that Mary and her family were unresponsive to Jesus' ministry (John 2:4; 7:5; Mark 3:31). Quite possibly they were resentful that he had left Nazareth to make his home in Capernaum, near the northern extremity of the Sea of Galilee (Matthew 4:13), and about a day's walk away. Nevertheless deep family ties may be discerned in the migration of Mary and her sons to Jerusalem at the time of the crucifixion (Acts 1:14). They became part of the community of one hundred and twenty Galileans who took up residence in Jerusalem under the leadership of the apostles and, in time, James was to succeed Peter as the leader of the Jerusalem church. (Acts 15:13 ff.) It is clear that Jesus was literate, able both to read and to write. At the commencement of his public ministry, he attended his own synagogue at Nazareth where "he stood up and read . . .the book of the prophet Isaiah" (Luke 4:16-17). When the woman taken in adultery was brought to him he "bent down and wrote. . .on the ground" (John 8:6). When he was only twelve he sat among the teachers of the law in the temple "asking" and "answering" questions, to the astonishment of those present (Luke 2:46-47). The gospels often portray Jesus engaged in technical legal debate with the teachers of the Jewish Law. Those who heard him were amazed that he had acquired his knowledge without having studied under the rabbis (see John 7:15). Jesus' own frequent references to "what is written" reveal an extensive knowledge of the Hebrew scriptures. Much of his teaching was conducted in synagogues, which implies that he read from the Hebrew Bible before commenting upon it in Aramaic. If Jesus was able to read and write, to quote from the Bible, to teach and to debate, where was he educated in these things and by whom?

The Jewish historian Josephus, who wrote in the last quarter of the first century, commented on Jewish education, "The education Jews underwent was confined to Torah (=scriptures). . .all learning was to that end."[2]

Josephus noted how seriously Jewish parents viewed the education of their children.

The law. . .enjoins sobriety in their upbringing from the very first. It orders that they shall be taught to read and shall learn both the laws and the deeds of their forefathers, in order that they may imitate the latter, and being grounded in the former, may neither transgress nor have any excuse for being ignorant of them.[3]

Another Jew, Philo, who wrote in about the middle of the first century, observed that Jewish education reflected their profound commitment to the scriptures. "[The Jews] consider their laws to be divine revelation and are instructed in them from their youth."[4]

Presuming that his upbringing was typical, Jesus would

have derived his education in the Torah from two principal
sources — his father and the synagogue. To quote once
again from Philo,

> . . .before any instruction in the holy laws and unwritten
> customs they are taught. . .from their swaddling clothes
> by parents, teachers and educators to believe in God, the
> one Father and Creator of the world.[5]

The more formal "instruction" referred to by Philo
began, according to the Mishnah (compiled in the second
century after Christ) at five years of age. "At five years old
one is fit for the scripture. . .at thirteen for the fulfilling of the
commandments."[6] At five, then, Jesus would have begun
his education at the synagogue where an attendant (Greek:
hyperetes) was employed to look after the scrolls of scripture,
to announce the beginning and ending of Sabbath by the
blowing of the trumpet and to teach children to write and to
know the Torah.[7] The "attendant" who handed Jesus the
scroll to read when he visited his home synagogue (Luke
4:17, 20) may have been the one who had taught him to read
and write as a boy.

It should not be overlooked that the Sabbath attendance
at the synagogue was primarily for instruction in the law.
Luke 4:16 specifically states that it was Jesus' "custom"
to attend the synagogue on the Sabbath. This educational
emphasis of the synagogue service is stated by Josephus.

> He [our law-giver i.e. God] made the law to be an excel-
> lent and necessary subject of instruction in that it is not
> to be heard but once, or twice, but frequently, but he
> ordained that every week the people should set aside their
> other occupations and gather together to listen to the law
> and learn it accurately.[8]

Apart from the *Shema* ("Hear O Israel, the Lord our God
is One" — Deuteronomy 6:4-9) the prayer which followed
and the blessing at the end, the synagogue service consisted
of readings from the Law and Prophets and a teaching
sermon based on a scriptural passage. The synagogue
meeting was strongly educational in character.

By the time Jesus was twelve and came to Jerusalem for
his first Passover, in preparation for "the fulfilling of the
commandments" or *Bar Mitzvah*, he had been exposed to

considerable formal and informal education in the Hebrew
scriptures. So far as we know, Jesus did not receive any
formal education beyond this. Unlike Saul of Tarsus, for
example, who had been for many years the pupil of a rabbi
(Gamaliel), Jesus did not become a student of a rabbi.
Indeed Jesus was critical of the rabbis' interpretation of the
law and accused them of destroying the true meaning and
intention of the Law of God. (Mark 7:3-9)

Beyond the influence of home and synagogue it appears
that Jesus was self-educated. Nevertheless when he commenced his ministry at "about thirty years of age" (Luke
3:23) Jesus was called "rabbi" (e.g. John 6:25) and allowed to
teach in the synagogues of Galilee. (Luke 4:16 ff.; Mark 1:21,
39)

Mark records that Jesus created tremendous interest
when he first taught in the synagogue in Capernaum. He
gave "new teaching. . .with authority" (Mark 1:27). It was
radically different from the teaching of the rabbis. This may
be discerned from Jesus' twin parables of the new wine
and the new cloth. His teachings were like new wine which
would burst the old wine skins; or like new cloth, which
would tear away from an old garment. (Mark 2:21-22)

Jesus taught in Jerusalem and Judaea, as well as in
Galilee. He said, in reply to the question of the high priest,
"I have spoken openly to the world; I have always taught
in synagogues and in the temple, where all Jews come
together. . ." (John 18:20)

His visits to Jerusalem for the feasts were occasions
of controversy which created ever-growing anticipation.
His arrival for what would be for him the last Feast of
Tabernacles was awaited with excitement both by the
Pharisees and the ordinary people. Their question was: Is
Jesus "a good man" or one who is "leading the people
astray?" When in the middle of the week-long feast Jesus
finally appeared, the Pharisees expressed amazement. "How
is it that this fellow has learning [Greek: *grammata*,
"letters"] when he has never studied?" (John 7:15)

They were astonished that a man, who had not attended
the rabbinic schools, could be a teacher and debater of
the law, equal, if not superior to, the most highly trained

professionals. Jesus probably debated with them, not in vernacular Aramaic, but in Hebrew, the formal language of the religious establishment. Jesus' explanation of his ability was, simply, "my teaching is not mine, but his who sent me" (John 7:16). His expertise in the technicalities of legal debate may be contrasted with the high priests' later scornful dismissal of Peter and John as "unlettered" and "laymen" (*agrammatoi* and *idiotai*). (Acts 4:13)

The wealthy Galilean landowners and members of the Herod family lived in or near the two cities of Sepphoris and Tiberias. (Sepphoris was on the next hill three miles to the north of Nazareth and clearly visible to it. Tiberias was on the Sea of Galilee, half a day's walk from Nazareth.) These landowners were an élite group, socially remote from the Galilean peasants.

Members of these wealthy families had received considerable exposure to Greek culture and philosophy. The parables of Jesus reveal that such people travelled abroad frequently, presumably to Greece and Rome, so their theology was probably Sadducaic, that is, deeply influenced by Greek views of the remoteness of God.

The ordinary people from the Galilean towns and villages, however, had as little as possible to do with these cities of the aristocracy. They looked to the temple in Jerusalem as the focus of their loyalty. As required by the Law (e.g. Exodus 23:15-16) they made three annual pilgrimages to Jerusalem — in the spring for Passover, in summer for First Fruits and in winter for Tabernacles. Many weeks each year were taken up for Galileans in these visits to Jerusalem. The gospels and Josephus make numerous references to Galileans coming to Jerusalem to observe these great festivals. Luke states that Joseph and Mary went to Jerusalem every year at the Feast of Passover (Luke 2:41), as did Jesus and his disciples. To avoid passing through Samaria, Galileans would have travelled down the Jordan valley, past the Gentile city of Scythopolis, through the bleak Judaean desert, through the oasis-city Jericho, ascending approximately 4000 feet through the desolate ravines up to Jerusalem. If, as Josephus says, the direct route from Galilee to Jerusalem through Samaria took three days, then the longer journey probably took twice that time.[9]

Although the pharisaic movement was concentrated in Jerusalem it is clear that they had some influence in Galilee. Their aim was to train the common people to observe scrupulously the Sabbath, the ritual purifications, the fasting and the tithing. In this they were only partially successful, especially in Galilee.[10] The gospels depict the Pharisees of Galilee in debate with Jesus over such matters.[11] References to scribes "from Jerusalem" (Mark 3:22; 7:1) suggest that local Pharisees needed assistance in dealing with him. Sean Freyne writes of a "pharisaic presence in Galilee and a scribal mission from Jerusalem to support it".[12]

The pharisaic leaders in Jerusalem had a low view of Galilee. In their eyes Galileans typified ordinary people of the land who were ignorant of the law and slack in fulfilling it (John 7:47-52). These scholars were certain that neither the Messiah nor any prophet would come from Galilee (John 7:41-52). Later Rabbi ben Zakkai was to declare: "Galilee, Galilee you hate the Torah".

The Mishnah recognised that Galilee was not one, but three, separate regions, "Galilee is divided with upper Galilee, lower Galilee and the valley".[13]

Upper Galilee is high and mountainous country to the north and the north-west of the Sea of Galilee. Its difficult terrain made it inaccessible to regular troops and a natural haven for brigands and revolutionaries who were active throughout the Roman period. The "valley" relates to the Sea of Galilee and to the Jordan which flows out of it to the south. Lower Galilee is the elevated and stepped plateau-land between the Sea of Galilee and the Mediterranean. Nazareth is located near the southern extreme of lower Galilee, in the mountain range that rises abruptly from the beautiful valley of Jezreel.

Nazareth, the village to which Joseph and Mary brought Jesus as a small boy, is estimated by archaeologists to have had a population of between 1500-2000.[14] It is located about fifteen miles west of Lake Galilee and twenty miles east of the Mediterranean. Sited on a range of hills 1150 feet above sea level, Nazareth has commanding views of the Plain of Jezreel to the south, Mount Carmel to the west, Mount Tabor to the east and Mount Hermon to the far north. Joseph Klausner, the noted Jewish New Testament scholar, first visited Nazareth in 1912 describing it as having perhaps the finest view in the world.

Josephus had been a military commander in Galilee in AD 66 and was well qualified to describe the countryside and people. He wrote that,

Galilee, with its two divisions known as Upper and Lower Galilee, is enveloped by Phoenicea and Syria... With this limited area and although surrounded by such powerful foreign nations, the two ‘Galilees have always resisted any hostile invasion, for the inhabitants are from infancy inured to war, and have at all times been numerous: never did the men lack courage nor the countrymen. For the land is everywhere so rich in soil and pasturage and produces such variety of trees that even the most indolent are tempted by these facilities to devote themselves to agriculture. . . The towns too are thickly distributed and even the villages. . .are so densely populated that the smallest of them contains above fifteen thousand inhabitants.[15]

Galilee was and remains a fertile and beautiful region, whether around the lake or in the high country. Its soil supported a wide variety of fruits — citrus, grapes, figs, walnuts and dates, olives, for example. Wheat, barley and flax were sown in abundance. The pasture lands supported numerous flocks of sheep and goats. The waters of the superb lake teemed with more than forty varieties of fish. Galilee was a rich and fertile area, especially when compared to the barren desert regions of Samaria and Judaea.

Nazareth was quite close to important roads. The *Via Maris*, the main route from Egypt to Syria, passed a mere six miles to the east of Nazareth. The main road from Sepphoris, the old capital of Galilee, passed through Nazareth to Jerusalem. A major road from the Mediterranean to the Sea of Galilee passed a few miles to the north of Galilee.

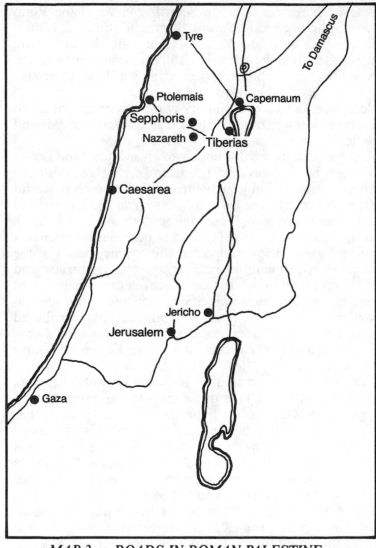

MAP 3 — ROADS IN ROMAN PALESTINE.

Nazareth was a small rural hamlet with so little claim to fame, that a cynic from nearby Cana could ask, "Can any good thing come out of Nazareth?" (John 1:46; 21:2) Nevertheless it was by no means remote or unimportant. While there is no reference in literature to Nazareth prior to Jesus, travellers from distant places would often have been seen in its streets. Greek speaking visitors, for example, must have passed through the village.

From the time of Alexander the Great, three centuries earlier, the Greek language had been spoken throughout the Middle East. Certainly Greek was known to wealthy people, bureaucrats and administrators, including Jews. During the years of Jesus' early life it is certain that he would have heard Greek spoken in and around Nazareth.

A few years after Jesus, while Claudius was emperor (AD 41–54), a Greek inscription was erected in Nazareth forbidding the removal of bodies from tombs.

It is my pleasure that sepulchres and tombs, which have been erected as solemn memorials of ancestors or children or relatives, shall remain undisturbed in perpetuity. If it be shown that anyone has either destroyed them or removed them with malicious intent to another place, thus committing a crime against those buried there, or removed the headstones, I command that against such person the same sentences be passed in respect of solemn memorials of men as is laid down in respect of the gods. Much rather must one pay respect to those who are buried. Let no one disturb them on any account. Otherwise it is my will that capital sentence be passed upon such person for the crime of tomb spoliation.[16]

Scholars have wondered why this edict prohibiting the removal of bodies from graves should have been preserved only in Nazareth. Were attempts made to find the body of Jesus and so rebut claims that he had risen from the dead leaving the tomb in Jerusalem empty? Apart from that interesting possibility, the significance of this inscription in Nazareth is that it is in Greek. Clearly some people at Nazareth were presumed able to read it.

In the latter part of his ministry Jesus visited the northern coastal region of Tyre and Sidon, to the north, which had long been exposed to Greek culture. There he conversed with a Greek woman, Syro-Phoenician by birth (Mark 7:26). This is often seen as evidence that Jesus could speak Greek. His use of the word "hypocrite" or play-actor is thought also to indicate his familiarity with the Greek language. Plays were forbidden to the Jews; the word "hypocrite" does not appear in Hebrew or Aramaic. Some scholars suggest that when Jesus addressed Galilean crowds he spoke Greek. They point out that on the few occasions Jesus' Aramaic words are recorded they occur in private conversations where the language of the home would have been more appropriate (Mark 5:4; 7:34). His reference to *mammon*, apparently spoken to a crowd, is an exception. (Matthew 6:24)

Despite the Hellenization of the general region and the probability that Greek was known to many people it seems likely that Nazareth remained a conservative Jewish village. After the Jewish war with the Romans from AD 66–70 it was necessary to re-settle Jewish priests and their families. Such groups would only settle in unmixed towns, that is towns without Gentile inhabitants. According to an inscription discovered in 1962 in Caesarea Maritima the priests of the order of Elkalir made their home in Nazareth.[16] This, by the way, is the sole known reference to Nazareth in antiquity, apart from written Christian sources.

Some scholars had even believed that Nazareth was a fictitious invention of the early Christians; the inscription from Caesarea Maritima proves otherwise.

Although there is no record of Jesus visiting Sepphoris or Tiberias, the two major cities of Galilee, both were close to Nazareth.

Sepphoris, the old capital, lay at the centre of Lower Galilee and was, according to Josephus, "the strongest city of Galilee",[17] being almost impregnable. Nevertheless it had been destroyed by the Roman General Varus in 4 BC and its citizens sold into slavery. Soon afterwards, when Jesus was a small boy, Herod Antipas rebuilt Sepphoris as "the ornament of all Galilee",[18] a comment which implies Greek town planning and architecture. Although Galileans generally were anti-Roman, the people of Sepphoris adopted a pro-Roman stance during the war

AD 66-70, doubtless on account of their experiences in the time of Varus. Wealthy and aristocratic Jews who owned large estates in the area lived in or near this city. Although it was to lose its pride of place to Tiberias the new capital, Sepphoris remained the largest city in Galilee. Nazareth was only three miles south of it, less than an hour's walk away.

In about AD 20, about a decade before Jesus emerged as a public figure, Antipas built a new capital, Tiberias, in honour of the Roman Emperor Tiberius. The site of the new city had been used as a graveyard. It was necessary to use force to make some Jews live there since Jewish law forbade contact with the dead. Antipas planned and built his new capital on the lines of a Greek city with a Greek stadium, and a palace decorated with representations of animals — also contrary to Jewish law. Antipas was imitating his father Herod but, due to financial restraints, Antipas' building programme was more modest.

Nonetheless Tiberias had a population of approximately forty thousand people. Administratively the new city followed the Greek pattern with an *archon* (=ruler), *dekaprotoi* (=panel of ten leading men), a *boule* (=senate) and an *ekklesia* (=assembly of citizens). Tiberias became a centre of Greek education and culture. Because Tiberias was his administrative centre Antipas minted coins for his tetrarchy there. Large properties near Tiberias were owned by relatives of Antipas and the wealthy people.

Apart from the cities Sepphoris and Tiberias there were two hundred and four towns in Galilee,[19] each with a local chief citizen, who may also have been the Ruler of the Synagogue. They were grouped in five districts[20] or *"toparchies"* each administered by an official known as a *"Toparch"* who would have been responsible to Antipas, the Tetrarch. This subdivision of Galilee went back almost three centuries to the period when Palestine was part of Egypt, under the rule of the Ptolemies.

The *Toparch* and other officials, together with Antipas' relatives and the wealthy aristocrats, represented a small ruling class who held absolute power within Galilee. This small élite, who stood to gain from Herod Antipas' continuing rule, were probably the group identified by Mark as "the Herodians" who sought Jesus' life (Mark 3:6; 12:13). The "official" from Capernaum whose son Jesus healed is called *basilikos*, a "royal" person — probably an official or soldier. This man may also have belonged to the Herodian faction. (see John 4:46)

This small aristocratic ruling class owned most of the land in Galilee. The remainder, in diminishing quantities, was owned by peasant farmers and subject to the perennial uncertainties of inclement weather and pestilence. In good seasons there was over-production and low prices; in bad seasons there was famine. Either way the peasant farmer was subject to a battery of harsh taxes and strict bureaucratic control. It has been estimated that peasants were taxed at the rate of between 30% and 40% of their produce. They very easily fell into debt and were forced into debt-slavery, tenant farming or day labouring.[21] The instruments of their suffering — the market-controller (*agoranomos*), the debt records (*archeia*) and the money-lenders (*trapezai*) were located in the capital of Galilee — first in Sepphoris then, after AD 20, in Tiberias.

Thus the peasants had two good reasons for hating these cities and their inhabitants. Those who collected the taxes, controlled the prices and recorded their debts lived there as part of the web of power surrounding Herod Antipas. And they were, generally speaking, both pro-Roman and influenced by Gentile religious culture.

This resistance to influence from pro-Roman Sepphoris and Tiberias reinforced the peasants' loyalty to Jerusalem and its temple.

Some people have commented that the parables of Jesus imply that Jews of his time were all either wealthy land-owners or poor peasants constantly in debt. We read of the wealthy man (and his steward) and the debtor who owes one hundred measures of oil and wheat (Luke 16:1-6), a vineyard owner with his tenant farmers (Mark 12:1) and labourers hired by the day Matthew 20:1-16). A two-class society seems to be on view — the wealthy and the poor.

There are exceptions, however. In the story of the prodigal son, the sons work the farm, along with hired labour (Luke 15:11-31). The fisherman Zebedee has employees as well as the assistance of his sons (Mark 1:20). It is conceivable that the family of Joseph, the builder-carpenter of Nazareth, belonged to this lower middle/upper peasant class, composed of borker-entrepreneurs of modest means.

The boy Jesus settled in Nazareth a year or so after Herod the Great died and his son Antipas assumed control of the Tetrarchy of Galilee; his crucifixion in AD 33 preceded Antipas' fall from grace by about six years.

When he described Herod Antipas as "that fox" (Luke 13:31) most of his hearers would surely have considered it an apt description of the shrewd and crafty Antipas. Born in 20 BC to Malthace, a Samaritan woman, and then educated in Rome, Antipas was a mere sixteen years old in 4 BC when his father Herod the Great died. He travelled to Rome to persuade the Emperor Augustus to accept the earlier of Herod's two wills, in which he inherited the entire realm. Augustus, however, ratified the more recent will; Antipas had to be content with the lesser title "Tetrarch" as ruler of a quarter of Herod's kingdom.

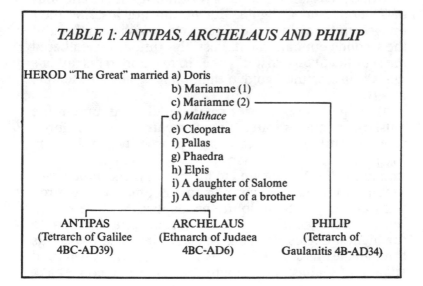

TABLE 1: ANTIPAS, ARCHELAUS AND PHILIP

HEROD "The Great" married a) Doris
                          b) Mariamne (1)
                          c) Mariamne (2) ——————
                        ┌ d) *Malthace*
                          e) Cleopatra
                          f) Pallas
                          g) Phaedra
                          h) Elpis
                          i) A daughter of Salome
                          j) A daughter of a brother

ANTIPAS	ARCHELAUS	PHILIP
(Tetrarch of Galilee 4BC-AD39)	(Ethnarch of Judaea 4BC-AD6)	(Tetrarch of Gaulanitis 4B-AD34)

On his return to Galilee in 4 BC he immediately rebuilt Sepphoris and Betharamphtha, shrewdly naming them in honour of members of the Roman Imperial family ("Autocratis" and "Livias" respectively). In about AD 20 Antipas built his new capital Tiberias (after the Emperor Tiberius) on the shore of the sea of Galilee, and astride a major trade route between Egypt and Syria. The Tetrarch's building programme was designed both to strengthen fortification of the region and to enhance its commercial strength which would, in turn, enable him to pay his taxes to Rome.

A further example of Antipas' "fox"-like shrewdness may be seen in his marriage to the daughter of Aretas IV, king of the Nabataean or Arabian kingdom on the eastern border of Galilee. By marrying their princess the Tetrarch secured his border with the Nabataeans, who were as much trouble to him as they had been for his father Herod the Great.

There is no record of civil disturbance within Antipas' tetrarchy, although the Galilean people were renowned for their volatile character. Judas the Galilean (from Upper Galilee?) led an uprising in AD 6 over the imposition of Roman taxation, but in Judaea not Galilee. Antipas cultivated his Roman masters by minting coins in honour of Tiberius and Caligula. But he did not inscribe their images on the coins, in deference to Jewish scruples and the second commandment. Possibly Antipas remembered the significant civil disturbances in reaction to his father's mistake in erecting a golden eagle on the gate of the temple in 4 BC.

Although his region was small, landlocked and on the outskirts of the empire, history records Antipas' forty-three-year rule to have been one of prosperity and strength. Josephus records that Antipas was "content with his tranquility".[22] He appeared to have been preoccupied with keeping the peace. According to Josephus the Tetrarch was "alarmed" about John the Baptist, because of his "eloquence" and that "the crowds. . .were aroused to the highest degree".[23] Later, when Antipas heard of Jesus through the mission of the twelve disciples to the towns and villages of Galilee, he thought that John had come back

from the grave to create more problems in his tetrarchy.
(Mark 6:14-17)

Jesus warned the disciples against "the leaven of Herod
Antipas", that is, his malicious jealousy towards any threat
to his rule (Mark 8:15). On a number of occasions Jesus
prudently withdrew out of the public eye to escape the
stated intention of Antipas and his "Herodian" supporters
to kill him (Luke 13:31; Mark 3:6; 6:45; John 6:15;
Mark 9:2). Clearly the activities of Jesus had been noticed
by Antipas.

Luke states that Antipas had for a long time sought to
meet the famous Nazarene, hoping to witness a miracle
sign. His opportunity did not come until Jesus was arrested
and handed over to him by the Roman prefect, Pilate. Jesus,
however, did not perform a sign for Antipas nor answer
him, despite mockery and contempt. The ever "fox"-like
tetrarch sent Jesus back to Pilate for judgement rather than
be associated with the death of another popular prophet.
(see Luke 23:6-12)

For some years, however, Antipas seemed secure in
his tetrarchy. His undoing was almost entirely due to the
woman he took as his second wife. Some time in the
late twenties Antipas divorced the Nabataean princess in
order to marry his half-sister Herodias who was already
married.[24] This started a chain of evil consequences
for Antipas.

John the Baptist publicly denounced Antipas and
Herodias for acting against the Law of God (Mark 6:18).
Incensed by the insult, Herodias had John beheaded at
Antipas' birthday banquet (Mark 6:25-28). This in turn
led to widespread and long lasting resentment against the
ruler; John the Baptist had been very popular.[25]

When opportunity came the Nabataean king took his
revenge for the divorce of his daughter and, in a military
engagement, Antipas' army was wiped out. His credibility
with the Romans would have suffered as a result.[26]

Herodias goaded Antipas to have himself promoted to
"King" by the mad emperor, Caligula. Herodias' brother
Agrippa had recently been appointed "King" over the
tetrarchy of the now-deceased Philip. Antipas' request to

Caligula was a fatal mistake. In AD 39 the Tetrarch was dismissed from his position and he and his wife were sent into exile. His long and largely successful rule was abruptly and ignominiously terminated. The "fox"-like Tetrarch, who had twice sought unsuccessfully to be king, thus stepped out of the spotlight of history to live out his days in obscurity.

Jesus' boyhood, youth and ministry were lived out within the Galilean rule of this crafty, dangerous Herod Antipas, the man he called "that fox".

The references in the parables to courtiers with soft clothes, to banquets, to divided kingdoms, to warring kings and to the completion of buildings may well have been inspired by Herod Antipas and his court. It was, after all, a small realm, accessible to observation.

Jesus must also have spent considerable time in Jerusalem and Judaea and acquired an understanding of political and religious life there. The gospel of John reveals that Jesus visited Jerusalem for three major feasts, which had probably been his practice from the age of twelve.

The Galilee from which he came was stable and quiet throughout the long rule of Antipas (4 BC–AD 39); the Judaea he visited was subject to periodic turbulent upheaval.

The basic reason for the turmoil arose from Augustus' decision in AD 6 to make Judaea a Roman province. Archelaus' ten-year rule since the death of Herod the Great had been marked by immaturity, inefficiency and cruelty. Those who successfully secured his dismissal were the Jewish aristocrats whose support Archelaus, unlike Antipas in Galilee, did not enjoy. So, instead of appointing Antipas as King of both Judaea and Galilee, Augustus chose to annexe Judaea as a Roman province. Over it he set a military governor. This fateful decision precipitated the civil disturbances in Judaea and led ultimately to the catastrophic Jewish War of AD 66–70, the climax of which was the destruction of the temple. The course of Jewish and Christian history may have been different if Augustus had found an indigenous client king to keep order in turbulent

Judaea. The problem was that successful client kings also had expansive territorial ambitions. Perhaps Augustus discerned that Antipas was truly his father's son in that regard and therefore too dangerous to appoint as King of Judaea.

The annexation of Judaea to Rome meant significant changes. The contrast with Galilee in the years following the fall of Archelaus would have been sharp.

Roman troops were stationed in Jerusalem, with their barracks in Herod's former palace and in the Antonia fortress adjoining the temple. Their main garrison was at Caesarea Maritima on the coast, which became the capital of the Roman Province of Judaea and the base of the governor whose title was "Prefect". He was responsible for overall military security and peace keeping, for judging and executing those guilty of capital crimes, and for the gathering of the taxes which, significantly, were now paid direct to Rome. Because Judaea was a minor province the governors were drawn from the equestrian order, an upwardly mobile "middle class" group, whose members could be put in the emperor's debt by a provincial appointment of this kind.

In spite of the obvious military presence, the day-to-day running of Judaea now became the responsibility of the High Priest and the Sanhedrin. Under Roman rule, the aristocrats of Judaea, long repressed by Herod and Archelaus, enjoyed new freedom and power. The Sanhedrin, a governing senate of seventy-one members, was chiefly drawn from wealthy Judaean landowners. So too was the high priest, who was appointed or dismissed by the Roman prefect. The major administrative positions in the temple were allocated to members of the high priest's family. To win the high priesthood was a rich prize and it is quite probable that large bribes were paid to the prefect to secure and keep this position.

The first prefect, Coponius, appointed Annas as high priest. Apart from a brief interregnum in AD 16-17 he, his son Eleazer and his son-in-law Caiaphas were able to keep that position in the family and so dominate Judaean public life for the next thirty years. Something of the shrewdness of

TABLE 2: RULE IN JUDAEA 37 BC – AD 37

Emperor		Ruler in Judaea	High Priest	Date of Appointment
Augustus (27 BC - AD 14)	H	Herod	Ananelus	37 BC
	E	(King 37 BC	Aristobulus	36
	R	d.4 BC)	Ananelus reappointed	35
	O		Jesus, son of Phabi	?
	D		*Simon, son of Boethus	?
	I		*Matthias, son of Theophilus.	
	A		(related by marriage	
	N		with Simon)	
			Joseph, son of Elam (relative	For one day during
	M		of Matthias)	Matthias' term
	O			
	N		*Joazar, son (?) of Boethus	4
	A		*Eleazar, brother of Joazar	4
	R	Archelaus		
	C	(Ethnarch 4 BC		
	H	deposed AD 6)		
	Y			

Roman Annexation of Judaea: (Uprising led by Judas the Galilaean)

	R	Coponius	*Joazar reappointed	AD 5/6(?)
	O	Prefect 6-9	#Ananus, son of Seth	6
	M			
	A	Ambibulus		
	N	Prefect 9-11		
		Rufus		
	P	Prefect 12-14		
Tiberius (14-37)	R		Ishmael, son of Phabi	15
	E	Gratus	#Eleazar, son of Ananus	
	F	Prefect 15-26	Simon, son of Camithus	
	E		#Caiaphas, son-in-law of	26
	C	Pilate	Ananus	
	T	Prefect 27-36		
	S			

Note that high priesthood was
dominated by just a few families.
*Member of Boethus family
#Member of Ananus family

the Annas dynasty, as well as the inherent nepotism of the system, can be seen from the lament of Abba Saul, a contemporary.

Woe is me for the house of Hanin [=Annas]
Woe is me for their whisperings! . . .
For they are the high priests;
Their sons are the treasurers;
Their sons-in-law are temple-officers
And their servants beat the people with cudgels.[27]

It was this high-priestly dynasty which issued the warrant for Jesus' arrest, recognising in him a threat to their continuing incumbency (John 11:45-53). It was they who bullied the prefect to execute Jesus. Nor was this the end of it. Less than two years later they had Stephen the Hellenist Christian leader stoned and issued warrants to Saul for the arrest of Christians in Jerusalem and even in foreign cities (Acts 7:1, 54-58; 9:1-2; 22:5; 26:11). The vendetta against Jesus continued for decades. It was Annas' son, also named Annas, who in AD 62 had James the brother of Jesus executed.[28]

A further indirect consequence of Augustus' decision in AD 6 was the shift of the balance of religious power from the Pharisees to the Sadducces. The decision effectively put great power in the hands of a few wealthy Judaeans whose families now occupied the high priesthood and dominated the Sanhedrin. Since the majority of these aristocrats followed Sadducaic teaching, the Sadducees now became very powerful in Judaea.

Although this small aristocratic faction had been in existence throughout the previous century they had not been prominent in the previous half century because both Herod and Archelaus had suppressed the Judaean aristocracy. It is not certainly known how they came to be called "Sadducees" and no writings from members of the faction have survived. Unlike the Pharisees, there is no evidence of the existence of the Sadducees after the war AD 66-70.

The Sadducees are known to have differed from the Pharisees in the following ways.

1 The Sadducees confined their religious teaching to

the Old Testament scriptures whereas the Pharisees
regarded the continuing traditions of the rabbis as
authoritative. The Sadducees therefore tended to be
inflexible and unbending in their interpretation. There
is no early evidence to support the widely held belief
that Sadducees only accepted the first five books of the
Bible and specifically refuted the prophets.

2 "The Sadducees say that there is no resurrection, nor
   angel, nor spirit; but the Pharisees acknowledge them
   all" (Acts 23:8). Since these doctrines arose in the
   period after the Old Testament it was consistent with
   the more fundamentalist approach of the Sadducees to
   reject them.

3 The Sadducees, unlike the Pharisees, rejected any belief
   in an after-life, of either body or soul.[29]

4 The Sadducees, again unlike Pharisees, "do away with
   fate [=providence] and remove God beyond not only
   the commission but the very sight of evil".[30] The
   Greek philosopher Plato taught that God was unknow-
   able and uninvolved in human affairs. Possibly the
   Sadducees as wealthy Jews educated in Greek
   language and thought derived this belief from Plato.

5 Josephus observed that the Sadducees were rude to one
   another and aloof from the community whereas the
   Pharisees cultivated harmonious relationship with the
   community and were affectionate to each other.[31]

It should be noted that while Jesus and the Pharisees
debated with one another they probably had much in
common. Their differences may have arisen, in part from
their separate visions for the kingdom of God and about
how to enter it. It was the Sadducees, however, who were
responsible for the execution of Jesus, and for the opposition to the apostolic community in Jerusalem, including
the deaths of Stephen and James the brother of Jesus.

Augustus' momentous decision and the three direct
consequences discussed above — a Roman tax-collecting,
military presence, the rise to power of the aristocracy in
Sanhedrin and high priesthood and the new dominance
of Sadducees over Pharisees — were to unleash massive
reactions within Judaea.

According to Josephus, one consequence of the Roman annexation of Judaea in AD 6 was the emergence of what he called the "Fourth Philosophy".[32]

Roman rule meant the physical, visible presence of pagan soldiers in the sacred precincts of Judaea and Jerusalem. Roman money bearing the portrait of Caesar was now in circulation, something deeply offensive to Jews whose law forbade images of humans and animals. Above all, each Jew was forced to pay tax direct to Caesar, a symbol that the hated Gentile was now master in place of God. The "Fourth Philosophy" was different from the other three — the Essenes, as well as the Pharisees and the Sadducees[33] — in that it was determined to take direct, violent action against the Gentiles.

When Coponius the first prefect began to register the names of Judaeans for the new tax, a major uprising occurred led by the first exponents of the "Fourth Philosophy," Judas the Galilean and a Pharisee named Saddok. Judas was killed and the revolt subdued by the Romans. The youthful Jesus may well have seen the crucified bodies of Judas and his partisans. Nonetheless, the source of bitterness which provoked the rise of the "Fourth Philosophy" remained. Many Pharisees appear to have adopted its commitment to violence. Doubtless they were grieved not only by the Roman presence but by the new dominance of the Sadducees. The Roman military forces and the tight grip of the Sadducees and the Annas dynasty combined to hold down revolutionary forces for thirty years after the failure of Judas' revolt.

The Roman author Tacitus made the interesting remark in *The Histories* that in "Tiberius' time [AD 14–37] all was quiet".[34]

One reason for the "quietness" was that Tiberius lengthened the tenure of prefects from three to ten (or more) years. He explained this change of policy in his cynical allegory of the flies — a bleeding man suffers less from bloated flies who have long gorged themselves on his wounds than from constantly arriving, hungry flies. It may well have been that long-serving prefects and a long-serving high priestly dynasty contributed to the "quietness" of Judaéa of which Tacitus wrote.

There was one major exception to this quietness which is not noted in Tacitus but which is described by Josephus and the writers of the gospels.

One prefect came to Judaea with the express purpose of de-stabilizing Judaism.[35] His name was Pontius Pilate. His actions provoked major disturbances especially during his first five years (AD 26–31) when Rome and the provinces were controlled, not by Tiberius the Emperor but by his sinister Praetorian Prefect, L. Aelius Sejanus.

Many scholars suspect that Sejanus, unlike Augustus and Tiberius, was anti-semitic. They further believe that he sent Pilate to Judaea specifically to overturn Judaism. It is noted that once Sejanus was removed by execution in AD 31 and Tiberius had regained the reins of power, Pilate ceased provoking the Jews. During those first five years, Pilate brought images of the emperor attached to military standards into Judaea; issued coinage with even more offensive pagan symbolism than before; robbed the sacred temple treasury to build an aqueduct and slaughtered a number of Galileans in Jerusalem during Passover. The gospels refer to an "insurrection" which had occurred sometime before the arrest of Jesus and to the two men crucified with Jesus who had taken part in it. (Mark 15:7) It is probable that this insurrection was an expression of the "Fourth Philosophy", provoked by the actions of Pontius Pilate.

The public ministry of Jesus in Judaea occurred in a period of simmering revolt after the annexation to Rome. The violence which had erupted in AD 6 was suppressed by the Romans and the long-ruling high-priestly Annas family. But the actions of Pilate in Judaea while Sejanus and his Praetorian Guards were supreme in Rome caused violence to break out once more. It was at this time that John the Baptist followed by Jesus of Nazareth began their public ministries.

So, who was Jesus of Nazareth? While we have extensive information about his brief public career there is almost nothing known about the years beforehand. All we can say is that he was raised in Nazareth, a builder, the son of a builder, the eldest in a family of five brothers whose names we know and unnumbered, unnamed sisters. We may speculate that he moved into public life at a point when the next brother, James, was capable of providing for Mary, the mother, and the family. This, however, is the limit of our direct knowledge of his early years.

We do, however, have extensive background data about the historical period through which he lived and the educational, social and economical conditions which prevailed during his lifetime. Jesus was too independent and powerful a personality to be explained merely in terms of his background and context. Nonetheless they do throw light upon what he did and said and the reactions of the people he influenced or provoked.

What is significant is that the widening and deepening of our knowledge through modern archaeological and historical research has not only filled in the context of Jesus' life and ministry; it has served to support and illuminate the New Testament records. The course of the river of New Testament story is clarified rather than blurred or changed as our knowledge of the terrain through which it flows increases.

Further reading to Chapter Two:
A.W. Argyle, "Greek Among the Jews of Palestine in New Testament times." *NTS* 20 (1974) 87-89.

M. Avi-Jonah, *The World History of the Jewish People: The Herodian People*, Masada Publishing, Jerusalem, 1975.

J. Finegan, *The Archaeology of the New Testament, The Life of Jesus and the beginning of the Early Church*, University Press, Princeton, 1969.

S. Freyne, *Galilee from Alexander the Great to Hadrian 323 BCE – 135 CE*, Glazier, Willington/Notre Dame, 1980.

H.E. Hoehner, *Herod Antipas*, Zondervan, Grand Rapids, 1980.

J. Klausner, *Jesus of Nazareth,* Collier-Macmillan, London, 1929.

P.L. Maier, "Sejanus, Pilate and the Date of the Crucifixion", *Church History,* 37, (1968), 3-13.

Y. Meshorer, *Ancient Jewish Coinage,* Amphora Books, New York, 1982.

E. Meyers and J. Strange, *Archaeology, the Rabbis and Early Christianity,* SCM, London, 1981.

E. Schürer, *The History of the Jewish People in the Age of Jesus Christ,* I and II, T. & T. Clark, Edinburgh, Revised and Edited 1973, 1979.

J.N. Sevenster, *Do You Know Greek?* E.J. Brill, Leiden, E.T., 1968.

E. Stauffer, *Jesus and His Story.* A. Knopf, New York, 1974.

M. Wilcox, "Jesus in the Light of his Jewish Environment", *Aufstieg und Niedergang der Römischen Welt II,* 1982, pp. 131-195.

Notes

[1]E.H. Meyers and J.F. Strange, 57.

[2]*Apion,* ii, 178.

[3]*Apion,* ii, 204.

[4]*Legatio,* 210.

[5]*Legatio,* 115.

[6]*Aboth,* 5:21.

[7]E. Schürer, *The History of the Jewish People in the Age of Jesus Christ,* Volume II, 415-463.

[8]*Apion,* ii, 175.

[9]*Vita,* 269.

[10]See S. Freyne, 319.

[11]Mark 2:18-22 (fasting); 2:23-28 (Sabbath); 7:23 (purification); 10:2-10 (divorce).

[12]S. Freyne, 322.

[13]Mishnah, *Shebiith,* 9:2.

[14]E.M. Meyers and J.F. Strange, 56.

[15]*BJ,* iii, 40-43. Perhaps Josephus means 1500 not 15000 inhabitants!

[16]E.M. Meyers and J.F. Strange, 57.

[17]*BJ*, ii, 510.

[18]*AJ*, xviii, 27.

[19]*Vita*, 235.

[20]See H.E. Hoehner, 46.

[21]See, e.g. Matthew 20:1-16.

[22]*AJ*, xviii, 245.

[23]*AJ*, xviii, 118.

[24]There is a conflict between Mark 6:17 and Josephus *AJ*, xviii, 136. For discussion see H.E. Hoehner, 131-136.

[25]*AJ*, xviii, 116.

[26]*AJ*, xviii, 114-115.

[27]Babylonian Talmud, *Pesahim*, 57d.

[28]*AJ*, xx, 200.

[29]*BJ*, ii, 165.

[30]*BJ*, ii, 164.

[31]*BJ*, ii, 166.

[32]*AJ*, xviii, 23-25.

[33]*AJ*, xviii, 11-22, *BJ*, ii, 119-166.

[34]Tacitus, *Histories*.

[35]*AJ*, xviii, 55.

3
Nazareth to Jerusalem:
Jesus' Movements (c. AD 29-33)

The "hidden years" are now past and the river of the New Testament story comes into full view. After living quietly and unnoticed for the past twenty years, Jesus emerges into the blaze of public attention. The events of the next three years will, in time, make him the most famous person in history. All dates in European and, ultimately, world history will be calculated from his birth date.

For our purpose, chronology is important in a way that it was not for the writers of the gospels. So, for the sake of convenience, we will separate Jesus' movements and their timing from his teaching.

Our major sources for Jesus' movements will be the Gospels of Mark and John. Unlike Matthew and Luke which depend on and are derived from Mark, these gospels are independent of each other.

Careful study of Mark and John reveals that they have in common, and in the same order, five important reference points about Jesus.

	John	Mark
1 The baptism of Jesus	1:32-33	1:9-11
2 Jesus' ministry in Galilee after the imprisonment of John the Baptist	3:24 4:3,43,47	1:14-15
3 Jesus' feeding of the multitude at Passover time	6:1-15	6:30-45
4 Jesus' final journey from	7:9-10	10:1

Galilee to Jerusalem		
5 Jesus' arrest and execution in Jerusalem at Passover	12:1	14:12

It is not suggested that both authors give equal emphasis to each of these reference points. Reference points 3 and 5, the second last and last Passovers respectively, are prominent in both gospels. However, the baptism of Jesus is explicit in Mark and only implicit in John. Mark's account of the beginning of the Galilean ministries is explicit in Mark and only implied in John. John's description of Jesus' journey from Galilee to Jerusalem is not so obviously final as it is in Mark's account. Despite these qualifications, however, the five reference points, in the same sequence, are present in our two primary sources.

A word of caution before we continue. The Jesus-history which we are attempting to reassemble from the available New Testament evidence can never be complete in every respect. The gospel writers all had different styles and purposes. And they were not writing to provide raw research data to be processed by modern historians into an authorized biography of Jesus.

As we consider the five reference points we may be surprised to discover that Jesus' ministry was more extensive in time than either Mark's or John's gospel taken on its own would suggest.

In Mark's account *Reference Point 1*, John's baptism of Jesus, is followed directly by *Reference Point 2*, the beginning of the Galilee ministry. If we depended only on Mark we would assume that the baptism in the Jordan River, the temptation in the wilderness, the arrest of John the Baptist and Jesus' return to Galilee followed in swift succession.

John's account, however, shows us that a significant period of time elapsed between Jesus' baptism and the commencement of his Galilean ministry. The gospel of John relates how Jesus gathered a core of disciples from John the Baptizer's circle and returned with them to Galilee, presumably to his home at Nazareth. Jesus and these disciples accompanied Mary to the marriage in nearby Cana, after which they all went to Capernaum for a short period.

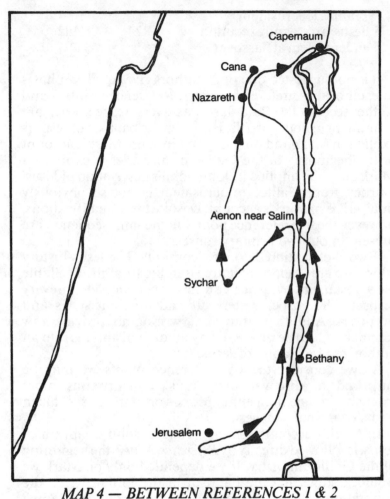

MAP 4 — BETWEEN REFERENCES 1 & 2

The earliest part of Jesus' ministry overlapped the latter of John's ministry. According to John, Jesus visited: Bethany, [Nazareth], Cana, Capernaum, Jerusalem, Aenon, Sychar, [Nazareth], Cana.

Then they journeyed to Jerusalem for the Passover where Jesus dramatically cleared the temple and met Nicodemus. Some time was then spent in Judaea near the Jordan where many people were baptized. To avoid the Pharisees who had come to investigate John and Jesus, Jesus stayed briefly with the Samaritans at Sychar. It is probable that the arrest of John the Baptist occurred at about that time. All this activity means that a considerable period of time, probably more than a year, elapsed between Reference Points 1 and 2, and it is to John, not Mark, that we are indebted for the information.

Reference Point 2, the beginning of Jesus' ministry in Galilee following the arrest of John the Baptist, is dramatically narrated in Mark 1:14-15. Mark gives a vivid and detailed account of the early days of the Galilee ministry in Capernaum. While his account is episodic and incomplete, Mark's numerous brief stories give us a good idea of Jesus' proclaiming and healing activities in Galilee, both in the synagogues and among the multitudes. Because of the extensive character of the ministry in Galilee it is unlikely to have occurred within too brief a period. In my opinion it must have stretched between the summer it began to the spring of a year and a half later.

In John's version only two incidents are related, the healing of the nobleman's son in Galilee and the healing of the cripple at the feast (unspecified) in Jerusalem. We are

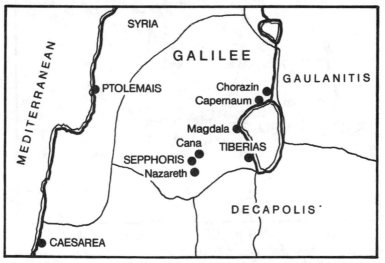

MAP 5 - BETWEEN REFERENCES 2 & 3

The great Galilee ministry lasted about one and a half years, as described in Mark 1-6

given no idea of the passage of time between *Reference Points 2 and 3.*

Reference Point 3, the feeding of the multitude, represents the end and the climax of Jesus' ministry in Galilee. It was the mission of the twelve disciples to the Galilean towns which led the five thousand men to converge on Jesus in the wilderness. Their attempt to force the kingship upon him was greeted with displeasure. The Galilean mission had failed to provoke repentance and had succeeded in making it unsafe for Jesus to remain in the suspicious Herod Antipas' tetrarchy of Galilee. He became a fugitive, constantly on the move — now in the east, now the west, now in the north — in what is sometimes called the "period

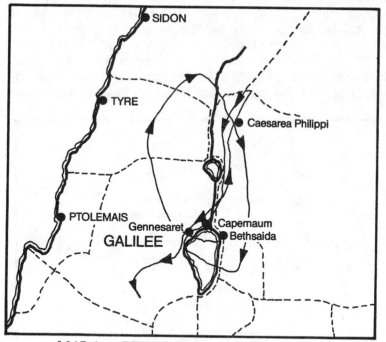

MAP 6 — BETWEEN REFERENCES 3 & 4

Jesus was a fugitive from Herod Antipas for six months after the Galileans attempted to make Jesus King at the Feeding of the Multitude (John 6:14-15). In Mark 6-9 Jesus visits east side of Sea Galilee, Territories of Tyre, Sidon, Decapolis, Dalmanutha, Bethsaida, Caesarea Philippi, Mountain[?Hermon], Capernaum [Nazareth].

of the wanderings". John's account gives no information at all about this part of Jesus' ministry, which was probably of six months' duration.

The last part of the story, between *Reference Points 4*, the final journey from Galilee to Jerusalem, and *5*, Jesus' departure for and death in Jerusalem, is the most difficult of all to reconstruct. The two major sources both contribute information which is not easily reconciled. They agree about Jesus' departure from Galilee (John 7:1,9-10; Mark 9:33; 10:1) and his climactic entry to Jerusalem (John 12:1,12; Mark. 11:11). The problem is: what occurred in between these events? According to Mark, Jesus moved continuously and purposefully from Galilee to Peraea through Jericho up to Jerusalem (9:30-33; 10:1,17,32,46; 11:1,11), in what seems like a period of no more than a few weeks.

John's overall narrative, which must be preferred because of its greater detail, represents a period of about six months, from the feast of Tabernacles (7:2), in the autumn, to the Passover in the following spring. Within that period Jesus went to Jerusalem no less than three times. The first visit (Reference Point 4) was from Galilee to Jerusalem where Jesus stayed, apparently continuously, for the two months between the Feast of Tabernacles and the mid-winter Feast of Dedication (John 7:2-10:22). After the attempt to stone him, he withdrew in hiding to Bethany-in-Peraea (10:40). Jesus' second visit to Jerusalem (Bethany) was on account of the death of his friend Lazarus (11:17). At that time the high priests issued a warrant for his arrest (11:47,53,57) and Jesus withdrew to Ephraim in the wilderness, north-east of Jerusalem. From there he made his final journey (via Jericho?) to Jerusalem shortly before the Passover (11:55-12:1).

It has to be admitted that it is not possible to reconcile exactly John's and Mark's accounts of what happened between Reference Points 4 and 5. In attempting to make sense of the two accounts we suggest that we start by making a cut in Mark's account at the point of Jesus' arrival in Peraea (10:45 cf. 10:1) and the insertion of John's report of Jesus' two visits to and withdrawals from Jerusalem (7:14-

11:54). Both narratives would then proceed together in portraying Jesus making his final journey to Jerusalem, in Mark's case describing Jesus passing through Jericho (John 12:1; Mark 10:46-11:1).

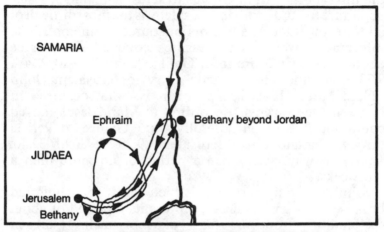

MAP 7 — BETWEEN REFERENCES 5 & 6

Jesus' final six months were spent in Jerusalem (winter) and the Judaean wilderness (spring). According to John 7-11/Mark 10 Jesus visited [Nazareth], Bethany beyond Jordan, Bethany near Jerusalem, Ephraim [Jericho], Jerusalem.

Our next suggestion relates to the events in Jerusalem between Jesus' public arrival there and his arrest a few days later. Mark and John both describe Jesus' triumphal entry, the latter indicating that it occurred five days before the Passover. (Mark 11:1-11; John 12:1,12-19)

John passes over those five days prior to the Passover in silence, apart from the accounts of the Greeks' enquiry about Jesus (12:20-26) and of the voice from Heaven (12:27-50). John then takes us, without further comment, to the meal on the night of the betrayal at which Jesus gave extensive teaching about the way things would be in his prospective absence (chapters 13-17). Clearly there are significant omissions from John's account as compared to Mark's.

Mark narrates in some detail the events of these days. Indeed he makes it clear that Jesus returned from Jerusalem each evening to Bethany. On the first day he arrived in Jerusalem and went into the temple; on the second day he drove out the merchants who traded there. The third day he engaged in debate with the chief priests, Pharisees and Sadducees and prophesied the destruction of the temple. It is not clear from Mark where the third day ended and if, or at which point, a fourth began. What is clear from Mark, unlike John, is that Jesus was very active in the days between his arrival and his arrest.

The major historical problem is that Mark places the exclusion of the temple traders on Jesus' second day in Jerusalem whereas John describes it occurring three years earlier!

The positioning of the clearing of the temple in Mark at Jesus' *last* visit to Jerusalem following his description of the triumphal entry seems secure, and is favoured by most. Nonetheless John's location of the event on the occasion of Jesus' *first* public visit has had its persuasive advocates, most notably J.A.T. Robinson.[1] Is it possible that Jesus cleared the temple twice? Perhaps Jesus spoke against the temple on his first as well as his final visit to Jerusalem; and took some symbolic action against its merchants on both occasions. It may be that the first such clearing was less public, less dramatic than the second. By the time of the final visit, however, Jesus was very well known, not least in view of the dramatic manner in which he entered the city the previous day.

It is entirely feasible that on his first visit to Jerusalem Jesus signalled by word and action the end of the temple. Then, after extensive ministry in Galilee, interrupted by periodic visits to Jerusalem, he came finally to Judaea for a six-month period, which was climaxed by the fateful ride up to Jerusalem and the public clearing of the temple.

The end came swiftly. Within the week of his arrival the Jewish authorities had arrested him and the Roman military governor executed him.

How long was Jesus a public figure? What is the period of time covered by the five reference points we have mentioned? Although the New Testament writers do not specifically address that question, they do provide enough information about the celebration of annual feasts and the passing of the seasons for us to make a reasonably accurate calculation.

We begin by noticing that John refers to *three Passovers* — which occur in spring each year:

when Jesus first cleared the temple and spoke to Nicodemus (2:13, 23-3:21);

when Jesus fed the multitude in the wilderness (6:4); and

when Jesus came to Jerusalem for the "Passover of Death" (12:1).

Mark, far from being limited to a one-year ministry, also refers (by implication) to *three* Passovers or springs:

when Jesus' disciples plucked the grain in Galilee (late spring, early summer) (2:23);

when Jesus fed the multitude in the wilderness ("*green grass*" 6:39);

when Jesus was in Jerusalem for the "Passover of Death" (14:12).

It is immediately obvious that the second and third Passovers in John and Mark coincide. If we could establish that the first reference in both accounts also coincided we would conclude that Jesus' period as a public figure lasted about two years. This, however, is unlikely. According to John, Jesus went from the Passover in Jerusalem to Judaea where his disciples baptized (3:22-26) and from there to a ministry near and in the city of Sychar in Samaria (4:1-42). Jesus' reference to "fields white to harvest" (4:35) suggests late spring/early summer. Thus there simply would not have been time for Jesus to do all that is implied by Mark 1:14-2:22 for the grain-plucking episode to have occurred in the same year Jesus was in Jerusalem-Judaea-Samaria. The spring/summer of the grain-plucking incident must have been in the following year.

According to this reconstruction Mark and John when taken together imply *four* Passovers within the period of Jesus' public ministry, making it of three years' minimum duration. Since John refers to activities of Jesus prior to the first Passover (2:23) we conclude that the ministry of Jesus lasted between three and four years, as in the following table.

Jesus' ministry over summer, autumn, winter, spring seasons

```
SU  A  W  SP  SU  A  W   SP SU A W SP  SU    A   W SP
Peraea Galilee  Judaea    Great Galilee  Wandering   Judaea
  Jn 1-2        Samaria    ministry        Mk 7-9     Jn 7-
                Jn 3-4     Mk 1-6                      11


                First      [Second    Third       Fourth
                Passover   Passover?  Passover    Passover
                Jn 2:13    Spring/    Jn 6:4/     Jn 12:12
                           Summer     Mk 6:39     Mk 14:1
```

According to the Roman historian Tacitus, who wrote soon after the close of the New Testament period "Christûs …suffered the extreme penalty during the reign of Tiberius at the hands of one of our procurators, Pontius Pilate..."[12] With this the gospel writers agree. Each writes that Jesus was executed by the soldiers·of the governor, Pontius Pilate. Luke locates the ministry of John the Baptist, and therefore the ministry of Jesus, in the later part of Tiberius' reign — AD 14–37. (See Luke 3:1-2)

But can we be more precise? Pontius Pilate's prefecture of Judaea lasted from AD 26–36. Therefore the ministry of Jesus occurred within that period. Again we ask, can we pinpoint the dates more exactly?

Establishing New Testament chronology is quite technical and the interested reader is referred to more specialist works for detailed study.[3] Here we will establish the time-frame of Jesus' ministry in five steps.

The first step is to confirm that the day of the week on which Jesus was crucified was a *Friday*. On this each of the gospel writers agree. (Matthew 27:62; 28:1; Mark 15:42; Luke 23:54,56; John 19:31)

The second is to work out on which date in the month this Friday would have occurred. We know that Jesus' death occurred near Passover, and Passover always began with the killing of the lambs on the 14th day of the month of Nisan. The lambs were eaten that evening. The gospel of John indicates that the Friday would have been 14th Nisan in the official temple calendar (19:14,31). (Since Galileans used a different religious calendar, Jesus would have eaten Passover with his disciples earlier, on the Thursday evening, as Mark 14:12 indicates.)

The third step is a mathematical calculation based on the length of Jewish months to establish in which years 14th Nisan fell on a Friday. The relevant possible years are AD 27, 30, 33 and 36. We can eliminate AD 27 and 36 as being too close to the beginning and too close to the end, respectively, of Pilate's term of office (AD 26–36). By process of elimination we are left with either AD 30 or 33. Both dates have their champions.

The fourth step is to bring into focus Luke 3:2, which sets the beginning of John the Baptizer's prophesying in Tiberius' fifteenth year as emperor, and John 2:20 which fixes the date of the first clearing of the temple as forty-six years after its construction began. While the latter is difficult to calculate, there is some confidence in allocating the former to AD 28/29. If we add to AD 28/29 a three- to four-year length ministry we calculate that Jesus was crucified in the spring of AD 33.

The fifth step is to check this against Luke 3:23 which states that Jesus was "about thirty years of age" when he began his ministry. If he was born 7 BC, as suggested earlier, he would by Jewish internal counting method be in his mid-thirties in AD 28/29. Many scholars believe Luke 3:23 to be sufficiently elastic to permit the variance between "about 30 years" and 35/36 years.

Clearly this is a technical matter and one about which there will always be some disagreement. If we opt for Friday, 14th Nisan in AD 33 as the date of Jesus' death, the dates of his public ministry as set out earlier would be:

29				30				31		32			33		
SP	SU	A	W	SP	SU	A	W	SP	SU	W	SP	SU	A	W	SP
Peraea	Galilee			Judaea				Great Galilee		Wander-			Judaea		
				Samaria				Ministry		ing					
				First				[Second		Third			Fourth		
				Passover				Passover]		Passover			Passover		

If this option is correct — that Jesus died on 14th Nisan AD 33 — it follows that he was baptized by John in AD 29 and began his ministry in Galilee in the later summer of AD 30.

Having set the chronology of the Jesus-history, we can now proceed to establish the *historical* and *geographical* context.

The primary sources Mark and John contain considerable information which ties their respective gospels into the period and the landscape of Roman Palestine, when Pontius Pilate was prefect.

For example, in the gospel of Mark, there are references to details of known *historical events and people*:

1 The arrest of John the Baptizer (1:14) a prophet of the time known also through the writings of Josephus;[4]

2 The opposition of the Pharisees (2:16), a religious faction referred to by Josephus;[5]

3 The decision that Jesus must die was plotted by the Pharisees and the Herodians (3:6 cf. 12:13), a group not otherwise referred to, but whose existence as a political party is not seriously doubted;

4 The. former marriage of Herodias to Philip, brother of her new husband Herod Antipas (6:17) which Josephus confirms. (That Mark calls the former husband "Philip" and Josephus calls him "Herod"[6] may be a discrepancy more apparent than real. Descendants of Herod the Great were often called "Herod" in addition to, for example, Philip.)

5 The execution of John the Baptizer by Herod Antipas (6:16) is a detail confirmed by Josephus;[7]
6 The imprisonment of rebels, notably Barabbas, who were held in Jerusalem for murder committed in the insurrection (15:7) — public disturbances during Pilate's prefecture are referred to at length by Josephus.[8]

Not found in Mark but in the source peculiar to Luke ("L") are several further contemporary events.

7 The famous census in Judaea conducted by Quirinius, military legate of Syria (Luke 2:2);
8 Luke's reference to the beginning of the ministry of John the Baptizer in the fifteenth year of the emperor Tiberius' rule when Pilate was governor of Judaea and Antipas, Philip and Lysanias were tetrarchs respectively of Galilee, Iturea, and Abilene (Luke 3:1) is a detailed and precise historical statement;
9 Prefect Pontius Pilate's slaughter of Galileans while they were sacrificing Passover lambs in Jerusalem (Luke 13:1) is consistent with the problems encountered during Pilate's prefecture, as described by Josephus (see note 8);
10 The collapse of a tower at Siloam, killing eighteen people (Luke 13:4) is not at all improbable in that a watch tower would be needed in the vulnerable area of Siloam near the base of the Kidron Valley, to the south of the city.

The gospel of Mark also gives authentic geographical, topographical and architectural contexts for the *movements* of Jesus — in fact the detail is extraordinary when it is remembered that this is the shortest of the gospels:

1 The existence of Nazareth is now confirmed through archaeological discovery in 1962[9]. Prior to that time many scholars had doubted the existence of Nazareth;
2 The movements of Jesus from the banks of the Jordan river after his baptism (1:9) into Galilee (1:14),

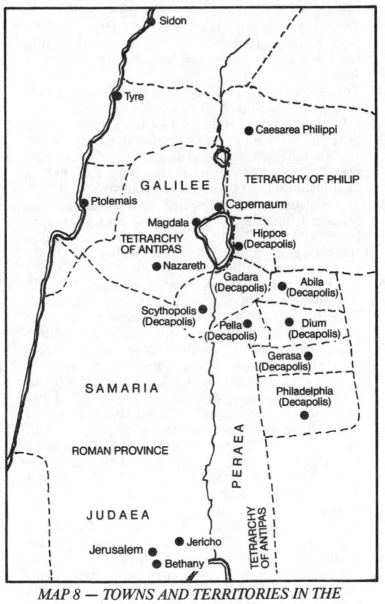

MAP 8 — TOWNS AND TERRITORIES IN THE GOSPEL OF MARK

specifically to Capernaum (1:21) near the Sea of Galilee (1:16), can be easily traced on a map;

3 There are ruins of a synagogue in Capernaum (1:21) from a later period, but it is more than likely that there was a synagogue there from before the time of Jesus;

4 The house of Simon and Andrew at Capernaum is frequently referred to in this gospel (1:29; 2:1; 7:17; 9:33) as the base for Jesus' Galilean ministry and the tradition that the lowest section of the Byzantine church adjacent to the synagogue in Capernaum was "Peter's house" rests on evidence that is circumstantial but by no means improbable;[10]

5 The tension which is implied between his natural Nazareth household and the adopted Capernaum household (3:21,31-34; 6:1-6) is a family detail which rings true as part of the background to Jesus' Galilean ministry;[11]

6 The various withdrawals from Capernaum (1:38; 3:7; 7:24) to regions out of Antipas' tetrarchy suggest that Capernaum was chosen as a base because it was near the border between Antipas and Philip's tetrarchies;

7 References to Jesus' travels throughout all Galilee preaching in their synagogues are remarkably coherent in relation to the known geography of Galilee. (Presumably most of the "two hundred and four cities and villages" referred to by Josephus would have had their own synagogues.[12] Three of these "cities", Chorazin, Bethsaida and Capernaum mentioned in the "Q" Source (Matthew 11:20-23 = Luke 10:13-15) are within four or five miles of each other near the northern extremity of the Sea of Galilee.);

8 Mark's fifteen references to the Sea of Galilee, to boats and to fishing (1:16) are consistent with the size of the sea and the known activities of the people living on its shores. (The ancient town on its southern shores, Tarichaea, has a name which means "pickled fish" suggesting that a fishing industry operated from there.);

9 While there is a problem with the location of the country of the Gerasenes (5:1) on the eastern shore of the sea, the presence of a herd of pigs (5:11,14) is entirely consistent with the Gentile Decapolis region (5:20). (Decapolis, which means "ten cities", was a Greek-speaking region located to the east of the lower part of the Sea of Galilee and to the west of the upper part of the Jordan River.);

10 A network of Herodian supporters and spies (3:6) reported all unusual or suspicious events to the tetrarch based in Tiberias. This is confirmed by the matter-of-fact report that the twelve disciples' teaching in the villages of Galilee (6:7) had come to Antipas' attention (6:14);

11 There are several positions on the north-eastern side of the Sea which fit in with the gospel references to the feeding of the multitude. This general area has mountains (6:46), is near the water (John 6:23), and is within running distance of Bethsaida, the rendezvous point after the mission of the twelve which attracted Antipas' attention (Luke 9:10). A technical point: to compensate for the current of the Jordan entering the north of the sea (in the spring), to have arrived at Gennesaret (6:53) it would have been necessary to steer initially towards Bethsaida (6:45) — the Greek *pros* means "towards" which doesn't necessarily mean "to". Bethsaida;

12 The attempt to make Jesus "king" (of Galilee) at the feeding of the multitude (John 6:15) made it necessary for him to avoid further public exposure in the tetrarchy of Antipas; from then on Jesus either travelled outside Antipas' region — Tyre and Sidon (7:24), the Decapolis (7:31), Bethsaida (Philip's capital 8:22), Caesarea Philippi (8:27) — or remained out of sight within it (9:30,33; 10:1) — the strange route taken from the region of Tyre through Sidon to the Sea of Galilee through the Decapolis (7:31), which is sometimes cited as evidence of Mark's inaccuracy, is actually quite logical in the circumstances. (Mark's frequent reference to "the

territory" (Greek: *horia*) of the Decapolis (5:17) of Tyre and Sidon (7:24 cf. 7:21) and of Judaea (Mark 10:1) relates accurately to the political boundaries of that region. Independent cities like Tyre and Sidon and the cities of the Decapolis like Gadara were centres of autonomous "regions", with their own boundaries. The writer of the gospel of Mark is aware of these boundaries. He does not say that Jesus went to Tyre and Sidon, but that he crossed the boundaries of their territories.);

13 Jesus' final move towards Jerusalem as recorded by Mark follows the route Galileans usually took to avoid passing through Samaria; Galilean pilgrims travelled down the Jordan Valley through Jericho up to Jerusalem, a much longer journey than the more direct route through Samaria. Thus from Caesarea Philippi in the north (8:27) he passed through Galilee (9:30), came to Capernaum (9:33), left there and went to the region of Judaea beyond Jordan (10:1), was on the road going up to Jerusalem (10:32) coming to Jericho (10:46) and, finally, leaving Jericho. . . drew near to Jerusalem (10:46; 11:1). The details of the journey from Caesarea to Jerusalem are geographically consistent;

14 The description of Jesus' last days in Jerusalem provides a wealth of geographical detail; approaching Jerusalem he passed the villages of Bethphage and Bethany towards the Mount of Olives (11:1). From there he entered Jerusalem and went into the vast temple area (11:1); each evening he returned the three miles to Bethany (11:11,12; 14:3) where presumably he resided with Lazarus, Martha and Mary (John 12:1); his followers commented on the *massive stones* and the wonderful buildings (13:1) of the temple and looking across from the Mount of Olives he prophesied the details of its destruction (13:2ff); Passover was observed in a large upper room (14:15), from which he walked to the Mount of Olives (14:26); from there he went to a garden across the Kidron (John 18:1) which presumably was

Gethsemane (14:32) where he was arrested; Jesus was interrogated in the house of the high priest (14:53) in the upper, south western part of the city, from which he was taken nearby to Herod's palace used by Pilate as his *praetorium* or barracks (15:16); Jesus was crucified outside the northern/western walls in a place of skull-like formation known as *Golgotha* (15:22,29).

The gospel of John is no less rich in specific details about people and places.

John's references to *people* include:

1   John the Baptizer whose activities, as we have already noted, were well known to Josephus — this gospel alone informs us that Jesus' first disciples had originally belonged to John's circle and that both John's and Jesus' baptizing activities ran in parallel for a period (3:22–4:2);

2   Nicodemus the leading Pharisee and Sanhedrin member (3:1,7,50; 10:38,39) is probably the same person as Naqdimon the notable rabbi referred to in later Jewish literature;[13]

3   Mark does not give the name of the high priest under whom Jesus was executed but John identifies him as Caiaphas and also notes tht he was the son-in-law of Annas, the founding patriarch of that high-priestly dynasty (18:13) (Neither Josephus nor any other New Testament source discloses this relationship.);

4   Pontius Pilate is now known to us as "prefect" of Judaea through an inscription discovered at Caesarea Maritima in 1962 — he had long been known from references in Philo and Josephus as a ruthless governor bent on harassing his Judaean subjects — but it is only John who reveals that the high priests actually blackmailed Pilate by suggesting that he would not be Caesar's friend if he released the self-styled "king of the Jews" (19:12 cf. 19:3); "Friendship (*amicitia*) to one's superiors, that is strict political loyalty, was well known in Roman political practice

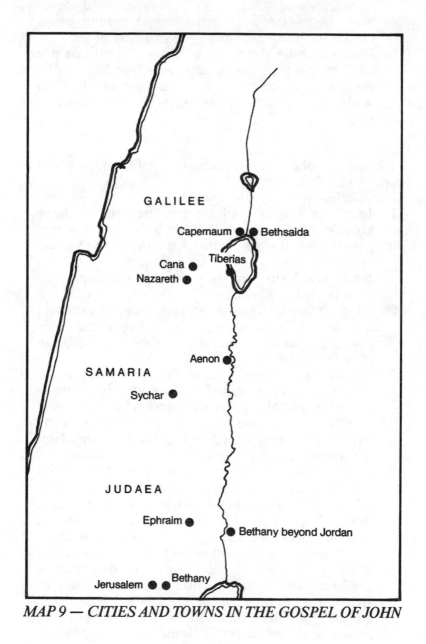

MAP 9 — CITIES AND TOWNS IN THE GOSPEL OF JOHN

— of the four evangelists John alone reveals that it was the obligations of *amicitia* rather than weakness of character which led Pilate to give in to the high priests.

John's *geographical* and *topographical* references are even more detailed:

1   He indicates that John the Baptizer engaged in his ministry in the Jordan River, specifically at "Bethany beyond Jordan" (1:28; 10:40) and at "Aenon near Salim" (3:23). The context in 3:26 suggests that if Bethany was on the further side of Jordan, Aenon was on the Judaean side;

2   John's description of Jesus' return to Galilee via Samaria in order to evade the Pharisees is remarkably detailed (4:1-4) — thus he came to the city of Sychar close by Joseph's field, Jacob's well (4:5) and Mt Gerizim (4:20) (The modern tourist is able to visit a well in a church in Nablus, a city under the shadow of Mt Gerizim, with the strong confidence that this is the very location of Jesus' encounter with the Samaritan woman. Mt Gerizim is, to this day, the cultic centre of the Samaritan high priest.);

3   The Cana of Galilee, referred to twice in the Gospel of John (2:1; 4:46) is also known to us in the writings of Josephus.[14] John's threefold reference to "coming down" from Cana to Capernaum (4:47,49,51) accords well with the topography. Cana is in the high Galilean plateau land, just north of Nazareth; Capernaum is by the Galilean Sea, two hundred metres below (Mediterranean) sea level;

4   John's indication that Jesus went "up to Jerusalem" from Capernaum (2:13) is exactly in accordance with the known topography;

5   The pool with five porches called Bethesda or Bethzatha "near the sheep gate" (5:2) has been confidently identified as the excavated pool complex with a surviving archway/porch within St Anne's monastery near the eastern wall of old Jerusalem;

6   The Pool of Siloam to which Jesus sent the blind man

    (9:11) is almost certainly located to the south of the temple mount at or near the exit of Hezekiah's tunnel;

7   Jesus' shelter from the wintry weather in the portico of Solomon in the temple precincts is entirely consistent with the occasion, namely the Feast of Dedication (10:22-23) or *Hanukah* which occurs in December; snowfalls in Jerusalem at that time of year are not uncommon;

8   Jesus' withdrawal from Jerusalem to the "country near the wilderness, to a town called Ephraim" (11:54) occurred at a time when his life was in danger (We may take it to have been in the general region of the tribe of Ephraim which was to the north-east of Jerusalem, towards the Jordan valley — this was and is "country near the wilderness".);

9   Bethany, the home of Lazarus, Martha and Mary said to be only two miles from Jerusalem (11:18), is the modern village of Eizariya on the road to Jericho;

10 John's topographic references in Jerusalem during Jesus' last days are specific — after the Passover meal he crossed the Kidron Valley, to a garden (18:1); on his arrest he was taken in turn to the house of Annas (18:13) and Caiaphas (18:28), both of which were located in the upper city, in the south-west quarter.

Jesus was then handed over to Pilate in the praetorium or barracks, located in what had previously been Herod's palace (18:28). Josephus describes a scene in front of this building thirty years later which bears a close resemblance to the trial of Jesus, as described by John.

Florus [the governor] lodged at the palace and on the following day had a tribunal [*bema* cf Matthew 27:19, John 19:13] placed in front of the building and took his seat; the chief priests, the nobles and the most eminent citizens then presented themselves before the tribunal.[15]

John's mention of the *Praetorium* (18:28 = "palace" Mark 15:16), the tribunal, the chief priests and other notables and the governor's decision to crucify is strikingly corroborated in Josephus' passage.

John, however, gives more detail than Josephus. Acc-

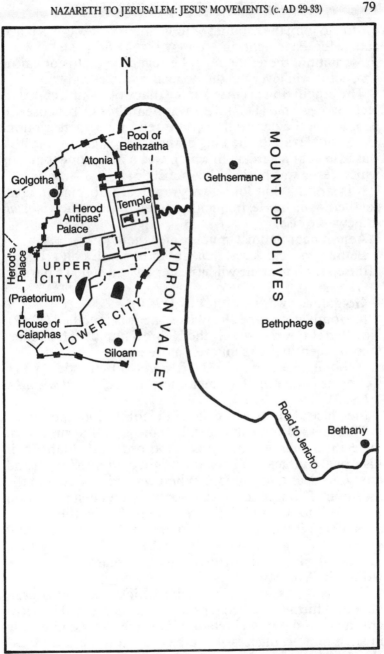

N

Pool of
Bethzatha

Atonia

Golgotha

Herod
Antipas'
Palace

Temple

Herod's
Palace

UPPER
CITY

(Praetorium)

House of
Caiaphas

LOWER CITY

Siloam

KIDRON VALLEY

MOUNT OF OLIVES

Gethsemane

Bethphage

Road to Jericho

Bethany

MAP 10 — JERUSALEM IN MARK AND JOHN

ording to John the tribunal or judgement seat was at a place called the Pavement, in Hebrew *Gabbatha* (19:13). John's presentation, therefore, must be regarded as historical in character, whatever the theological nuances may be.

The crucifixion occurred at the place of a skull, called in Hebrew *Golgotha* (19:17). This was near the city because the people (on the city walls?) could read the superscription, "Jesus of Nazareth, the king of the Jews" (19:20). Golgotha was also near a garden, in which was a new stone tomb, in which Jesus was buried. (19:41 cf 20:15)

It is striking that John's geographical information is as detailed as it is. He frequently notes that a place is *near* somewhere else,

Aenon near Salim. . .much water there (3:23);
Bethany. . .near Jerusalem, about two miles off (11:18);
the country near the wilderness. . .a town called Ephraim (11:54);
Golgotha. . .was near the city (19:20);
the tomb was near. . .the place. . .he was crucified (19:42).

He often chooses to supply the Hebrew name for locations, thereby identifying them even more exactly —

a pool in Hebrew called *Bethzatha* (or Bethesda) (5:2);
a place called the Pavement, and in Hebrew, *Gabbatha* (19:13);
the place of the skull. . .called in Hebrew *Golgotha* (19:17).

This mass of contextual detail in the gospel records must raise fundamental questions for those who doubt their historical character. What is the origin of this historical and topographical information? When was it inserted into the tradition? The sceptical would reply that it must have been inserted into the tradition later rather than earlier. If one asks where it was added the answer would be: in places outside Palestine. It is widely believed that the gospel named after Mark was written in Rome, whereas John's was written in Asia Minor.

How is it possible for material which was added even later and further away to reproduce in such detail the geographical and physical relationships of places and people in such remote, inaccessible areas as Galilee and Judaea? How would the inserters of such information know that one went "down" from Cana to Capernaum and "up" from the Jordan valley to Jerusalem? How would anyone but a witness writing in Rome or Ephesus decades later know of "the Herodians", or "the insurrection", or that Caiaphas was Annas' son-in-law? Such information is not found in Josephus or any other source known to us.

Details such as these — and we have only mentioned a few — simply could not be contrived later and elsewhere. The details are intrinsic to the context of the Jesus history as it was remembered by participants and told from the beginning.

Further reading to Chapter Three:

C. Blomberg, *The Historical Reliability of the Gospels*, IVP, Leicester, 1987.

A.E. Harvey, *Jesus and the Constraints of History*, Duckworth, London, 1982.

J. Jeremias, *Jerusalem in the Time of Jesus*, SCM: London, 1969.

J.A.T. Robinson, *Redating the New Testament*, SCM, London, 1976.

———*The Priority of John*. SCM, London, 1985.

G.N. Stanton, *Jesus of Nazareth in New Testament Preaching*, CUP, London, 1974.

E. Stauffer, *Jesus and His Story*, Knopf, New York, 1974.

G. Dalman, *Sacred Sites and Ways*, S.P.C.K., London, 1935.

Notes
[1] See J.A.T. Robinson, *Priority*, 123-157.

[2] *Annals*, 15, 44:2-5.

[3] e.g. J. Finegan, *Handbook of Biblical Chronology* (Princeton University Press, Princeton, 1964), H. Hoehner, *Chronological Aspects of the Life of Christ*, Zondervan: Grand Rapids, 1977.

[4] *AJ*, xviii, 116-119.

[5] *BJ*, ii, 162-163 *AJ* xviii, 12-15.

[6] *AJ*, xviii, 136.

[7] *AJ*, xviii, 119.

[8]*BJ*, ii, 169-177, *AJ* xviii, 55-62.

[9]See J. Finegan, *The Archeology of the New Testament I*, Princeton University Press, Princeton, 1978, p.29.

[10]"Has the House where Jesus stayed in Capernaum been found?" in *Biblical Archaeology Review* viii/6 1982, 26-37.

[11]See further P.W. Barnett, *Is the New Testament History?* Hodder & Stoughton, Sydney, 1986, 89-90.

[12]*BJ*, iii, 42, *Vita* 235.

[13]See J.A.T. Robinson, *The Priority of John*, 283-7.

[14]*Vita*, 86.

[15]*BJ*, ii, 301.

4
Nazareth to Jerusalem: Jesus' Teaching (c. AD 29-33)

None of the context or even the flow of the Jesus-story has any significance apart from the character, personality and significance of Jesus himself — without the power of his teaching and his example there would be no New Testament story to trace.

Jesus had an astonishing impact on those who heard him speak. Josephus, writing more than sixty years later, commented "He. . .was a teacher (*didaskalos*) of such people as accept the truth gladly".[1] According to the Talmud, "Yeshu. . .enticed Israel to apostasy".[2] Behind this negative comment we may discern a powerful teacher. However these are but faint echoes of the reactions recorded in the New Testament of those who heard Jesus speak — whether in the synagogue, in the open, or in the temple. In each gospel Jesus is characteristically referred to as "teacher" (*didaskalos*), or "rabbi".

Mark notes the effect of Jesus' speaking in the synaagogues of Capernaum and Nazareth. At Capernaum those present were "astonished at his teaching for he taught them as one who had authority, and not as the scribes" (1:22). In Nazareth, "Many who heard him were astonished, saying, 'Where did this man get all this? What is the wisdom given to him?'" (6:2). Jesus must have had exceptional qualities as a synagogue teacher to provoke this kind of reaction.

Mark also states that Jesus taught very large crowds of Galileans in the open, beside the Sea of Galilee. So great were the numbers that it was necessary, on one occasion, for Jesus to speak to them from a boat. (4:2 cf 3:9)

John refers to Jesus' debates with the religious leaders in the temple. The Judaeans looked forward to his coming to Jerusalem for the feasts (7:11) and they marvelled at Jesus' debating skills despite his lack of formal education from the rabbis (7:15). The temple officers were sent to seize him, which they were not able to do. They reported back to the chief priests and the Pharisees, "No man ever spoke like this". (7:46)

The evidence from the gospels reveals that Jesus was a very impressive public teacher, able to adapt his method to suit his audience, whether in the synagogue, in the open or in the temple.

Modern day readers of the Bible naturally wish to know how his hearers were able to remember and record what Jesus said in such detail. How do we know that what we read is what Jesus said? Several factors probably contributed to the disciples' recollection of Jesus' words.

First, unlike the scribes who quoted other scribes' opinions, Jesus spoke authoritatively. Characteristically he said "I say unto you". Mark notes that on a number of occasions Jesus looked right around at the group to which he was speaking.[3] Jesus had a commanding presence and he spoke simply and very directly.

Second, Jesus was a very skilful teacher. He used colourful images and seldom spoke in abstractions. More than seventy parables, long and short, have been preserved in the gospels. These testify to Jesus' brilliance as a communicator. Aramaic scholars believe that many of Jesus' teachings were delivered originally in poetic, easily memorable forms.[4]

Third, if the sayings of lesser rabbis than Jesus are found authentically in the Mishnah why should it be doubted that Jesus' words would have been accurately recalled in the gospels. The gospels are closer in time to Jesus than the Mishnah is to the leading rabbis, Hillel and Shammai, who are quoted so frequently. Hillel and Shammai lived before Jesus; the Mishnah was written more than a century after the latest of the New Testament books. It is a fact that rabbis, including Jesus, had skills of teaching and their hearers skills of remembering, the precise technical details of which are now lost. There is good reason to believe that many of the sayings of Jesus had been assembled as a body of oral teaching within two decades of his crucifixion. Certainly the apostle Paul's letters written in the fifties contain many allusions to the teachings of Jesus.[5]

A fourth reason Jesus' words were remembered may have been that they were so powerful in their impact on the living situation of the hearers. Jesus did not speak in generalities; he addressed people directly. He declared that God's kingdom was now upon them, present in his words and deeds and that life and death decisions had to be made then and there. It should be noted that Jesus was executed not so much for what he did, as for what he said about his identity and mission. His words provoked passionate loyalty or intense opposition.

Fifth, the earliest community of believers were aware of the presence of the Holy Spirit, promised by Jesus, helping them to remember and understand what Jesus had said. On several occasions John states that the disciples did not understand Jesus' actions and words at the time. It was only after the first Easter that the disciples understood what Jesus did and said at the clearing of the temple (2:22) and when he rode up to Jerusalem six days before the final Passover (12:16). This coincides with Jesus' teaching that the Holy Spirit, when he came, would bring to their "remembrance" all that he had taught them (14:26).

On view here, in the period after Easter, is the experience of the earliest Christians, remembering and understanding the words of the Lord. The significance and meaning of what Jesus taught was now understood by them — through the work of the Spirit of God among them.

As we have seen, the gospels state that Jesus was a teacher; they often portray him teaching and debating. But what did he teach? Our problem here is that so many parables, sayings and teachings are recorded for us in the gospels that we do not know where to begin. Not only are Jesus' teachings extensive, more significantly, his doctrines are so profound that it is extremely difficult for the human mind to encompass them. It is sufficient for our purpose to select six elements of Jesus' message which give some perspective on its almost immeasurable length, breadth and height. Even so we will focus on Jesus' words only as they relate to himself. His teachings on numerous other subjects will not be discussed here.

1 Fulfilment

Jesus declared that two closely related things were now fulfilled by his coming and ministry — the Law and the Prophets (our Old Testament) and Time. The Old Testament projected forward from its pages what the apostle Paul called in retrospect "the promises of God" (2 Corinthians 1:20). The prophets of Israel characteristically looked at the future when Yahweh their God would act decisively and finally. Thus, for example, Yahweh said through Jeremiah "Behold the days are coming when I will make a new covenant with the house of Israel" (31:31). Repeatedly Yahweh said "it will come about after this that I will..." or, "in that day I will..." or, "a day is coming when".

We know from incidental information in the New Testament that the period in which Jesus lived was a time of heightened expectation of the fulfilment of the promises of God. Men and women were "looking for" all that God had promised to come to pass at that time. The aged Simeon was "looking for the consolation of Israel" and the prophetess Anna was among those "looking for the redemption of Jerusalem" (Luke 2:25, 38). When John the Baptizer began his work the religious leaders in Jerusalem sent officials to enquire if he was the Messiah, Elijah or the Prophet, each of whom was expected to appear at the promised moment (John 1:19-21). There was great diversity of opinion among the Jews as to which of his prophesied agents Yahweh would send or what precisely would happen. However there was widespread agreement that God was about to send *someone* who would do *something* final in salvation and judgement.

It must have been an electrifying moment, therefore, when Jesus stood in his home synagogue in Nazareth, read from Isaiah 61, "The Spirit of the Lord is upon me because he has anointed me...sent me..." and then declared, "Today this Scripture has been fulfilled in your hearing" (Luke 4:21). Mark records that Jesus began his Galilean ministry by proclaiming "The time is fulfilled" (1:15). Matthew quotes Jesus as announcing "I have come to...fulfil" (the Law and the Prophets) (5:17). In other words, Jesus was convinced that at that very moment Yahweh was acting through him, Jesus, to bring to fulfilment all that had been promised in the Law and the Prophets.

It is illuminating to take note of the frequency with which Jesus quotes from or refers to the Old Testament. The gospel of Mark, for example, contains fifty-seven such quotations from or references by Jesus, to the Old Testament. We may notice, for example, that Jesus acknowledges Isaiah's writings on thirteen occasions (three of which come from Isaiah 53) followed by Daniel's writings on eight occasions (three of which come from Daniel 7:13). The Psalms and Zechariah are both quoted on six occasions each.

It is of the greatest importance to note that from the beginning of the post-Easter period the earliest Christians proclaimed Jesus as the fulfilment of the Law and the Prophets. In what is the oldest part of the New Testament, an oral fragment given to Paul on becoming a believer, but which preceded Paul's conversion, we hear the living voice of the primitive evangelists "Christ died for our sins, in accordance with the scripture...he was raised on the third day in accordance with the scriptures" (1 Corinthians 15:3-4). Later Paul wrote in his own words "For all the promises of God find their Yes in him [the Son of God, Jesus Christ, whom we proclaimed among you]" (2 Corinthians 1:19-20). How did these first believers become convinced that the scriptures were now fulfilled? This can only have come to them from Jesus' own teachings, which were confirmed to them by his resurrection from the dead.

2 Identity
One of Jesus' most striking sayings is, "Whoever receives me receives him who sent me." (Mark 9:37)

Jesus was convinced that he was "sent" by God, as God's

representative or "apostle" and that to receive him was to receive the One who sent him.

Jesus uses the "sent" vocabulary in other contexts. When asked by the chief priests for his authority in acting the way he did in clearing the temple Jesus replied in the pointed allegory of the vineyard. The owner of the vineyard (=God) sent servants (=prophets) to the tenants (=religious leaders). Then, Jesus continued, "He (=God) still had one other, a beloved Son; finally he sent him saying "They will respect my Son". (Mark 12:6)

Here Jesus is referring to himself. He is "sent" by God, as we have seen above. But more than that, he specifically discloses that he is, in God's eyes, "beloved Son...my Son". Jesus' awareness of himself as God's Son emerges at many points in his teachings. The day of the coming of the Son of man is not known to "the Son" but only to "the Father" (Mark 13:32). The "Son of God" was one of the ways of referring to Israel's messiah. But Jesus meant much more by his use of this word. He implied that an intimate and exclusive filial-paternal relationship existed between himself and God. He said, "All things have been delivered to me by my Father; and no one knows the Son except the Father and no one knows the Father except the Son (Matthew 11:26-27; see also John 5:19-20). How different Jesus' sonship was from that of the mystical rabbis Geza Vermes describes. Honi, for example, who lived in the preceding century, could only say "Lord of the Universe... I am as a Son of the house before thee".[5a] Neither Honi nor Hanina (a few years after Jesus) makes the unique, exclusive claim to be *the* Son that Jesus does.

The Aramaic word *Abba*, meaning "father" in an affectionate, domestic sense, is the very word Jesus used in conversation with God. It was used rarely by Jews, if at all, in reference to God. The word *Abba* as Jesus' actual means of address to God survives in Paul's letter to the Greek-speaking Christians in far away Galatia and Rome. (Romans 8:15; Galatians 4:6)

The Old Testament referred to the temple as the "House of the Lord". But Jesus — even as a twelve-year-old — referred to the temple as his Father's house (Luke 2:49;

John 2:16 compare Zechariah 14:21)
The writer of the fourth gospel shows special interest in and deep understanding of Jesus' identity, which he expresses in Jesus' own words. There is nothing in this gospel about Jesus as the Son, however, which is not found in other gospels. Perhaps the frequency of the references suggest that Jesus' words struck a particular chord with John. Jesus speaks of himself as, "him whom [God] has sent" (5:38; 6:29) and says that, "I came forth from God...he sent me" (8:42). In Jesus' understanding he was God's Holy One, "consecrated and sent to the world" (10:36). Jesus refers to God as "the Father who sent me" (5:36 cf 6:57; 10:36). On one occasion Jesus said: "I know him, for I come from him, and he sent me" (7:29).

Again it is of great importance to notice the attitudes of the earliest Jewish Christians on this matter. According to Peter, Jesus was the "Holy" and "Righteous One", God's "Anointed One", his servant or child whom he sent to Israel (Acts 3:14, 18, 26). From whom did Peter acquire these ways of speaking about Jesus? Again the answer must be that Peter learned to think of Jesus in these ways from Jesus himself. As we have seen, Jesus referred to himself as God's Son, "sent" into the world, his "Holy One" (see John 10:36). We conclude that what Jesus taught about his identity and mission was the source of what the early Christians said about him.

3 Purpose
Not only does Jesus say, "I was sent", on many occasions he also says, "I came". The two statements are closely related. Jesus "came" because he was "sent", as God's Son, to Israel. In turn, this is closely connected to Jesus' claim to be the fulfilment of Yahweh's many promises, spoken through the prophets. Within the timetable of God this was the divinely ordained moment. At precisely the right time Jesus *came* because he was *sent* by God, to do God's will and to fulfil his purpose.

Jesus, however, does not merely say "I came" but "I came that..." or "I came to..." His utterances are heavy with a sense of purpose and intention. For example:

I came. . .that I may proclaim [the kingdom of God]
(Mark 1:38, 15);
[The Lord] anointed me to preach good news to the poor.
He sent me to proclaim release to captives, recovering of
sight to the blind, to set at liberty those who are oppressed.
(Luke 4:18-19);
I was sent. . .to the lost sheep of the house of Israel.
(Matthew 15:24);
I came. . .to call. . .sinners. (Mark 2:17);
The Son of man came to seek and to save the lost. (Luke
19:10);
I came. . .to cast a fire upon the earth. (Luke 12:49);
The Son of man came. . .to give his life a ransom for many.
(Mark 10:45)

Clearly Jesus was a man of powerful purpose. But what
was that purpose? What did Jesus come to do? What mission did he believe God had sent him to fulfil?

It is no use simply to give a list of Jesus' statements of
purpose, as above. These must be placed within the context
of Jesus' carefully phased ministry. In broad terms, the
hinge on which that ministry turns is the fateful Passover
feeding of the multitude in Galilee. (Mark 6:30-45)
Everything Jesus said and did must be seen as coming
before or after that event.

During the earlier phase, Jesus summoned the people of
Israel to welcome and gratefully receive God's kingdom
(=His sovereign rule) which, in Jesus' announcement, had
now drawn near. This was a humbling message for the
Jewish people since Jesus did not refer to them in élitist or
triumphalist terms, as God's favoured people, but pitifully,
as "poor. . .captive. . .blind. . .oppressed" and as "lost sheep".
Unlike many of the Jewish writings of that period which
spoke of God's intervention for his people against the
Gentiles in terms of a great, last battle to be fought and won
by God's people led by a military messiah, Jesus used the
language of mercy, healing and reconciliation. He spoke of
himself as a physician, come to heal.

Jesus' friendship with social outcasts, the downtrodden
and the disabled and his numerous healings and exorcisms
show that the kingdom of God as proclaimed by Jesus was

one of grace and restoration, fulfilling in particular the great promises of the prophet Isaiah (27:17-20; 35:3-6; 42:1-7; 61:1-3; 65:17-20). Jesus' message, proclaimed first by him, then by his twelve disciples in their mission to Galilee, was widely heard but not welcomed by the people at large. From the beginning Jesus knew that death awaited him and that the people would not recognise him on his terms as the merciful king he truly was. The Parable of the Deceased Bridegroom, spoken early in his ministry, reflects Jesus' understanding that he would soon be taken away from them by death. (Mark 2:20)

During the latter, year-long phase of the ministry subsequent to the feeding of the multitude, Jesus spoke repeatedly about his imminent humiliation and death, which he said would be redemptive in its effects (Mark 10:45). At the same time Jesus pronounced the judgement of God on Israel since she failed to recognise the one who had been sent to her. The land would be invaded by the Gentiles, Jerusalem's walls would be trampled down, and her holy shrine, the temple, destroyed. The cursing of the fig-tree, the clearing of the temple and the splitting of the temple curtain were concrete signs pointing to the end of proud and unrepentant Israel. In the mercy of God, however, this would be the opportunity for the Gentiles to be incorporated in the people of God. The vineyard would be given to others (Mark 12:9), the gospel proclaimed to all nations (=Gentiles Mark 13:10).

It is clear, therefore, that Jesus did not come to bring some kind of political solution for Israel's problems with the inclusion of the Gentiles as an afterthought invented by the early church, as some scholars suggest. The kingdom of God proclaimed by and embodied in Jesus' concrete actions was for the restoration of humanity as a whole, beginning with God's historic people Israel, who paradoxically refused to recognise the identity and mission of the One sent by God for her salvation.

As we consider further these "I came to" statements we notice a very close relationship between Jesus' statements of purpose and his actions. His work embodied his words, as these four examples show.

First, Jesus not only said he came to fulfil the Law and the Prophets; he did certain things to bring that fulfilment to pass. His riding up to Jerusalem on a young ass and clearing of the traders from the temple actualized two prophecies from Zechariah (9:9 and 14:21). Jesus' actions deliberately and consciously fulfilled the Law and the Prophets; that is what he came to do.

Second, not only did Jesus come to proclaim the arrival of the kingdom of God he was himself, by what he did, the very presence of the kingdom of God among men and women. On one occasion, referring to his frequent expulsion of demons, he said, "If it is by the finger of God that I cast out demons then the kingdom of God has come upon you." (Matthew 12:28; Luke 11:20)

Again, when John the Baptizer queried whether Jesus was the "One who (was) to come" Jesus' reply was, "Tell John what you hear and see: the blind receive their sight and the lame walk, lepers are cleansed and the deaf hear, and the dead are raised up. . ." (Matthew 11:4-5). Jesus' deeds, about which he reminded John, were in fulfilment of Isaiah who prophesied ". . .your God will come. . .to save you. . .then will the eyes of the blind be opened. . .the ears of the deaf unstopped. . .the lame leap like a deer. . .the mute tongue shout for joy" (35:4-6)

In other words, Jesus claimed by these miracles that the long-awaited "coming" of God prophesied by Isaiah was now a reality. The exorcisms and miracle-healing of Jesus demonstrate the truth of his words that the kingdom of God had arrived.

A third example of Jesus' actions embodying his stated purpose was his deliberate fellowship with the outcasts and downtrodden of that society. He said, "I came to call not the righteous but sinners. . ." (Mark 2:17). Sinners were those who pursued immoral lifestyles (e.g. prostitutes) or who practised despised occupations (e.g. tax collectors). But it was probably applied by the Pharisees to those whom they regarded as undisciplined in the keeping of the Law. The Pharisees' attitude to such people is well expressed in their words recorded by John. "This multitude which does not know the law is accursed" (John 7:49). To Pharisaic leaders,

based as they were in Jerusalem, Galileans typified this
ignorance of the Law. A later tradition may well reflect
Pharisaic opinion from the time of Jesus, "Galilee, Galilee,
you hate the Torah."[6] But it was with these disreput-
able, despised, ill-educated and morally lax people, as the
Pharisees saw them, that Jesus identified himself.

At that time eating together was a sacred fellowship,
hallowed by thanksgiving to Yahweh. Thus Jews would not
eat with Gentiles (Acts 10:28 cf. Galatians 2:12) and even
to enter the house of a Gentile meant defilement (John
18:28). It was customary for Jews to purify themselves from
possible contact with Gentiles by washing their hands in
the purification water kept in large jars near the entrance of
the house (Mark 7:3-4; John 2:6). To strict Pharisees these
lawbreakers among the Jews were "sinners", Gentile-like,
impure and defiled. Yet Jesus not only conversed with them
but also ate with them. He was scornfully referred to as "the
friend of tax collectors and sinners" (Matthew 11:19).
The Pharisees were scandalized at his behaviour and said,
"This man receives sinners and eats with them." (Luke 15:2)

It is possible that these leaders saw in Jesus' friendship
with sinners an endorsement of their lifestyle. Since the
messiah and his kingdom would not appear until the nation
was a pure, law-keeping people it may have been thought
that Jesus' support of the sinners actually contributed to
the delay of the messianic age. If only these people had
understood that Jesus' friendship with sinners actualized
the kingdom and mercy of God among men and women
in their need. So far from Jesus' action being against the
kingdom of God, he was the kingdom of God present
among them. (Luke 16:16; 17:21)

Jesus was also a "friend" to those who were regarded
as undesirable or unfortunate. In the gospels we read of his
conversation with the Samaritan woman who suffered
from the triple liability of being a woman, Samaritan
and immoral! We also see Jesus blessing children although
they were thought to be inferior and unworthy of adult
companionship. He was constantly present with the
invalids, the diseased, the mentally ill and the demon-
possessed. Clearly these kind of people were an extension

of the "sinners" whom Jesus befriended. Jesus sought their company and relieved their sufferings. A contemporary illustration of the perceived inferiority of such needy folk may be seen in the exclusive membership rules of the Qumran community which stated, "No madman, or lunatic, or simpleton, or fool, or blind man, or maimed, or lame, or deaf man, and no minor shall enter the community".[7] Yet these were the very people to whom Jesus went. His friendship with them and care of them was the actual embodiment of the kingdom of God among them.

A fourth example of Jesus' actions fulfilling his stated purpose was in relationship to his death. On one occasion he said, "The Son of Man came...to give his life a ransom for many" (Mark 10:45). This was, it appears, Jesus' ultimate intention in coming — to die a death which would be a ransom to liberate others.

Early in his Galilean ministry he spoke of, "that day ...when the bridegroom is taken away" (Mark 2:20). In the twelve months following the dramatic Passover feeding of the multitude Jesus often spoke of his death, and in increasingly explicit ways (Mark 8:31; 9:30-32; 10:33-34). He went up to the next Passover in Jerusalem knowing that death was awaiting him there. In his mind it was no ordinary death but a "baptism" to be undergone, a "cup" to be drunk and "fire from heaven" to be endured (Mark 10:38; Luke 12:49). It was an "hour" which in prospect he dreaded profoundly (Mark 14:35); as he said at the Last Supper, "my blood of the covenant...is poured out for many" (Mark 14:24). Jesus knew that his "life" was to be "given", his "blood...poured out" for the benefit of, on behalf of and as a substitute for others. He knew that his death was cosmic and eternal in character, the last and final battle with Satan, a saving death. He would prevail ultimately in resurrection but only after enduring the God-ordained "cup", "baptism" and "fire". Jesus said it was for this, supremely, that he "came".

We may say, in summary, that Jesus had very clearly stated objectives. His oft-repeated "I came to . . ." sayings demonstrate this to have been true of him. However these were no empty sayings. Jesus came to fulfil Time and the Law and the Prophets: and he cleared out the temple traders and rode king-like up to Jerusalem. He came to proclaim the arrival of the kingdom of God; and he actualized that kingdom by casting out demons and healing the diseased. He came to call sinners; and he received them and ate with them. He came to give his life as a ransom; and he drank the cup, underwent the baptism and suffered the fire. By what he said and did Jesus of Nazareth was, to an extraordinary degree, a man of purpose.

Jesus' impact on his followers was profound. The deeds of this man in life, in death and in resurrection so thoroughly matched his words that his followers became convinced that in him God had acted finally and decisively for the salvation of mankind (Acts 4:12). Jews though they were, they now believed that the messianic age previously thought to belong to the distant future, had been actualized in time and history, in Jesus. (Acts 3:17-21)

The anonymous writer to the Hebrews, whose statements about Christ appear to represent the views of primitive Jewish Christians, declared that Christ "appeared once for all at the end of the age to put away sin by the sacrifice of himself". (9:26)

Paul stated that he and his contemporaries were those "upon whom the end of the ages has come". (1 Corinthians 10:11)

As the writers of the New Testament literature wrestled with the significance of Jesus, it became clear to them that all the blessings of God which he would bestow on his people at the end of the ages — forgiveness of sins, deliverance from death, the presence of God's Spirit — all these and other blessings were their *present* possession at that very time, in Jesus. This radical re-thinking of God's timetable was due entirely to the impact of Jesus upon them. They remembered and knew that everything he said he came to do he did in fact accomplish — before their very eyes. Because of Jesus, what he said and did, the future of God actually now lay *behind* them, fulfilled and completed. Henceforth the future would hold no surprises, bring no new revelation or new action. The future would merely unveil the new permanent reality. This conviction arose because of the coming of Jesus to them.

4 Authority

Jesus' teaching was universally recognised as profoundly authoritative. At the commencement of the Galilean ministry the members of the synagogue at Capernaum were amazed that "he taught them with authority and not as the scribes" (Mark 1:22). The scribes interpreted and debated the sacred Law of God and appealed to the various opinions which had been given by other scribes. Jesus, however, brought a new revelation from God. Characteristically he prefixed his utterances with the solemn "amen" by which, in effect, he claimed to be the true witness of God. Jesus' use of "amen" to introduce his own words is without parallel in Jewish literature. It is very close in power and effect to the divine utterances in the Old Testament introduced by the words "as I live, says the Lord". Scribes quoted other scribes. Prophets as mouthpieces of God said "thus says Yahweh. . .", but Jesus said, "Amen I say unto you". Mark's gospel records this form of words fourteen times. John's gospel recorded them twenty-five times, but always as "Amen, amen, I say to you". The words also occur frequently in Matthew and Luke. Clearly this distinctive mode of speech was often used by Jesus.

Later in the synagogue service in Capernaum, comment was again made about Jesus' "new teaching, with authority" (Mark 1:27). His teaching was regarded as authoritative and new — a new revelation regarding the arrival of the kingdom of God (cf. Mark 1:14-15). The confirmation of his authoritative, new message could be seen in his accompanying actions, "He commands even the unclean spirits and they obey him" (Mark 1:27). Near the end of his ministry the chief priests, scribes and elders, recognising his extraordinary powers, demanded to know, "By what authority are you doing these things. . .who gave you this authority?" (Mark 11:28). Clearly Jesus was widely regarded as having an authoritative manner.

It would be incorrect to regard Jesus' "authority" as merely "charisma" or a "commanding presence", though he doubtless possessed these qualities. Rather, it is important to understand that "authority" meant legal power given by someone in ultimate authority to his representative. The Greek word for "authority" is *exousia* - meaning "delegated authority". This may be illustrated by Pilate's statement to Jesus, "I have authority to release you and authority to crucify you" (John 19:10). Pilate referred to the "authority" given him by the Roman Emperor Tiberius by which, as his legal representative, he was empowered to release or crucify a prisoner.

A further illustration is Jesus' bestowal of authority on his "apostles" (Mark 6:30) who represented him in their mission to the towns of Galilee. He appointed/sent them out "to have authority to cast out demons" (Mark 3:15; 6:7). The disciples represented Jesus as his apostles, sent forth bearing his authority in a manner analogous to Jesus who represented God as his "apostle", sent forth bearing his authority.

This helps us to understand one of Jesus' most significant statements. A paralysed man had been placed before him clearly seeking to be healed. Quite unexpectedly Jesus said to the man, "My son, your sins are forgiven" (Mark 2:5). The scribes who were present understandably protested that this was blasphemy for who could forgive sins except God alone? For his part the paralysed man was probably puzzled that forgiveness of sins was pronounced whereas he was looking for healing. Then Jesus made the astonishing statement, "but that you may know that the Son of Man has authority on earth to forgive sins. . .I say to you take up your bed and go home" (Mark 2:10-11). The gospel records that the man took up his bed and went off, visibly demonstrating the truth of Jesus' invisible claim to have authority to forgive sin. Jesus' use of the word "authority" indicates that he represented God on earth, bearing all the authority of God in his place as his representative. The idea of Jesus as the bearer-on-earth of the authority of God is, of course, very similar to Jesus' teaching that he was the Son of the Father sent into the world, which we have already considered.

The scribes were correct: God alone can forgive man's sins. But Jesus brought new teaching, namely, that God's representative, the Son of man, has the authority of God to forgive sins. The miracle of the man's healing was the proof of that authority. But this strongly implies that the bearer of the authority to forgive sin is himself without sin and moreover that he is a divine figure. We may and do say, on the basis of this passage, that "Jesus is God", so long as we understand that Jesus represents God. We may not say that Jesus is God in the sense that Jesus replaces God, that because Jesus was with man God somehow no longer existed. God was still there; Jesus prayed to him as "Abba", dear Father. But as the Son of God sent unto the world to fulfil his mission, as the Son of man bearing the authority of God to do what only God can do, we do indeed truly see, in Jesus, God his Father.

5 Divinity

Did Jesus lay claim to divinity, to be "God"?

Certainly he was prepared to be regarded as God. It will be remembered that after the resurrection the disciples "worshipped" him and that Thomas called him "my Lord and my God" (Matthew 28:17; John 20:28). Given the Jewish devotion to the creed "Hear, O Israel, Yahweh your God is one. . ." it is not surprising that the disciples' attitude to Jesus is without parallel. As Jews they must have come to very powerful conclusions about Jesus to treat him as "God".

But did Jesus himself make such claims? The answer is "Yes", but implicitly rather than explicitly. As we have noted already, he declared the crippled man's sins to be forgiven (Mark 2:5). On another occasion he told a wealthy man, in effect, that to follow him was to keep the commandments including those which repudiate all other gods except Yahweh, Lord of Israel (Mark 10:21). Jesus put himself in the place of Yahweh.

Moreover, on several occasions he spoke of himself as "I am", the very words by which Yahweh disclosed his identity to Moses (Exodus 3:14). When he walked on the water he told the disciples "Do not be afraid, I am". This statement is all the more remarkable because it occurs in two sources, John and Special Matthew (=M), which are quite independent of each other. (John 6:20; Matthew 14:27)

Several times in the eighth chapter of the gospel of John, Jesus referred to himself in this way. Once, he warned his hearers "...you will die in your sins, unless you believe I am ..." (v.24) predicting, "when you have lifted up the Son of Man, then you will know that I am..." (v.28), concluding, "...before Abraham was, I am" (v.58).

Clearly the fourth evangelist portrays Jesus declaring himself to be Yahweh among his people, the Jews. The "I am" statements leave us with no other alternative. But do these words occur in any other source? The answer is "Yes". There is the "Be not afraid, I am" of Special Matthew, already mentioned. Additionally, Jesus told the high priests "I am" whereupon they accused him of blasphemy (Mark 14:62-63). Further, the false messiahs who come in Jesus' name will be identified because they will say "I am", in imitation of his words (Mark 13:6). Clearly Jesus used the divine words "I am" of himself.

On the basis of the above there can be little doubt that Jesus claimed to be divine, and that the disciples came to the astonishing conclusion that he was, indeed, Yahweh among them. Certainly they proclaimed him as such after the resurrection. The apostolic declaration was: Jesus is "Lord" (Greek: *Kyrios*) and it was by that divine name Jesus was worshipped and confessed by the earliest Christians (Acts 2:36; 1 Corinthians 16:22). *Kyrios* is the Greek for the Hebrew *Yahweh*, the name of Israel's God. But this was not a belief which came to them at some later stage in the history of the early church. Even within his ministry they had asked, "Who then is this, that even wind and sea obey him?" (Mark 4:41). His resurrection from the dead gave them the answer and this is reflected in their worship of him as God. The earliest Christian proclamation of his divinity is a natural continuation of that.

6 The Future

In the months following the Passover feeding of the multitude in Galilee Jesus spoke, and spoke increasingly, of the future. Jesus now began to use verbs in the future tense, frequently with his self-designation as the "Son of man".

Certainly Jesus spoke of himself this way early in the ministry as, for example, when he said "The Son of man has authority...to forgive sins" or, "The Son of man is Lord even of the Sabbath" (Mark 2:10,28). Why did Jesus call himself "Son of man"? In the early part of his public ministry Jesus may have adopted this enigmatic self-description to signal that he was indeed God-sent, but not to fulfil the expectations of a military messiah, current at that time. The so-called Psalms of Solomon, written approximately a century before Jesus, give us a good idea of the nationalistic hopes of Israel. Psalm of Solomon 17, in particular, pleaded with Yahweh that he "raise up unto them their King, the Son of David. . .that he may shatter unrighteous rulers. . .that he may purge Jerusalem from nations. . ." (1-5)

It is striking that whenever Jesus was called "King of Israel" or "Messiah" he did not accept such nationalistic titles, referring to himself instead as "Son of man" (Mark 8:29,31; John 1:49,51). The climax of this was his negative reactions to the attempt to impose the kingship on him after the feeding of the multitude, an incident which effectively ended his public ministry in Galilee (John 6:15). The title, "Son of man" appears to have been chosen by Jesus deliberately as a substitute for nationalistic titles like "King" or "Messiah".

From the time of the feeding of the multitude, then, Jesus noticeably used the Son of man reference with verbs of the future tense. Basically they fall into two categories:

The death and resurrection of the Son of man — "The Son of Man will be delivered into the hands of men, and they will kill him; and when he is killed, after three days he will rise." (Mark 9:31 cf. 8:31; 10:33-34)

and the glorious coming of the Son of man — "...whoever is ashamed of me. . .of him will the Son of Man be ashamed, when he comes in the glory of his Father with the holy angels. . ." (Mark 8:38)

On the one hand Jesus describes the humiliation of the Son of man; on the other he speaks of his glory. The former will occur in Jerusalem, in the immediate future. But *when* will the Son of man come in glory? The most direct answer is that Jesus himself didn't know. "But of that day or that hour no one knows, not even the angels, nor the Son, but only the Father." (Mark 13:32)

Not only does no one know when the Son of man will come in glory, Jesus added that there would be no warning beforehand. To establish the point he told the parable of the absent house owner who would return unexpectedly (Mark 13:34). The one thing Jesus did indicate was that the coming of the Son of man would occur *after* the destruction of the temple. The temple would indeed be demolished within a generation and there would be due warning (Mark 13:28-30) but there would be nothing to signal the coming of the Son of man. It would occur after the temple destruction and it would be sudden and unannounced. (Mark 13:24,32-37)

While some scholars believe Jesus saw the humiliation and glorification of the Son of man as the one event, it is obvious that he envisaged the passing of a period of time between them. Attention is sometimes drawn to Jesus' statement that (some of) his hearers would not taste death before they saw the kingdom of God come with power (Mark 9:1), suggesting that this refers to the glorious coming of the Son of man. It seems to me more likely, however, to refer to Jesus' post-resurrection exaltation as prefigured in the Transfiguration incident immediately following his words.

The fatal problem for the belief that Jesus saw the humiliation and glorification of the Son of Man as one event, with no lapse of time between them, is that Jesus gave extensive teaching about behaviour for the period after his death. Even as he made his way to Jerusalem and to death we see Jesus teaching his disciples about the necessity for life-long loyalty to their husbands/wives and about the grave danger to them of riches (Mark 10:10-11, 23-31). He taught them that the community of his people was not to be marked by the self-aggrandizement of the Gentiles but by humility and sacrificial service, in imitation of him (Mark 10:43-45). On the eve of his death he took loaf and cup declaring that his people were to re-enact this meal, in remembrance of him (1 Corinthians 11:23-26). His exhortations to watchfulness (Mark 14:37,38) in the face of suffering and persecution add to the strong conviction that Jesus foresaw a historical period of some length between humiliation and glorification of the Son of Man. It is Mark's gospel which places his humiliation and glorification side by side, which also reports Jesus making elaborate provision for the lifestyle of his followers *after* his death.

Jesus' contemporaries would not have been surprised that Jesus spoke parables, or that they were the vehicle for some of his most important teachings. Parable-telling was commonplace at the time of Jesus. The following is attributed to Rabbi Eleazar ben Azariah (AD 50-120),

Whosoever wisdom is in excess of his works, to what is he like? To a tree whose branches are abundant, and its roots scanty; and the wind comes, and up roots it, and overturns it. And whosoever works are in excess of his wisdom to what is he like? To a tree whose branches are scanty, and its roots abundant; though all the winds come upon it, they stir it not from its place.[8]

It was customary for the teacher to address his disciples as they walked together, something we can envisage Jesus doing. Some of his parables use overlapping imagery, as in the parable above where the wind is critical to the story. (see Matthew 7:24-27)

There is, however, a fundamental difference between the rabbis' parables and the parables of Jesus. It is that the parables of the rabbis were directed to rabbis-in-training and for the purpose of explaining or applying the sacred law. Jesus' parables, however, were directed to whoever he was with and always for the purpose of explaining and applying his radical, new teaching. This probably explains why the rabbis' parables are often arid and uninspiring whereas Jesus' parables are simple, direct and vivid.

It wasn't just that Jesus was a skilful story-teller; his parables were also vigorously and directly applied in terms of the context of his ministry at the time of speaking. Let us briefly mention three ministry contexts reflected in Jesus' parables.

First, we observe that Jesus' parables of the kingdom were spoken to Galileans, sinners and those regarded as "unfortunate" or "inferior". They are simple and direct, easy to understand. So Jesus tells of a farmer sowing his field, and of a crop growing unnoticed before harvest, and of grain receptacles large and small and of a light suddenly brought into a room. He told of a merchant's search for the ultimate pearl and of the chance discovery of buried treasure. A basic element in this method, is a demand for radical self-evaluation and decision making. Repeatedly Jesus says, "He who has ears to hear, let him hear". The "hearer" is forced to ask: What kind of soil am *I*? What will happen to *me* at the harvest, or when the light is brought in? How much of myself am *I* opening up to the kingdom? Would *I* sell everything for the pearl or for the buried treasure? Thus Jesus' parables serve to illuminate the honest seeker and draw him into the kingdom and at the same time to baffle and confuse the sceptic and push him further away. The parables of Jesus do not leave anyone where they found him.

Second, many of Jesus' parables are his lively response to those who criticized his ministry to the unworthy and his own alleged slackness in keeping the Law. The parable of the bridegroom was in reply to those who complained that he did not observe the Law on fasting (Mark 2:19). The parables of the physician, the lost sheep, the lost coin and the lost son were in direct answer to those who said Jesus was the "friend of sinners" (Mark 2:17; Luke 15:1-32). His parable of the children who are never happy expressed Jesus' reaction to those who were unhappy with both John the Baptist and Jesus (Matthew 11:16-19). Quite possibly the parable of the labourers in the vineyard was Jesus' response to those who rejected his kindness to the unworthy (Matthew 20:1-16) and the parable of the new patch and the new wine represented his insistence that his was indeed a new, radical message not a re-hash of existing beliefs (Mark 2:21, 22). The parables of the divided kingdom/household and the struggle specifically declared Jesus' response to those who accused him of casting out demons by the power of Satan (Mark 3:20-30). His parable of the wicked tenants is a direct answer to those who accused him of lacking any authority for his actions (Mark 12:1-11). These response-parables often contain very distinctive teachings and give us an excellent idea of what Jesus believed while bringing us into the midst of the furious debate with the Pharisees over his ministry to sinners.

A third group of parables arose out of that last year of Jesus' ministry when he addressed the future. The parable of the budding tree taught that there would be warnings for everyone to see that the temple was doomed (Mark 13:28-31) whereas the parable of the absent house-owner taught that the coming of the Son of man will be un- heralded (Mark 13:34-37). Other parables such as the pounds (Luke 19:12-27) and those relating to stewards (Luke 12:41-48; 16:1-13) are directed at believers' behaviour in the period before the Lord comes. Parables like the ten virgins (Matthew 25:1-13) and the wedding garment (Matthew 22:11-13) warn the people to be ready for his coming, whereas the sheep and the goats portrays the reality of the judgement of the Son of man. (Matthew 25:31-46)

Jesus was a master story-teller, whose parables were simple, direct and challenging in a way that the rabbinic parables were not. The astonished response of the Galileans — "He teaches with authority and not like the scribes" — sums up the difference between the rabbis' parables and those of Jesus.

The sayings of Jesus, read in the context of his actions, reveal him to have been a man powerfully convinced that he was God's Son, sent by God into the world, with divine authority, to fulfil a God-given mission to call and to save the lost. Despite the passing of so many years between his era and ours, we who read the gospels continue to be confronted by a person of extraordinary power and authority. The words of Jesus are so profound that this writer, at least, feels dwarfed by them.

The question, "Who is he?", which was asked at the time, continues to be asked today including by many who are not Christians. Every year or so a new book appears claiming at last to explain who Jesus really was. According to Samuel Brandon he was a zealot for Jewish nationalism.[9] Geza Vermes portrays him as one of the gentle pious Jewish mystics of those times.[10] For Morton Smith Jesus was a magic-worker, a man of dubious morality.[11] Albert Schweitzer saw him as a mistaken, broken-hearted prophet.[12] So the theories continue to be proposed, usually based on only a small part of the data available to us.

The belief that Jesus was agonizingly uncertain of his identity and mission is the most untenable of all. Nothing could be further from the truth. On the contrary we see in the gospels one who was in control of each situation and indeed of the whole of what he set out to accomplish. That is not to say that he did not agonize over the failure of his fellow Jews to respond to what he called their "visitation", their time of God-given opportunity (Luke 19:44). Unquestionably he approached his own death with profound apprehension., Nevertheless he was purposeful and convinced both of his identity and mission throughout his public ministry.

The gospels themselves relay to their readers what people at the time thought of Jesus. The common people regarded him as one of the great prophets of the past come back to the people of God (Mark 8:28). The religious leaders on the one hand demanded to know if he claimed to be the Messiah (John 10:24) while on the other reviling him as false teacher (John 7:12), law-breaker (John 9:16), blasphemer (John 10:33) and demon-possessed maniac (John 10:20.) Against such vilification Jesus continued to insist that he was the Holy One of God, the Son of God sent into the world (John 10:36). He replied that if they were in any real sense descendants of Abraham (John 8:39-47) or followers of Moses (John 5:46) they would recognise Jesus for who he was.

One attitude Jesus did not encourage was that of Nicodemus (John 3:2) who wanted to treat Jesus as a God-inspired miracle-worker and teacher — akin to Vermes' presentation in *Jesus the Jew*. Jesus did not permit himself to be classified in polite inoffensive terms; he is the One sent from heaven to save the world. (John 3:14-16)

Further reading to Chapter Four:

G. Bornkamm, *Jesus of Nazareth*, Hodder & Stoughton, London, 1960.

R.T. France, *Jesus and the Old Testament*. Baker, Grand Rapids, 1982.

A.M. Hunter, *The Work and Words of Jesus*, SCM, London, 1950.

J. Jeremias, *New Testament Theology FI*, SCM, London, 1950.

I.H. Marshall, *I Believe in the Historical Jesus*, Eerdmans, Grand Rapids, 1977.

H.K. McArthur, *In Search of the Historical Jesus*, Scribner, New York, 1969.

H. Zahrnt, *The Historical Jesus*, Harper & Row, New York, 1963.

J.M. Robinson, *A New Quest of the Historical Jesus*, SCM, London, 1959.

G.N. Stanton, *Jesus of Nazareth in New Testament Preaching*, Cambridge University Press, London, 1974.

E. Stauffer, *Jesus and His Story*, Knopf, New York, 1974.

Notes

[1] *AJ*, xviii, 63.

[2] b. Sanh. 43a.

[3] Mark 3:5,34; 5:32; 10:23; 11:11.

[4] J. Jeremias, *New Testament Theology* I, SCM, London, 1963, 1-37.

[5] D.C. Allison, "The Pauline Epistles and the Synoptic Gospels", *NTS*, 28, 1982, pp. 1-32.

[5a] G. Vermes, *Jesus the Jew*, Collins, London, 1973, 202-210.

[6] Y. Shab 15.d.

[7] Damascus Rule XV, *The Dead Sea Scrolls in English*, trans. G. Vermes, Penguin Harmondsworth, 1975, p. 109.

[8] *Pirkge Aboth*, III 18 quoted in A.M. Hunter, *Interpreting the Parables*, SCM, London, 1960, p. 113.

[9] S.G.F. Brandon, *Jesus and the Zealots*, Manchester University Press, Manchester, 1967.

[10] G. Vermes, *Jesus the Jew*, Collins, London, 1973.

[11]M. Smith, *The Secret Gospel*, Gollancz, London, 1974.

[12]A. Schweitzer, *The Quest of the Historical Jesus*, A. & C. Black, London, 1910.

5

Why Jesus Was Remembered

Those familiar with the New Testament will recollect the advice of the great Rabbi Gamaliel to his fellow-members in the Sanhedrin. Referring to early Christianity he said, "If this plan or understanding is of men it will fail. . ." (Acts 5:38). Gamaliel had just given examples of two leaders of earlier times — Theudas[1] and Judas — both of whom were killed and their movements came to nothing.

These were but two of the revolutionary leaders in that general period. Thanks to the Jewish author Josephus who wrote his historical works between AD 70–95, we know about a number of men and movements of that time. (Josephus, the military governor of Galilee, was captured by the Romans during the war AD 66–70. He served members of the imperial Flavian family — Vespasian, Titus and Domitian — until his death in the mid nineties).

Who were these revolutionaries and why are they almost forgotten while Jesus is remembered?

The death of Herod the Great in 4 BC was followed by a period of grave uncertainty. Herod's will had divided his kingdom into three parts, each to be ruled by a Herodian prince. But these princes were very young. Archelaus, who was nominated to rule Judaea, was only twenty-one when his father died; Antipas, the ruler-designate of Galilee, was seventeen. Moreover, since there was a dispute over the will, the parties had to travel to Rome for the Emperor Augustus to resolve the matter. In the absence of firm and authorized leadership civil war broke out in each of the main regions in Herod's realm. Josephus wrote that three men arose, each of whom claimed the title "King" Judas in Galilee, Simon in Peraea, Athronges in Judaea.

According to Josephus:

...in Galilee *Judas*, Son of Ezekias...raised a considerable body of followers...became an object of terror...in his desire...for royal rank.

...in Peraea *Simon*...assumed the diadem...burnt down the royal palace at Jericho.

...[in Judaea]...a shepherd had the temerity to aspire to the throne...*Athronges*...[with] four brothers resembling himself...their principal object was to kill Romans and royalists...this man kept his power for a long time, for he had the title King.[2]

Josephus summed up that turbulent period after 4 BC:

And so Judaea was filled with brigandage. Anyone might make himself King at the head of a band of rebels...[3]

Law and order was re-established by the Roman army from Antioch commanded by Varus. After a period of bloody warfare Simon was killed, Athronges captured and their respective followers dispersed, allowing the Herodian princes at last to take over their respective sections of Herod's kingdom. The "Kings" Simon and Athronges are long forgotten apart from Josephus' brief descriptions.[4]

In John 10, Jesus described himself as the "good shepherd" in contrast to the "thieves and brigands" (Greek *lestai*) who came before him. Did Jesus have in mind *brigands*, as Josephus described them, like Judas, Simon and Athronges? It should be noted that they too could be referred to as "shepherds" since they, like Jesus, *led* their followers (see verse 27). Unlike them, however, Jesus said he was a "good" shepherd who protected and gave his life for his sheep.

Unlike Simon and Athronges whose end Josephus describes, we do no know what happened to Judas, son of Ezekias, who was "King" in Galilee.[5] About ten years later in AD 6 a Judas is referred to by the Acts of the Apostles as "Judas the Galilean" (5:37) and by Josephus as "a Galilean named Judas".[6] Since the earlier Judas led his uprising in Galilee, and apparently survived there is good reason to identify this "Judas the Galilean" with "Judas, son of Ezekias"?

Sixty years later Menahem, the son of Judas the Galilean, with his supporters, captured Masada and, duly armed, "returned like a veritable king to Jerusalem (as leader of the revolution) and directed the siege of the palace".[8] If Judas proclaimed himself "king" in 4 BC and his son Menahem "returned like a...king to Jerusalem" in AD 66 might not Judas in AD 6 also have aspired to the throne of Israel? Admittedly, however, this must remain a suggestion.

What we are specifically told is that the first Judas was a teacher or rabbi (Greek: *sophistés*) who, in league with the Pharisee Saddok,led an uprising against the Roman annexation of Judaea as a Roman province. According to Josephus, Judas and Saddok established a new, activist, zealot-like Pharisaism which advocated violent action rather than submission to Gentile rule, which the payment of taxes to Rome was seen as implying. Their watchword was "God alone is leader and master" and their passion, the "liberty" of the people of God.[9]

Until that time, most Pharisees would have been prepared to accept the Roman annexation and taxation as a punishment of God to be patiently suffered until the great apocalyptic reversal at the end of the world when evil would be condemned and patient endurance rewarded. With Judas and Saddok, however, came a new line of Pharisaic thought which demanded of God's people violent and immediate action in zeal for the name of God. Josephus stated that "Judas and Saddok started among us an intrusive fourth school of philosophy (which) agrees in all other respects with the opinions of the Pharisees."[9a]

Approximately two decades before Jesus' public career, therefore, there had arisen within Israel a group committed to zealous, violent action against Roman rule, which was apparently supported by many Pharisees. While the violent "Fourth Philosophy" was checked at the time of its initial manifestation, by the Romans' overthrow of Judas and Saddok, its beliefs and convictions simmered beneath the surface through the following decades. The "insurrection" led by Barabbas, in the context of which Jesus was crucified, may have been a sporadic eruption of the "Fourth Philosophy". (Mark 15:7)

In the fifties and sixties, when relationships between the Romans and their Judaean subjects had deteriorated even further, there would be increasing manifestations of the "Fourth Philosophy" from revolutionary factions like the *Sicarii* and the Zealots. Unlike the self-serving Simon and Athronges back in 4 BC these factions and their various leaders fought and died for the freedom of Israel, a hoped for freedom under the lordship of God. Like Simon and Athronges, however, they crumbled before the military might of Rome, and indeed, destroyed one another in bloody cross-factional struggles. Historically neither the leaders, their followers nor their "Fourth Philosophy" survived the Jewish war of AD 66–70 with the Romans. Apart from Josephus' cynical and self-righteous accounts the only traces in history of their heroism for the cause of God are the coins they minted during the war, the ashes from the Sicarii stronghold at Masada and the remains of the Jerusalem temple — and the arch erected in Rome by Titus their conqueror, celebrating their defeat! No literature expressing their hopes or beliefs has come down to us.

What then of the other three "philosophies", as Josephus calls them, which were current in the time of Jesus?

The third "philosophy", the Essene, apparently derived in name from the Aramaic word *hasa* meaning "pious". In addition to Josephus there is also extensive information about the Essenes in Philo and Pliny the Elder.[10] In 1947 the so-called "Dead Sea Scrolls" were discovered at Qumran and subsequently the nearby remains of a sectarian community settlement. Most scholars identify that community and the numerous scrolls as "Essene" or "Essene-like".

While Josephus, Philo and Pliny describe the Essenes from the viewpoint of outsiders, the scrolls give us an inside view of this movement. From all accounts the sect arose about the middle of the second century BC during the early days of the Maccabean rule. It is one of the ironies of history that the Maccabean rulers despite their initial zeal for God in driving their Greek masters out of Israel, immediately became heavily influenced by Hellenism. This dynasty seized the high priesthood and appointed to that position senior members of their family who were corrupt and godless. The scroll mentions a "Wicked Priest", referring to one or more high priests of this family. The other critical person in the genesis of the movement was "the Teacher of Righteousness", a genuine priest of the Zadokite line, but who was persecuted and driven off by the "Wicked Priest". "The Teacher of Righteousness" with his devout followers established a new separatist Israel in the wilderness, at Qumran near the Dead Sea. Here the movement grew and flourished, surviving the persecutions of the "Wicked Priest", the eventual death of the "teacher" and an earthquake in 31 BC. In AD 68, however, the Romans came to Qumran, put the community to flight and destroyed their buildings. The scrolls were presumably hidden in the face of the Roman assault.

What happened to the community? Some members appear to have fled south to Masada where they would have perished six years later in the Roman siege; others may have returned to mainline Judaism; possibly some converted to Christianity. In AD 68, despite a history of more than two hundred years, once the members had been dispersed, the buildings destroyed and the scrolls hidden the community came to an end. Apart from the chance discovery of the scrolls in 1947, the references to the Essenes in Josephus, Philo and Pliny would have attracted minimal attention from scholars.

Josephus' second "philosophy", the Sadducean, had few supporters. Its members were drawn from the small number of wealthy, land owning families. Their natural connections were with the Romans rather than with the indigenous people of Judaea and Galilee. It is probable that they were well educated in Greek language, literature and thought. The Sadducean disbelief in God's active involvement in history may be attributed to the Greek doctrine of a remote, uninvolved deity. Like the Greeks they believed that man was entirely free to do good or evil. The Sadducees rejected any notion of a future life — of body or soul. They rejected any "tradition" of interpretation of the scriptures insisting that only the scriptures themselves were to be the basis of religion. Although they had scribes and teachers no first hand Sadducean literature survives. The Sadducees were swept away, like so much in Israel, by the war with the Romans AD 66–70.

Josephus' first "philosophy", the Pharisaic, was the dominant one in New Testament times. It was a lay movement based in the middle and lower classes. According to the noted Jewish authority J. Neusner, the Pharisees were a "cult-centred piety, which proposed to replicate the cult in the home. . . The Pharisee was a layman pretending to be a priest making his private home into a model of the Temple."[11]

Judaism survived the devastating war of AD 66–70 through the leadership of rabbis like the Pharisee Johanan ben Zakkai who escaped Jerusalem and founded a rabbinic academy at Jamnia. They shifted their devotion from temple and priesthood to the oral law, that is the traditions interpreting the Old Testament. The rabbi became the "priest"; study of the scriptures became the "cult". The synagogue, as well as the home, became important. The people were ruled by rabbis according to rabbinic law. The pluralistic Judaism of the New Testament period did not survive after AD 70. Rabbinic Judaism became the sole representative of the Jewish religious heritage. Herbert Danby, translator of the Mishnah into English, noted that,

Until the destruction of the second temple in AD 70 [the Pharisees] had counted as one only among the schools of thought which played a part in Jewish national and religious life; after the destruction they took the position . . .of sole and undisputed leaders. . .Judaism as it has continued since is. . .a faith and a religious institution largely of their fashioning. . .[12]

After the disaster of AD 70 the rabbis began to collect and systematize the oral traditions of the previous centuries. Yet another war, the so-called Bar Cochba Revolt of AD 132-135 which saw the utter destruction of Jerusalem, accelerated the process. By AD 200 Rabbi Judah produced the Mishnah, the collected, edited teachings of the great scribes, in written form. Danby comments, ". . .while Judaism and Christianity alike venerate the Old Testament as canonical scripture, the Mishnah marks the passage to Judaism as definitely as the New Testament marks the passage to Christianity".[13]

We may say, on the basis of this survey, that, apart from Christianity, the only movement within Judaism to survive the Jewish war with Rome AD 66–70 was Pharisaism, transformed into Rabbinic Judaism.

Violence in one form or another, mostly from the Romans, was directed against all of these movements — Simon and Athronges in 4 BC; Judas and Saddok in AD 6; the Essenes and the various factions of the "Fourth Philosophy" AD 66–70. The Sadducees disappeared from Jewish life, one suspects, because of disapproval of their collaboration with the Romans during the war.

It would not be correct to assume that the Christian movement survived through lack of violent opposition. Far from it. Within two years of the beginnings of the movement, Stephen had been stoned and the "Hellenist" Christians driven from Judaea. Within ten years, James Zebedee had been beheaded and Peter forced to quit Jerusalem, at least for the time being. James the brother of Jesus was stoned to death in Jerusalem in AD 62. Paul was constantly in danger, finally losing his life, along with Peter, during the midsixties, along with great numbers of Christians who were butchered in Rome at the command of Nero. Christian Jews were to be killed during the Bar Cochba revolt from AD 132–135 because they declined to join the struggle against Rome.

Why is it, then, that while all other Jewish groups of the first century crumbled and disappeared in the face of great violence, Rabbinic Judaism and Christianity survived into the next century?

Judaism survived, apparently, because its leaders realised that the way of armed conflict with Rome could only spell destruction.[14] Two tragic wars (66–70 and 132–135) surely burnt that message into the souls of all thinking Jews. The survival of Judaism at that time was due to the attention the rabbis gave to Jewish religion, not to religious nationalism. The canon of Jewish scriptures was formalized and the Synagogue service reached a more fixed liturgical form. Special prayers, known as the Eighteen Benedictions, were created. The deep sense of nationhood, of being God's chosen people, could only have been confirmed by massive suffering at the hands of the Gentiles on the one hand, and by the growth of that hated heretical schism Christianity, on the other. Something of the national pride, expressed with bitterness, can be seen in Benediction 12, a prayer devised for use in the synagogue in about AD 80.

> For the renegades let there be no hope, and may the arrogant kingdom soon be rooted out in our days, and the Nazarenes and the minim perish as in a moment and be blotted out from the book of life and with the righteous may they not be inscribed. Blessed art thou, O Lord, who humblest the arrogant.[15]

The "renegades" may have been traitors like Josephus who went over to the Romans during the war 66–70. Almost certainly the arrogant kingdom was Rome. "Nazarenes" and "minim" clearly are Christians. All these were "the arrogant" who, this synagogue prayer, recited each week, asked to have excluded from the book of life. Clearly Benediction 12 indicates an intense loyalty to Judaism on the one hand and an intense hatred of its enemies — Rome and Christianity — on the other. It helps us see how Judaism as *Rabbinic* Judaism survived after the war AD 66–70.

But how did earliest Christianity survive as a movement after the death of its founder? We ask the question deliberately of *earliest* Christianity. Clearly, once a movement develops an institutional and cultural momentum, its survival may possibly be explained in sociological terms. But institutions and culture did nót develop significantly within Christianity until the latter part of the first century when the movement began to lose living contact with Jesus through the death of the followers of the original disciples. So, why did Christianity survive within that first, critical century, when all other movements except Rabbinic Judaism did not?

The answer lies in the unique character of its leader and in his resurrection from the dead.

It cannot be seriously questioned that Jesus made a massive personal impact on his followers. The Teacher of

Righteousness, Judas the Galilean and Eleazar founder of the Zealot faction each made a great impact on his followers, who made life and death commitments to their leaders. The difference was that each of these leaders embodied a *national* or *ideological* cause. The leaders of the "Fourth Philosophy", in particular, were followed, because of their leadership in religious and nationalist zeal which each articulated and exemplified to an impressive degree. (We need not consider further the leadership of Simon or Athronges, who led uprisings for personal gain.)

But, the utterly astonishing difference of Jesus lay in his personal qualities, which we attempted to sketch in the previous chapter. He went to extraordinary lengths to *avoid* being followed in the cause of nationalistic or messianic zeal, which was in each other case their *raison d'être*. Jesus taught that in him God's Time had come and that the Law and the Prophets were now fulfilled. Jesus was convinced that he was God's apostle, God's Son sent to Israel; that he was the Son of Man with a cluster of clearly articulated goals and uniquely the bearer of God's authority on earth; that the future, both immediately in terms of his redemptive death and resurrection, and more distantly in terms of his glorious return in judgement and salvation, was in his hands. These astonishing convictions were confirmed in his miracles of healing, in dramatic actions like the clearing of the temple and in gracious friendship offered to the outcast and downtrodden. This personal impact, it is submitted, is what remained with his followers, and caused his movement to survive his death.

But for how long would that impact, great as it was, have remained in the memory of his followers? Ten years, or twenty — perhaps thirty? The Acts refers to a group of John the Baptist's followers, twelve in all, located in Ephesus twenty or so years after his death (19:1-7). They were absorbed into Christianity, and disappeared from view, never to reappear. There must have been something else and, of course, that something else was the resurrection of Jesus from the dead. Doubtless his personal impact did remain with his first disciples. It was not this, however, which they proclaimed but his resurrection from the dead.

W. Künneth states that, "the primitive Christian message
. . .did *not* make general statements about Jesus, but
concentrated upon one singular event [the resurrection] as
the essential content of faith and as the ground of faith" [16] It
seems to me that it was his resurrection which caused his
astonishing personal qualities to be remembered and his
sayings to be treasured and written down. It was because he
rose from the dead that the gospels were ultimately written.
If Jesus had not been raised from the dead, his remarkable
person and teachings would have faded from their minds,
would not have been remembered, would not have been
committed to writing. Jesus would have been just another
mistaken Utopian, not remembered beyond his immediate
generation.

What, then, is the evidence for the resurrection of Jesus?

One hesitates to add to the volumes that have been
written about the resurrection of Jesus, especially as they
are, for the most part, based on lengthy specialized research.
The reader is referred, for example, to the scholarly
but eminently readable work of Murray Harris, *Raised
Immortal* (Eerdmans, Grand Rapids, 1983), as well as to
other titles listed at the end of the chapter.

I was tempted, then, to make no comment of my own.
However, that would have meant leaving out what is
perhaps the most critical part of the New Testament story.

So here are four pieces of evidence which this non-
specialist in resurrection studies finds personally compelling.

1 The example of Peter
The various other Jewish movements we have considered
did not survive the deaths of their leaders. Even the
non-Christian sources, however, reflect the continuance
of Jesus' followers. Writing in the midnineties in Rome
Josephus commented that,

When Pilate. . .had condemned [Jesus] to be crucified,
those who had in the first place come to love him did not
give up their affection for him. . . And the tribe of the
Christians, so called after him, has still to this day not

disappeared.[17]

By the mid-nineties it was possible to speak of "the tribe of the Christians".

Another non-Christian author, Tacitus, who wrote a decade or so after Josephus, observed that,

Christus...suffered the extreme penalty...at the hands of ...Pontius Pilate, and a deadly superstition, thus checked for the moment, again broke out not only in Judaea but also in the city [=Rome]...an immense multitude was convicted... [18]

Tacitus reveals that the death of Jesus did not mean the end of his movement but that it again "broke out in Judaea". Like Josephus, Tacitus clearly shows that the movement which arose during Jesus' lifetime continued after his death. The movement again broke out and did not disappear because of the resurrection.

As it happens we have detailed personal knowledge of someone who was involved at every point in the progress of early Christianity as described by Tacitus — from its fresh outbreak in Judaea after the death of Christus, to its passage to Rome where many of its adherents died at Nero's command. That someone was Peter, a small-time entrepreneur fisherman from remote Capernaum on the northern shore of the Sea of Galilee.[19]

Peter was a loyal but somewhat obtuse follower of Jesus, seeing him as the long-awaited messianic leader, so badly needed in Israel (Mark 8:29; John 6:69). At the Passover when Jesus was taken into custody and other disciples had fled, Peter attempted to follow his leader, but at a distance. However, under pressure he denied any knowledge of Jesus (Mark 14:54,66-71 and parr). He does not appear to have been anywhere near the scene of the crucifixion.

The whole tragic sequence in Jerusalem seems to have utterly dashed the aspirations of Peter and the others, focused as they had been on Jesus as Israel's Messiah, the one to redeem Israel (Luke 24:21). Had Peter been a follower of Judas the Galilean the death of his leader in AD 6/7 would surely have been the last we would have heard of him. Not one name of Judas' followers in the period after his death has been preserved in the historical records.

The contrast with Jesus' follower Peter, is striking. There is considerable information about Peter's career over the next thirty years, which raises questions like: Why did he migrate from Galilee to Jerusalem, becoming the leader of a growing sect and its spokesman to the wider community? Why did he engage in what appears to have been supervisory and pastoral visits throughout Samaria and the coastal towns of Judaea? How was it that he, an uneducated man with limited knowledge of the Greek language, is then seen travelling to Jewish-Christian communities in Syria, Greece and Italy? What can explain this astonishing career which began in far away Capernaum and ended by death in Rome during Nero's onslaught on the Christians? Peter was involved in every phase of Tacitus' description — with Jesus prior to the "extreme penalty", as part of the "deadly superstition. . .which again broke out in Judaea", and which spread to "Rome" where, under Nero, "an immense multitude were convicted" and killed.

Mindful of the veil of silence that fell over the followers of failed revolutionaries we ask: Why is it that Peter's career took such a striking re-direction after the death of his leader? How is it that we know about Peter's career? The answer surely is that the crucified Jesus did in fact rise from the dead. There are no less than four separate, independent references to this,[20] including the earliest historical statement of all (1 Corinthians 15:5) which declares that Peter saw Jesus after his resurrection from the dead.[21] Thus, it is not merely that Peter's career was subject to a surprising change of geographical direction. It was the change in vocation, that he, a fisherman, should have become an international witness to the resurrection of Jesus, that is so dramatic and significant. Peter not only became a verbal witness to the resurrection; in the period after the crucifixion his very life-direction is witness to the resurrection of Jesus from the dead. How else can the Peter-phenomenon be explained? It must be remembered that Peter's commitments were not nationalistic and ideological in character, as commitments would be during the early years of Islam. They were personally focused on Jesus and his resurrection.[22]

2   Early gratuitous references by Paul

Paul nowhere seeks to prove that Jesus rose again from the dead. Paul knew this had happened; there was no need to argue the point. In one of his earliest letters written in AD 50 no later than seventeen years after the crucifixion Paul reminded the Thessalonians that, "Since we believe that Jesus died and rose again even so through Jesus God will bring with him those who have fallen asleep". (1 Thessalonians 4:14)

Paul and his readers all believed Jesus died and rose again. Based on that agreed information Paul adds something the Thessalonians did not yet properly grasp — God would bring back the now deceased believers with Jesus at his return. It is clear from the words quoted below that the Thessalonians had come to believe in the death and resurrection of Jesus through Paul's proclamation of them:

The word of the Lord sounded forth from you...how you turned to God from idols, to serve a living and true God and to wait for his Son from heaven whom he raised from the dead, Jesus who delivers us from the wrath to come. (1 Thessalonians 1:8-10)

This is indisputable proof that in AD 50 it was Paul's practice publicly to proclaim that Jesus had died but was risen again from the dead.

Fortunately we have a fuller statement by Paul of the message he publicly proclaimed. Writing to the Corinthians in c. AD 55 he declared, "I would remind you...in what terms I preached to you the gospel... For I delivered to you as of first importance what I also received" (1 Corinthians 15:1, 3). Here we notice three moments of time for Paul: the present, AD 55 "I would remind you", the earlier time in AD 50 "I preached to you the gospel", and the time of Paul's reception of the message "what I also received". Clearly Paul must have received the gospel which he later preached, some time between his conversion in c. AD 34 and his first visit to Corinth in AD 50. But when?

Later in this passage he states with respect to the gospel he had received, "So we preach and so you believed" (1 Corinthians 15:11). The "we" who preach the same message are identified in this passage as Paul and "the apostles", including two who are named Cephas and James. As it happens we know from Paul's letter to the Galatians that three years after his conversion on the road to Damascus he returned to Jerusalem "to visit *Cephas* and remain with him fifteen days. . .I saw none of the other apostles except *James* the Lord's brother" (Galatians 1:18-19). The only two persons named as preaching the same gospel message are the very ones Paul visited in Jerusalem three years after his conversion. It seems probable, therefore, that the first "moment", the occasion when Paul received the gospel message, was his first visit to Jerusalem c. AD 36 when he "visited" Cephas and "saw" James. Please notice that this is not more than four years after the crucifixion/resurrection of Jesus.

It should be noted that this gospel message consists of four statements each commencing with "that". The Greek for "that" is *hoti* which really serves here as a punctuation signal that what follows lies within quotation marks. In other words it is a basic formula of the new movement, summarized as four statements or quotations.

Furthermore the words "delivered" and "received" were used of the rote-learned legal judgements of the great rabbis, judgements which were passed on intact from scribe to disciple, generation by generation.[23] Paul explained that before his conversion he had been "extremely zealous. . . for the traditions of my fathers" (Galatians 1:14). As a Christian he now used the word "tradition" in its noun and verb form to refer to the gospel message and to the Lord's Supper as a body of teaching handed over to him which he in turn, rabbi-like, handed over to those converted by him (1 Corinthians 15:1-3; 11:23). In other words, although Paul "received" the "tradition" about the gospel message in AD 36, the form of words he quoted went back even earlier than that, perhaps to the first months after the crucifixion/resurrection of Jesus.

What then was this fourfold quoted statement which became fixed in the brief time between Jesus and Paul, which Paul received in AD 36 and which he in turn passed on to the Corinthians in AD 50? He writes,

For I delivered to you as of first importance what I also received

that Christ died for our sins according to the scriptures *that* he was buried. . .

that he was raised on the third day in accordance with the scriptures and

that he appeared to Cephas, then to the twelve. . . (1 Corinthians 15:3-5)

Two observations on this passage are appropriate. The first is that Christ's *death, burial, resurrection* and *appearances* to people are referred to as historical facts. The *burial* confirms the fact of the *death*; the *appearances* confirm the fact that he *was raised*. Further evidence for his resurrection is provided by "he was raised on the third day". "Was raised" is technically known as a divine passive and means that God raised him. He did not rise and come, apparition-like, to them. "On the third day" specifies the point of time, three days (according to Jewish internal counting), after his death/burial. That he "was raised", by God, "on the third day", is a specific statement which is intended to be taken seriously. Moreover, the verb "appear" (*horao*) means "see" (literally) although it is correctly translated "appear" because the noun following the verb is in the dative case (*to* Cephas, *to* the twelve). The gospels use literal verbs of seeing *horao* and *theoreo* to denote that the witnesses really did "see" Jesus alive from the dead. If the writers had wanted to present Jesus as an apparition they would have used another verb like *phainomai* ("appear, show oneself") or a noun like *horama* ("vision"). They are stating as a fact that Peter, the twelve, more than five hundred brothers, James all the apostles and Paul, at various times physically saw Jesus who had been "raised on the third day".

It is sometimes pointed out that Paul does not specifically refer to the "empty tomb" in this passage. Nonetheless, his summary of the "received" gospel — Christ *died*, was *buried*, was *raised, appeared* to particular people who are still alive — should not be taken as evidence that Paul did not know about or believe in the "empty tomb". He says nothing here about Christ as the "Son of God". Yet 2

Corinthians 1:19 specifically gives that as the summation of the message he proclaimed when first at Corinth. It is naive to expect that 1 Corinthians 15:3-5 as part of a letter to the people at Corinth should summarise the whole of Paul's initial proclamation to them.

A second observation to be made is that Christ's death "for our sins" and his resurrection are both stated to be "according to/in accordance with the scriptures". This is consistent with the great concern among the earliest Jewish Christians to understand Christ as the fulfilment of the Old Testament promises and is further, though indirect, evidence for the resurrection. Why would the first believers have spent the time in establishing lists of Old Testament scriptures now seen to be fulfilled unless Jesus had been raised from the dead? It is difficult to imagine that such extensive, scholarly industry would have been invested in a dead Jesus if he was in fact dead. They surely would have concluded that he was just another failed leader of what would prove to be a non-movement, and forget all about Jesus.

In reviewing 1 Corinthians 15:1-11 we should note, once more, that Paul regards the fact of the resurrection of Jesus as settled. He is using this agreed fact to assure believers that they also will rise from the dead (see 1 Corinthians 15:12 ff.). Along with 1 Thessalonians 4:14 and 1:8-10, 1 Corinthians 15:1-11 are gratuitous, early — indeed exceedingly early — references to the resurrection of Jesus as an established fact.

We may assume that Paul checked carefully about the empty tomb and the authenticity of the resurrection appearances. Humanly speaking he had everything to lose and nothing to gain by converting to Christianity. It is inconceivable that so intelligent and logical a person as he was would have turned his whole life upside down if he had any lingering doubts about the resurrection — and Paul was one of the main human instruments for the survival of the Christian movement.

In addition to these early, gratuitous references to Jesus' resurrection, Paul's letters contain other information which encourages belief in the resurrection. I refer to a number of Aramaic words which are embedded within the Greek text of Paul's letters. There is clear evidence that the words *amen* and *Abba*[24] were used by Jesus. He often introduced weighty sayings with, "truly (amen) I say unto you. . ."[25] His preferred form of address to God was *Abba* which, according to Joachim Jeremias, was never used in Jewish literature as a way of speaking to God.[26] *Abba* was distinctive to Jesus. But where did Paul learn of these words, except through contact with the earliest community of Aramaic-speaking believers in Jerusalem whose leaders Cephas and James he first met in AD 36? (Galatians 1:18-19). Would the words *amen* and *abba* have been treasured in the Jerusalem church if Jesus was merely the deceased leader of a failed movement?

Another Aramaic expression used by Paul is *Marana tha*, an Aramaic phrase which means, "Our Lord, come" (1 Corinthians 16:22). It is highly probable that Paul here is reproducing some key words of the liturgy of the earliest Aramaic-speaking Christian believers in Jerusalem. The invocation, "Our Lord, come!" implies that Jesus is the *risen* Lord.

These words take us back to the earliest period of the Jerusalem church, as depicted in the first chapters of the Acts of the Apostles. We ask: How would these expressions, *amen, Abba* and *Marana tha* have found their way into Paul's vocabulary except by being handed on to him by Aramaic-speaking disciples before him? We ask further: would these words have had any meaning in that community if they referred to a dead Jesus? Do they not imply the early conviction, within that community, that he, the one who said "amen" and "Abba" during his historic life, was now their heavenly "Mara" (Lord) whose coming they invoked, "tha" (come)?

3   Zeal for Jesus the Son of God: the Letter to the Hebrews

The so-called Letter to the Hebrews — which is accepted as being written by someone other than Paul — is invaluable evidence of the transfer of allegiance by some Jews from temple and Torah to Jesus.

From the days of Alexander's invasion of the eastern Mediterranean and the subsequent spread of Greek civilization, the Jewish people were forced to develop clear *foci* for their faith. Put simply, they believed that their *Torah* or scriptures and their temple were sacred. From the second century BC there developed a notion of "zeal" or "jealousy" for Yahweh which was expressed as a life or death commitment to the sanctity of Torah and temple. The temple, as rebuilt by Herod, was a massive structure dominating Jerusalem, an imposing visible reminder of Yahweh, their Lord. In addition to the upper hierarchy of high priests, some seven thousand two hundred priests participated by roster in the temple ceremonies each year. The hundreds of thousands of pilgrims who visited Jerusalem each year came on account of the temple.

Zeal for Torah and temple often meant the giving of one's life. When Herod erected a golden eagle on the door of the temple he was in breach both of the Torah's second commandment and of the sanctity of the temple. The rabbis Judas and Matthias, who with their disciples in 4 BC removed the offending image, must have known this action would cost them their lives. The escalating violence between Jews and Romans after AD 44 and the eventual outbreak of war in AD 66 arose from Jewish "zeal" for Yahweh expressed in utter loyalty to Torah and temple.

It is therefore quite astonishing to read the Letter to the Hebrews which was evidently written before the war with Rome left the temple in ruins. This epistle makes sense only if it is read with the understanding that the temple is in full use with high priests, sacrifices and offerings.[27] All the references to the sacrificial activities are in the present tense. Yet the main thrust of the epistle is to persuade a persecuted and demoralized group of Jews that one man, Jesus, had abolished the temple, the priesthood and the sacrifices! They are being exhorted not to be absorbed back into the flourishing system of Judaism for just one reason — that Jesus Christ the Son of God was their great high priest and that he was *exalted* above the heavens (7:26). These Jewish readers were asked to hang on to that belief in the face of suffering and hostility (12:2-3) on account of that one man, a crucified man, who was seen infinitely to outweigh the fundamentals of their faith, Torah and temple, at a time when the temple was still in use and nationalistic loyalty was at its height!

How could the writer conceivably have made this appeal or hoped to be taken seriously, except for one incontestable fact? He and his Jewish readers had no doubt that the man who had been crucified had also been raised alive from the dead. How otherwise could their zeal be greater than the religious/nationalistic Jewish zeal for temple and Torah? The content of the epistle and its historical context virtually require that the Jesus who demanded the greater loyalty, the greater zeal, was a *resurrected* Jesus.

4   The empty tomb of Jesus

What happened to the body of Jesus of Nazareth, executed by crucifixion on the Passover Friday of AD 33, and buried in the tomb provided by Joseph of Arimathea? There are good reasons to believe that when it was examined on the Sunday the tomb was empty and the body gone.

Each of the four gospels and also the underlying, discrete sources — Special Matthew (M-Matthew 28:11-15), Mark (16:1-8), Special Luke (L-Luke 24:1-12) and John (20:11-18) report the empty tomb.

Each of the four gospels also indicates that the first witnesses to the tomb's emptiness were women. Since the evidence of female witnesses was inadmissible in Jewish Law,[28] any late or fabricated evidence inserted would surely have made the first witnesses men.

The fact that this *Jewish* sect changed its day of worship from Saturday to Sunday is also consistent with an authentic empty tomb tradition. So important was the Sabbath to Jews that the Romans did not require public duties of them on that day. Sabbath-keeping was very important, so why did the Jewish Christians change their Sabbath to the "first day of the week"? (Acts 20:7; 1 Corinthians 16:2 cf. Revelation 1:10) It is significant that, while Jesus was said to be raised on the third day, the discovery of the empty tomb is associated with the first day of the week. (Mark 16:2 parr. John 20:1)

Even scholars who stand outside the Christian faith are struck by the empty tomb tradition. The noted Jewish scholar Geza Vermes, for example, has referred to, "the one disconcerting fact: namely that the women who set out to pay their last respects to Jesus found to their consternation, not a body, but an empty tomb".[29]

Of what significance is it that the tomb of Jesus was empty? By itself it means little. However when taken along with the post-resurrection appearances of Jesus it indicates that Jesus was raised *bodily* from the dead. He was no apparition, resurrected in some merely mystical or spiritual sense within the subjective experience of his disciples.

5 The appearances of Jesus

There are many different strands of evidence for the resurrection appearances of Jesus. In 1 Corinthians 15:5-8 Paul notes that, as "raised on the third day" Christ "appeared" to Cephas, to the twelve, to a group of more than five hundred, to James, to all the apostles and to Paul.

Independently of Paul and of one another the other primary sources, Special Matthew (M-Matthew 28:1-10), Special Luke-Luke 24:13-42) and John (20:11-29; 21:1-23) also attest the resurrection appearances of Jesus on many occasions, to different people throughout a forty day period.

The multiplicity of independent written sources indicates a corresponding multiplicity of independent oral sources which in turn suggests numerous independent eyewitnesses.

The various accounts of the sightings of the risen Lord are all marked by considerable restraint. It is quite remarkable, moreover, that none of the four accounts mentioned above describes the actual resurrection itself. There were eleven different reported occasions when individuals or groups saw the Lord alive from the dead, but there is not one report of an eyewitness of the resurrection event. The sobriety and restraint of the New Testament writings speak eloquently for their veracity.

Gamaliel's words about Christianity have been proven true by the test of history. The "plan or understanding" about which he spoke, has not failed and this is evidence that it is not "of man" but "of God".

The primary reason for the survival and growth of Christianity is the conviction of the first Christians that Jesus rose again from the dead which men and women have confirmed and re-confirmed in every generation between the time of Jesus and today.

It is not to be found primarily in the profundity of his teachings or in his remarkable personality. It is doubtful that these qualities would have been remembered more than a decade or so after his death. It was his resurrection which caused every other thing about him to be remembered.

Further reading to Chapter Five:

P.W. Barnett, *Is the New Testament History?* Hodder and Stoughton, Sydney, 1986.

W.L. Craig, "The Empty Tomb of Jesus" in *Gospel perspective* II (eds) R.T. France and David Wenham JSOT Press, Sheffield, 1981, pp. 173-200.

M.J. Harris, *Raised Immortal,* Eerdmans, Grand Rapids, 1985.

R.J. Sider, "The Pauline Conception of the Resurrection Body" in 1 Corinthians XV 35-54", *NTS*, 21, 1975, pp. 428-439.

R.H. Gundry, *SOMA in Biblical Theology,* Cambridge University Press, Cambridge, 1976 (see in particular pp. 159-183).

Notes

[1] The only Theudas known to Josephus came after Jesus, subsequent to the time Gamaliel addressed the Sanhedrin (*AJ*, xx, 97-98). Many scholars believe that Luke's reference to Theudas is, therefore, anachronistic. It is possible, however, that the Acts is referring to another Theudas, not otherwise known.

[2] For Judas see *BJ* ii, 56, *AJ* xvii, 271-72. Simon see *BJ* ii, 57, *AJ* xvii, 271-72, Tacitus, *Histories,* v.9. Athronges see *BJ* ii, 60-65, *AJ* xvii, 278-84.

[3] *AJ,*xvii, 285.

[4] Simon is also mentioned by Tacitus, *Histories,* v.9.

[5] *BJ*, i, 204.

[6] *BJ*, ii, 118.

[7]Not all scholars make this identification. For the argument in favour of this opinion see S. Kennard, "Judas of Galilee and his Clan", *Jewish Quarterly Review*, 36, 1945, 281-86.

[8]*BJ*, ii, 433-34.

[9]*BJ*, ii, 118, vii, 253, *AJ*, xviii, 4-10, 23-25; Acts 5:37.

[9a]*AJ*, xviii, 9.

[10]*BJ*, ii, 119-161, *AJ*, xviii, 18-22. Pliny, *Natural History* V 15.73. Philo, *Hypothetica* xi, 1-18, *Quod Omnis* xii-xiii.

[11]J. Neusner, "Pharisaic-Rabbinic Judaism: A Clarification", *History of Religion* 122 1972-3 151.

[12]H. Danby, *The Mishnah*, Oxford University Press, Oxford, 1972, p. xiii.

[13]*Op. cit.*, p. xiii.

[14]Rabbi Akiba, who supported Bar Cochba in his revolt against Rome AD 132-135 in the belief that he was the Messiah, is clearly an exception.

[15]*In* C.K. Barrett, *The New Testament Background: Selected Documents*, S.P.C.K., London, 1956, p. 167.

[16]W. Künneth, *The Theology of the Resurrection*, SCM, London, 1965, p. 117.

[17]*AJ*, xviii, 64. While there is doubt concerning some of Josephus' statements about Jesus (*AJ*, xviii, 63-64), the general drift of the words quoted here appears to be authentic.

[18]*Annals* 15:44, 2-5.

[19]Luke 5:10.

[20]Mark 16:7; Luke 24:34; John 21:7; 1 Corinthians 15:5.

[21]P. Barnett, *Is the New Testament History?* Hodder and Stoughton, Sydney, 1986, pp. 81-98.

[22]See 1 Peter 1:3,8.

[23]See Mark 7:1-13; Galatians 1:14.

[24]2 Corinthians 1:20; Romans 8:15; Galatians 4:6.

[25]e.g. Mark 3:28.

[26]Mark 14:36; cf. J. Jeremias, *The Prayers of Jesus*, SCM, London, 1967, pp. 1-65.

[27]See Hebrews 5:1-4; 8:13; 9:6,9; 10:1-3; 13:10-14.

[28]H. Strack and P. Billerbeck, *Kommentar zum Neuen Testament aus Talmud und Midrash*, Beck, Munich, 1922-28, Vol. 3, pp. 217, 559-60.

[29]G. Vermes, *Jesus the Jew*, Collins, London, 1975, p. 41.

6

Jerusalem between Jesus and Paul
(c. AD 33-34)

The crucifixion of Jesus, followed by his resurrection on the third day, occurred at the time of Passover in Jerusalem in the year AD 33.[1] The conversion of Saul of Tarsus, who later became Paul the apostle to the Gentiles, occurred soon afterwards — probably not later than 34/35. By this reckoning the period between the resurrection of Jesus and the calling of Saul was only about two years.

Within these few months there were extensive developments within the earliest Christian community in Jerusalem. Those few months were so significant to the continuation of the Christian movement (which was to become the New Testament story) as to be second in importance only to the period of Jesus' own public ministry.

As we turn to consider the Christian community "between Jesus and Paul" we encounter some difficulty in establishing a chronology or internal history for this short span. Our chief source, the Acts of the Apostles, simply does not say when things happened. Nonetheless, we are able to identify the historical context of the wider world. Tiberius was still the Roman emperor, and Pontius Pilate his prefect in Judaea, though both would be dead by AD 37. The high priesthood was still held by the Annas dynasty, specifically by Annas' son-in-law Caiaphas who would continue in office until his death in AD 37. The same menacing forces, Roman and Jewish, which had combined to assault and kill Jesus were still in place in these critical early years.

It appears that these earliest years were a period of great reflection for the Christian community.

While it is not possible to establish an internal chronology of events we are able to sketch a profile of five major characteristics of the community.

1   Its uninterrupted continuity with Jesus

We know from the Acts of the Apostles that the resurrected Jesus continued to "present himself alive" to his followers for a period of "forty days" after "his passion" (Acts 1:3). The twelve "apostles" with other Galileans now including Mary the mother of Jesus with his brothers, about one hundred and twenty persons in all, were instructed by Jesus "not to depart from Jerusalem" (Acts 1:4, 11, 14-15). These Galileans settled in Jerusalem at that time, forming the nucleus of the larger community which would soon develop around them. Not surprisingly, therefore, given Jesus' origins in Galilee they became known in the wider community as "the Sect of the Nazarenes" (Acts 24:5). Their own preferred designation, apparently, was "the way" (9:2; 24:14). The term "Christian" arose a decade later and not in Jerusalem but in Antioch. (Acts 11:26)

The twelve disciples, now referred to as "apostles" according to primitive and first hand evidence (Galatians 1:18-19), were the leaders of the community. Special care was taken to choose a twelfth apostle, to replace Judas the betrayer (Acts 1:21-26). The twelve apostles were meant to correspond with the twelve tribes of Israel. Here was the messianic community of Jesus, the re-foundation of Israel.

The overall leader and spokesman was Peter, although John Zebedee's name is often bracketed with Peter's. (Acts 3:1 *passim* 8:14; Galatians 2:9)

What is clear from the Acts of the Apostles is that there was no interruption, no space of time, breaking the continuity of the life together of the twelve disciples before and after the first Easter. Those who had been with Jesus throughout the three and a half years continued together in Jerusalem, without interruption despite his physical absence from them. This is a striking characteristic of the community, and marks it off from other first-century leader-led movements which all disappeared with the deaths of their leaders. (See Chapter Five)

2 Signs/witness, growth and lifestyle

The first five chapters of the Acts of the Apostles portray the brief period of about two years between Jesus and Paul. There is a close relationship discernible between the apostles' signs and wonders, their witness to the risen Jesus and the enlargement and lifestyle of the community of believers.

Three such "signs and wonders" by the apostles are singled out for detailed description in the earliest period, though others are referred to in a generalized way (Acts 2:43; 4:30; 5:12). The three signs/wonders are:

a) "they. . .all. . .began to speak in other tongues". (2:4)

b) Peter's healing of the man "lame from birth". (3:7)

c) The deaths of Ananias and Sapphira after talking with Peter. (5:5,10)

Sign/wonder (a), the speaking in foreign tongues, was followed by Peter's "witness" on the day of Pentecost to the resurrection of Jesus and led to the significant growth of the original community (2:47). The Acts provides extensive description of the life together of this now-enlarged group. (2:43-47)

Sign/wonder (b), the healing of the crippled man at the "beautiful gate" to the temple, was followed by two occasions of "witness" by Peter — one to the bystanders (3:11-26), the other to the chief priest (4:1-22). Immediately the Acts relates the community's prayer of thanksgiving at the release of the apostles Peter and John (4:23-31) with further information about the life together of the community. (4:32-37)

Sign/wonder (c), the deaths of Ananias and Sapphira, was not accompanied by any statement of apostolic "witness". The Acts does note, however, that the community of believers was enlarged by "multitudes of both men and women". (5:14)

This dynamic triangle — signs/wonders, witness and enlargement and distinctiveness of the community — is portrayed by the Acts as the evidence in history of the exaltation of the resurrected Jesus of Nazareth to the right hand of God. It was because he the risen Lord had poured out his Spirit that this triad of interacting forces was set in motion.

3   A mixed community

Toward the end of the two-year period which separated the historical Jesus from the conversion of Saul, the Acts draws attention to the existence of the two racial sub-groups within the community — the "Hebrews" and the "Hellenists". (Acts 6:1)

The "Hebrews" evidently were Palestinian-born, Aramaic-speaking Jewish believers, composed initially of the one hundred and twenty Galileans who settled in Jerusalem after the resurrection of Jesus. It is reasonable to assume that in time other "Hebrews" were added to the rapidly growing community. Towards the end of the period the "many priests who were obedient to the faith" (Acts 6:7) would have been "Hebrews", members of the tribe of Levi who lived in and around Jerusalem.

The identity of the "Hellenists" has been much debated by scholars. The term appears only twice in the New Testament, both in the Acts of the Apostles (Acts 6:1; 9:29). There can be little doubt, however, that Hellenists were Greek-speaking Jews, probably originating ultimately from Hellenized parts of the Mediterranean world. John Chrysostom, a fourth century Christian leader from Antioch, stated that, "[Luke] uses Hellenists for those who speak Greek."[2] To most Palestinian Jews the word "Hellenist" would have been equivalent to "Gentile". "Hellenist", therefore, was probably a term of abuse.

The first of the two usages of the word "Hellenist" applies to Hellenists who had been converted to Jesus (Acts 6:1). It is commonly and rightly held that there were "Hellenists" among the national groups who heard Peter speak on the day of Pentecost and who became baptized members of the community from its inception (see Acts 2:9-11), in particular the Jews and proselytes from Pontus, Asia, Phrygia, Pamphylia, Egypt, Cyrene and Rome. But it is also possible that the Greeks who, according to John 12, sought Jesus were Greek *Jews*, that is Hellenists (vs. 20-21). Josephus mentions that Jesus, within his lifetime, "won over many . . .of the Greeks".[3] It is probable, therefore, that there were "Hellenist" Jews side by side with "Hebrew" Jews as believers in the Jerusalem church from the beginning of its history. It is also probable that the one hundred and twenty Galilean "Hebrews" were soon in a minority; most of the three thousand added to the church on the day of Pentecost would have been "Hellenists". Perhaps the "Hebrew" numbers were only increased by the later addition of the "priests", as mentioned above.

The second of the usages of "Hellenist" (Acts 9:29), however, relates to certain people who attempted to kill the now-converted Saul of Tarsus in about AD 36. Clearly these are non-converting Hellenist-Jews, who may have felt under considerable pressure to establish their distance from the converting Hellenists. The non-converting Hellenists are probably to be identified with the members of the synagogue to whom Stephen went in the course of his ministry. This synagogue, the so-called synagogue of the freedmen, may have derived its name from the Jewish slaves in Rome a century earlier who had been freed by Pompey.[4] According to this opinion these Jewish "freedmen", or some of them, made their way to Jerusalem where they established a synagogue. The reference to "of the Cyrenians", "of the Alexandrians" and "those of Cilicia and Asia" suggests that Jewish freedmen from these Greek-speaking regions had, over a period of time, been drawn into membership of this synagogue.

Of great interest is a synagogue inscription belonging to this very period, discovered in Jerusalem. Possibly it is from the same synagogue of the freedmen referred to in Acts.

Theodotus, son of Vettenus, priest and archisyna-gogue, son of an archisynagogue, grandson of an archisynagogue built the synagogue for the reading of the law and the teaching of the commandments, and the guest house and the rooms and the water supplies as an inn for those who have need when they come from abroad; which [synagogue] his fathers founded and the elders and Simonides.[5]

Since *Vettenus* is a Latin name it is possible he was a "freedman" who took his name from the former owner who had liberated him, as was customary. His son Theodotus, whose name is Greek and whom the inscription honoured, was both a priest and a synagogue ruler. Thus Theodotus was identified with both the temple (a priest) and the law (an archisynagogue) respectively. It may be significant that Stephen attacked, or was alleged to have attacked, both temple and law (Acts 6:13). Therefore we have the fascinating possibility, not only that Theodotus' synagogue was the synagogue of the freedmen, but also that Theodotus may have been the instigator of the high priests' opposition to Stephen. If so, it is equally possible that the Hellenists' opposition to Saul of Tarsus some years later came from the same quarter. (Acts 6:11-14; 9:29)

The Acts of the Apostles, therefore, points to the existence of a racial-linguistic component of Jerusalem society, known as "Hellenists". Some were converted to the faith of Jesus the Nazarene and quickly became a dominant part of the rapidly growing community of believers. Others, however, who were approached first by Stephen, then some years later by Saul, were violently antagonistic to the converting "Hellenists" and their radical message.

Is this the last we hear of the "Hellenists"? By no means. As we shall see the assault of Saul on the believing "Hellenists" led to their scattering along the Greek cities of the eastern seaboard of the Mediterranean and the creation of many congregations of believers, including ultimately the church of Antioch which would quickly rival the church of Jerusalem. Historically the mission to the Gentiles began not with the Apostle Paul in c. 47 but with the "Hellenists" twelve years earlier.

What then of the non-converting "Hellenists"? There is no explicit reference to them after their attempt to kill Saul of Tarsus in Jerusalem c. 36. It is, however, possible that they figure in the New Testament story in two related ways. First, they may be the source of the persecution of the community

of believers as recorded in the "letter to the Hebrews".
(The word "Hellenist", however, appears nowhere within
the letter, nor does "Hebrew".) This was a community
of believers who apparently lived in Palestine, and were
both Jewish and Greek-reading. (The letter is written in
sophisticated Greek.) It is possible that they were the
surviving believing "Hellenists" who did not emigrate from
Palestine in 34/35 and who were under ongoing pressure,
arguably from the antagonistic "Hellenists".

A second possibility is that the Jerusalem-based Jews
who launched successive missions against the Greek-
speaking churches established by Paul in Galatia, in
Corinth and in Philippi may have been non-converting
Hellenists. Clearly these unidentified opponents must
have been competent in the Greek language, at least as
competent as Paul, to visit the Gentile churches in
those regions. Did they feign true belief and somehow
ingratiate themselves with the Aramaic Christian community in Jerusalem, led as it was by James after c. 43?
Paul calls these opponents "pretended-brothers" and
"pretended-apostles", *pseudadelphoi, pseudapostoloi* (2
Corinthians 11:26; Galatians 2:4; 2 Corinthians 11:13),
implying perhaps that he saw through their pretence
whereas James did not.

But we have now come forward many years from the
critical period under review — the two or so years between
Jesus and Paul. What we have discovered is that this earliest
community was, from the beginning, a racially mixed
community. We should not conclude, however, that these
racial-linguistic lines were too sharply drawn — at least not
at the beginning. We must not suppose that the "Hebrews"
spoke only Aramaic and the "Hellenists" spoke only Greek.
Bi-lingualism must be taken into account. Among the
Aramaic-speaking "Hebrews" we know that Barnabas also
must have spoken Greek since he taught in the church of
Antioch and was bracketed with Paul for the mission to the
Gentiles (Acts 11:25-26; Galatians 2:9). We presume that
Peter knew at least some Greek since he travelled in
the Greek coastal cities and spoke in the household of
Cornelius where Greek would have been spoken (Acts 10:1-

48). Silas (=Silvanus), a prophet in the Aramaic-speaking, Jerusalem church in the late forties, delivered the decree of the Jerusalem church to the Greek-speaking congregations of Syria, Cilicia and Galatia (Acts 15:22; 16:4). Silas/Silvanus later accompanied Paul and Timothy on the missionary visit to Greece where, in partnership with them, he evangelized the Corinthians (2 Corinthians 1:19) and wrote to the Thessalonians (1 Thessalonians 1:1; 2 Thessalonians 1:1). In all probability he is the same Silvanus who, as Peter's amanuensis, wrote the elegant Greek of 1 Peter (1 Peter 5:12). (An amanuensis was a scribal assistant who wrote on behalf of someone else.)

What of the believing "Hellenists"? It is likely that they would have learned something at least of the language of the city in which they lived. Consider, too, the example of Saul who originated from the Greek city of Tarsus. We know that he spoke Aramaic, probably with considerable fluency since he was a leading Pharisee (Acts 22:2; Galatians 1:14). It is possible that among the converting "Hellenists" there were those who, like Saul from Tarsus in Cilicia, spoke Aramaic as well as Greek.

We have placed considerable emphasis on the mixed though integrated nature of this Hebraic-Hellenist community at the beginning of this brief period because scholars adopt an overly rigid format of four separate stages between Jesus and Paul: first the Aramaic phase; second the Palestinian Hellenist-Jewish phase; third the non-Palestinian Hellenist-Jewish phase; and, finally, the Hellenist/Gentile phase. These stages are introduced to explain how the (allegedly) simple Hebraic faith of Jesus became the (allegedly) Hellenistic theology of Paul. But, as we have seen, this is both artificial and untrue. The Christian community in Jerusalem was, from the beginning, a mixed Hebraic-Hellenist community. If anything the Hellenist Jews were greater in number near the beginning than the Hebraic Jews. The theological understanding of this mixed community must have been, to a degree at least, inter-dependent and inter-related. Jesus was regarded as "Lord" by both language groups — whether as *Mara* by the Aramaists or as *Kyrios* by the Hellenists. The integrated bi-partisan nature of the confession is surely reflected by Paul's sentences in 1 Corinthians 16:22 where he refers to Jesus as "Lord" in both Aramaic (*Marana tha* = "Our Lord, come") and Greek (. . ."if any one has no love for the *Kyrios* =Lord"). This integrated confession, Hebraic and Hellenist, was probably an established fact when Paul returned to Jerusalem in AD 36. It did not develop evolution-like, phase-by-phase, as the history-of-religion scholars suggest.[6]

4   A theologically reflective community

The earliest Christian community reflected on the great theological issues raised by the teaching, deeds and resurrection of Jesus of Nazareth. This is implicit in the Acts of Apostles' description of those who were baptized on the day of Pentecost, "they devoted themselves to the apostles' teaching and fellowship, to the breaking of bread and to prayers". (Acts 2:42)

There are at least four areas in which the post-Easter community engaged in theological reflection, some of which we have already touched on. This is not to suggest that the community was somehow monastic, withdrawn from Jerusalem society as, for example, the Qumran community was. On the contrary, the community members observed the Jewish hours of prayer and participated in the temple services.

It seems probable, therefore, that theological reflection occurred within a praying, worshipping community which was at the same time vigorously involved in signs/wonders and in Jesus-"witness" to the people of Jerusalem. These four activities would have overlapped.

It is evident, first, that the community, led by those disciples who had been companions of Jesus, reflected deeply on *Jesus himself* — what he said and did and the Old Testament scriptures he saw as fulfilled in himself. Consider, for example, the following passages from the gospel of John:

When therefore [Jesus] was raised from the dead his disciples remembered that he had said this ["destroy this temple and in three days I will raise it up"] and they believed the scripture ["you shall not make my father's house a house of trade" — Zechariah 14:21] and the word. . .Jesus had spoken ["destroy this temple . . .etc."] (John 2:22)· ·

This text gives us a window into the inner workings of the early church. We see these early disciples remembering that Jesus said, "destroy this temple, . . ." and the Old Testament scripture he used at that time, "You shall not make my father's house a house of trade" (Zechariah 14:21). But we see something further, another activity. These believers, in searching the Old Testament for prophecies about Jesus, located Psalm 69:9, "Zeal for thy house will consume me". This was judged specially appropriate since it foreshadowed that zeal of Jesus which would consume him, in his death. And it contained the word "house", which also appeared in the text from Zechariah which Jesus used at the time. Clearly the earliest believers both remembered Jesus' words and deeds and sought for scriptural prophecies which would further explain them.

Another example from John relates to Jesus' words and the Old Testament scripture he used during the Feast of Tabernacles, "If any one thirst let him come [to me] and let him drink who believes in me. As the scripture says, from within him shall flow rivers of living water." (John 7:38)[7] Jesus here portrays himself in terms of the new temple from which water would flow, as prophesied in Ezekiel 47:1-12. Later on, and upon further reflection, the disciples saw Jesus' word and the Old Testament text as fulfilled in the historic outpouring of the Spirit after the first Easter. "This [Jesus] said about the Spirit which those who believed in him were to receive; for as yet the Spirit had not been given because Jesus was not yet glorified." (John 7:39)

Clearly John's understanding arose as he and the other disciples in the community reflected upon the original words of Jesus, and the passage of scripture he used, in the light of their experience of the historic coming of the Holy Spirit.

Yet another example is John's description of Jesus' action riding up to Jerusalem five days before the Passover which was, he said, in accordance with Zechariah 9:9, "Fear not, daughter of Zion; behold your king is coming sitting upon an ass's colt." John continues immediately, "His disciples did not understand this at first; but when Jesus was glorified, then they remembered that this had been written of him and done to him." (12:16)

These three examples from the gospel of John show that the early Christians reflected on what Jesus said and did and upon the scriptures he saw as being brought to fulfilment by his ministry. When did these early Christians engage in this theological reflection? According to John his disciples "remembered" what Jesus said and the Old Testament texts he cited "when he/Jesus was raised from the dead/glorified" (2:22; 12:16), that is, soon after his resurrection. This is confirmed by a converging comment in John's gospel about the Holy Spirit, ". . .the Counsellor (*paraklétos*). . .whom the Father will send. . .will teach you all things and bring to your remembrance all that I have said to you" (14:26). This suggests that the disciples engaged in remembering, that is in Spirit-led reflection, in the immediate aftermath of the day of Pentecost.

The second, and closely related, area of community reflection was directed to *identifying and collecting* Old Testament passages which were seen to be fulfilled in the light of Jesus' ministry and exaltation, as several examples will indicate.

In Psalm 110:1, David wrote, "The LORD says to my Lord sit at my right hand until I make thy enemies the footstool at thy feet." Just prior to his arrest Jesus quoted this text in a debate with the scribes to raise the question how the "Son of David" could also be David's Lord, the One who was at God's right hand. (Mark 12:35-40)

On the day of Pentecost Peter quoted Psalm 110:1 as now fulfilled by Jesus' exaltation, the outpoured Holy Spirit being the evidence. Peter concluded, "Let all the house of Israel know. . .that God has made [Jesus] Lord and Christ" (Acts 2:36). Peter's use of this psalm had been influenced by Jesus.

As the early Christians reflected on Psalm 110:1 their minds went to another psalm which had a number of

corresponding words. Psalm 8 says, "the son of man
...(God) has put all things under his feet" (verses 4, 6). This
psalm spoke of "all things under [the] feet" of the son of
man. Psalm 110:1 was obviously to be linked up with these
ideas and were to be quoted in the years to come by Peter,
Paul and the letter to the Hebrews.

1 Peter 3:18-22	[Christ] has gone into heaven and is at the right hand of God. (Psalm 110:1) with angels, authorities and powers subject to him. (Psalm 8:6)'
Ephesians 1:20-21	when [God] raised [Jesus] from the dead and made him sit at his right hand. (Psalm 110:1) ...and he has put all things under his feet. (Psalm 8:6)
Hebrews 1:3	he sat down at the right hand of the majesty on high. . .(Psalm 110:1)
Hebrews 2:6,7	Son of man . . .[crowned] with glory and honour. . . Everything in subjection under his feet (Psalm 8:4,6)

Psalm 110:1, as we have noted, was the subject of
Jesus' own teaching about himself. The probability is that
the linking of Psalm 110:1 with Psalm 8:4 occurred by
theological reflection within the earliest community. The
extracts from these psalms then apparently formed part
of a wider collection of Old Testament scriptures (or
"testimonies") upon which the various New Testament
writers drew.[8] Clearly the "Lord" of Psalm 110:1/8:4,6
became the *kyrios* and the *Mara* whom the Hellenist and
Aramaist believers worshipped at their gatherings in Jerusalem and whom they proclaimed among unbelievers (1
Corinthians 16:22; 2 Corinthians 4:5). The words of Psalm
110:1 run like a thread through the New Testament. We can
trace it back to Jesus himself. It was Jesus' sense that the
goal of the Old Testament scriptures had been reached in
his own person that led his first followers to search those
scriptures for texts and teachings which foreshadowed

his coming. Thus there were created, as C.F.D. Moule wrote, collections of biblical passages "drawn together round Jesus, as a magnet collects iron filings" [8a]

Another example of the community's use of Old Testament passages is Deuteronomy 21:22-23.

If a man has committed a sin worthy of death and he is put to death and you shall hang him on a tree...you shall surely bury him on the same day (for he who is hanged is accursed by God)...

It is striking how frequently the term "tree" is found in the New Testament. In the Acts of the Apostles it is referred to in speeches by both Peter and Paul (5:30; 10:39; 13:29). It is also found in Letters of Paul and Peter. In Galatians 3:13, Paul wrote "Christ redeemed us from the curse of the law having become a curse for us — for as it is written Cursed is everyone who hangs on a tree'." Peter in his first letter joins the "tree" of Deuteronomy 21:22-23 with the sin-bearing servant of Isaiah 52:13-53; 12:24 "[Christ] himself bore our sins in his body" (Isaiah 53:4,12); "on the tree" (Deuteronomy 21:22-23)

The Jewish audiences responding to early Christian preaching doubtless quickly pointed to Deuteronomy 21:22-23 to show that Jesus, far from being the Messiah, must have "committed a sin worthy of death". Was he not "hanged on a tree"? Didn't this prove he was the "accursed" of God? But the earliest community, by interpreting Deuteronomy 21:22-23 with Isaiah 52:13-53:12, were able to show that the Messiah's death was not for his sins but for the sins of others, for their redemption. That both Peter and Paul made use of the "tree" imagery in speeches and letters suggests that this was an exegesis arrived at within the earliest community as a response to Jewish objections to the proclamation of Jesus as Messiah.

These examples Psalm 110:1; 8:4,6, Deuteronomy 21:22-23 and Isaiah 52-53 give us some idea of the industry with which the earliest community searched the Old Testament scriptures to discover passages which were prophetic of Jesus. The reader is referred to C.H. Dodd, *According to the Scriptures* (London, 1952) for a comprehensive survey of the extent and use of these texts.

A third, also closely related area, of community reflection led to the early writing of a *narrative of Jesus' last days in Jerusalem*, including the account of his death and resurrection. The earliest Christians were, it seems, very interested in what happened to their Lord in Jerusalem at the end of his life.

Scholars are in general agreement that Mark chapters 11-16 existed originally as an early, self-contained record of Jesus' final week in Jerusalem, climaxed by his crucifixion and resurrection. How soon after his death/resurrection was this narrative written? Two characteristics of Mark 11-16 suggest that it may have been written very early in the life of the new community. One is that the text is remarkably detailed in regard to personal names, places and the passage of time.[9] See, for example, Mark 14:1,12, "it was now two days before the Passover and the Feast of Unleavened Bread. . ." ". . .On the first day of Unleavened Bread. . ."

The intensification of historical specifics in Mark 11-16 would be consistent with its early writing, possibly by collaboration between Peter and John Mark. Another characteristic suggestive of early writing is in the references to the high priest (14:53,54,60,61,63) but without the mention of his name. This may imply writing prior to AD 37, the date of Caiaphas' death, since before then it would not have been necessary to give his name. Significantly, Matthew, Luke and John each gives the name of the high priest, indicating post-AD 37 writing in their cases.

A fourth, also closely related, area of community reflection was in the *creation of two tradition-formulae*, given at a very early date to Paul by the Jerusalem church and reproduced by him in the first letter to the Corinthians. First there was the tradition about the Last Supper/Lord's Supper. "For I received from the Lord what I also delivered [="traditioned"] to you that the Lord Jesus on the night when he was betrayed took bread. . .the cup. . ." (11:23-25)

Then, there were the chief elements of the gospel which Paul "delivered" ("traditioned") to the Corinthians which he had also previously "received":

that Christ died for our sins in accordance with the

scriptures
that he was buried
that he was raised the third day in accordance with the
scriptures
that he appeared to Cephas, then to the twelve (15:3-5).

These tradition-formulae which Paul received, as I believe from the earliest Jerusalem church, were closely
related to two previously discussed areas of community
reflection.

(a) The tradition-formulae quoted by Paul resemble
elements of the narrative in Mark 11-16. The vocabulary
used by Paul in his Last Supper/Lord's Supper tradition
bears such a striking word for word similarity with Mark's
account of the Last Supper that a dependency of one
upon the other is demanded. Paul's account, which is
longer, appears to reflect a slightly earlier version, which
Mark appears to have shortened. Moreover in the gospel
tradition, the "he was raised" of the Pauline formula has the
same Greek root as the angel's word to the women on the
first day of the week: "He is risen". (Greek: *egeirein* in both
1 Corinthians 15:4 and Mark 16:6)

(b) The tradition-formula of the gospel-message is
closely related to the fulfilment motif in the earliest
community. Thus: "Christ died for our sins in accordance
with the scriptures"; ". . .he was raised the third day
in accordance with the scriptures. . ." Clearly, the
proclamation of the message about Christ was seen to arise
out of the prophecies and promises of the Old Testament.

Enough evidence has been produced to establish that the
earliest community of believers industriously reflected
upon Jesus. They "remembered" what Jesus said and did
and the Old Testament scriptures he quoted as now being
fulfilled. Additionally they searched the Old Testament
isolating and collecting texts which had been brought to
fulfilment by Jesus' coming and exaltation. Moreover,
they wrote a comprehensive narrative of the last days
of their master. Finally, they devised summary-statements
about Christ for the remembrance-meal and for evangelism, based on the previously mentioned narrative and

which were seen to be in fulfilment of scriptures. It should be stressed that what has been written here is no more than the barest summary of what must have been far-reaching theological reflection within the community. Moreover, it should be re-emphasized that this activity within the community was closely connected with a vigorous ministry to the wider Jewish community in Jerusalem.

But why should these earliest Christians have been so active in these matters? The only answer can be Jesus. It was Jesus' recent presence with them and his historic resurrection which inspired them to "remember" what he said and did, to discover Old Testament texts prophetic of him, to write a narrative of his last days and to create faith formulas. These activities could not have been self-generating and would not have occurred unless Jesus had been raised from the dead. Certainly no such activities occurred (so far as we know) in the aftermaths of the death of the Teacher of Righteousness or Judas the Galilean.

5   A community which cared for its needy members

The Acts of the Apostles bears witness to the unity of heart and soul of the earliest community. The members' devotion to the apostles' teaching, their corporate prayer life, their frequent breaking of bread together was also characterized by the absence of want among needy members. The Acts reports that "there was not a needy person among them" (4:34-35 cf. 2:45).

The reason for this is that those who owned lands or possessions sold them and brought the proceeds to the apostles for distribution as necessary. It was not that all members compulsorily handed over everything they owned, as was the practice in the Qumran community for fully fledged members. Rather, those members who owned some-thing of value voluntarily contributed for the poorer members.

The somewhat *ad hoc* character of contributing within the earliest Christian community may be compared with the rigorous rules for membership at Qumran:

After he has spent a full year in the midst of the community, the members are jointly to review his case, as to his understanding and performances in matters of doctrine. If it then be voted by the opinion of the priests and of a majority of their co-covenanters to admit him to the sodality, they are to have him bring with him all his property and the tools of his profession. These are to be committed to the custody of the community's "minister of works". They are to be entered by that officer into an account, but he is not to disburse them for the general benefit.

Not until the completion of a second year. . .is the candidate to be admitted to the common board, when, . . .if it then be voted to admit him to the community, he is to be registered in the due order of rank. . .and share in the common funds. . .

If there be found in the community a man who consciously lies in the matter of his wealth, he is to be regarded as outside the state of purity by membership, and he is to be mulcted of one fourth of his food ration. . .[10]

Clearly there are major dissimilarities between the lifestyles of the communities of Qumran and the Jerusalem Christians. In contrast with the Jerusalem church the Qumran community was highly structured, with careful procedures and tight control of transition from the first to the second year of membership. Pooling of all possessions was compulsory and there were clearly decreed penalties for lying abut one's wealth. In the coming centuries Christian monasteries would take on a rigidity not unlike the Qumran rule. At this early stage, however, the Christian community displayed a noticeable lack of fixity. It is, therefore, unlikely that the first Christians modelled their life together on the Qumran pattern. There was, in fact, little in common between the two groups.[11]

It was the growth in the community which led to critical problems, in particular the growth in latter times of the Hebraic component. As a result the integrated character of the community began to be lost. The Hellenists began to complain against the Hebrews because the Hellenist widows were neglected in the daily food distribution. Clearly the apostles were no longer capable of attending to these matters without neglecting their calling to pray and minister the word of God.

The whole community chose seven Hellenist men to administer the distribution to both groups of widows. Possibly the deacons who came into sight later in the New Testament owe their origins to the "service" of these seven men (see e.g. Philippians 1:1; 1 Timothy 3:8-13). It should be noted, however, that it is the verb "to serve" (*diakonein*) not the noun "deacon" (*diakonos*) which is used in Acts 6:2.

Stephen, the first named of the seven Hellenists, was a man of exceptional gifts as well as of radical views. Upon his performance of "great signs and wonders among the people" (Acts 6:8), the antipathetic Hellenists from the synagogue of the freedmen engaged in a bitter dispute with him. Worsted in the argument, the non-converting Hellenists instigated Stephen's arrest. He was charged before the Sanhedrin.

This man never ceases to speak words against this holy place and the law; for we have heard him say that this Jesus of Nazareth will destroy this place, and change the customs which Moses delivered to us. (Acts 6:13-14)

It is quite possible that Stephen did, in fact, speak along these lines against the temple and the law. While Peter is not recorded as criticizing these twin pillars of Judaism, Stephen may have had a deeper insight into the implications and significance of Jesus. Stephen, like Paul who came later, appears to have understood that temple and law were now fulfilled, overtaken by the new covenant of Christ and the Spirit. It is indeed conceivable that, historically speaking, Stephen was the first to understand this.

In his sketch of the increase in the number of disciples at that time, the author of Acts notes in passing that "a great many of the priests were obedient to the faith" (Acts 6:7). Quite possibly this may have led to an intensification of judaizing pressure within the community to which, perhaps, Stephen objected.

In his long speech to the Sanhedrin answering the charges made against him (Acts 7:7-56) Stephen drew attention to God's promise to Abraham that he would deliver the Hebrews from Egypt into the promised land where they would worship him (Acts 7:7). However, from that time the people refused to submit to their God-appointed leader Moses (7:27,35-37,39) preferring Aaron who led them to worship the calf-idol and the host of heaven (7:40-44). Although at first the people were content to worship God in a tabernacle, made according to God's directions, where they heard the living oracles of God from Moses, under Solomon they dispensed with it preferring the house made with hands, the temple. Stephen's point was that in fact they had rejected Moses and his God-given oracles and they had rejected God's provision of a meeting place, the tabernacle. In other words it is not he, Stephen, but they, who are against the temple and Moses/the law.

Stephen made several remarkable statements about Jesus in the course of his speech. Moses is introduced only as a type of the Christ who was to come, as the true leader of God's people. It is Jesus Christ, by this typology, who is the "ruler and judge" over the people, their "ruler and deliverer" (7:35), "the prophet" who speaks the ultimate "living oracles" of God (7:37-38). At the climax of the speech Stephen declared that he saw "the Son of man standing at the right hand of God." (7:56)

Stephen's vision of Jesus in those terms arises, as we have seen, from Psalms 8:4,6, "the *son of man*" and 110:1, "the *right hand of God*".

Stephen was not alone in portraying Jesus as the Moses-like prophet who was to come. Peter also saw that (Acts 3:22). Yet Stephen understood that such a Jesus, as a greater than Moses, really meant the end of both law and temple. It is quite possible that this idea lodged in the mind of Saul of Tarsus, who was present on that occasion. In years to come Paul would teach that the temple of God was now to be thought of as a body of believers gathered on earth and in heaven (1 Corinthians 3:16-17; Ephesians 2:21). He would teach that the Covenant and Law of Moses were now superseded by the all-fulfilling Covenant of Christ and the Spirit (2 Corinthians 3:7-11). It is quite possible.

that Stephen's words were sown, seed-like, in the mind and memory of Paul to bear fruit later in his theological exposition of Christianity.

Stephen concluded that the Jews of his day in their rejection of the Holy One, the new Moses, and in their obsession with a house made with hands, were perpetuating the stubborn disobedience to God which their forbears had habitually shown. This was too much. The trial of Stephen before the Sanhedrin degenerated into a lynching. The Hellenist "witnesses" from the synagogue of the freedmen seized Stephen, cast him down from the city wall and stoned him to death.

Saul of Tarsus, who is now mentioned for the first time, apparently had been in close consultation with the antipathetic Hellenists. The Acts of the Apostles makes the significant comment that, "the witnesses [those who had charged Stephen before the Sanhedrin] laid down their garments at the feet of a young man named Saul" (7:58). The stoning of Stephen triggered an assault on the whole Christian church at Jerusalem, led by Saul. This was to have far-reaching consequences, both for Saul and for the spread of the new movement.

Thus it was that the first period of Christian history — the two-year span between Jesus and Paul — was brought to an end by the death of the first martyr, the Hellenist Stephen. That event was, in the presentation of the Acts of the Apostles, the critical event which led to the spread of the faith to the Gentiles.

From this point, AD 34, to refer again to our "river" analogy, the course of the story divides, one branch proceeding as Hebraic Christianity, the other as Hellenist Christianity.

Further reading to Chapter Six:
M. Hengel, *Between Jesus and Paul*, SCM, London, 1983.
C.F.D. Moule, *The Birth of the New Testament*, A. & C. Black, London, 1973.

Notes

[1]For the year AD 33 in preference to AD 30, see Chapter 3.

[2]*Homily*, 21.

[3]*AJ*, xviii, 63.

[4]Philo, *Legatio*, 155-156.

[5]In C.K. Barrett, *The New Testament Background: Selected Documents*, SPCK, London, 1956, 51.

[6]On this important topic see M. Hengel, *The Son of God*, SCM, London, 1976; *Between Jesus and Paul*, SCM, London, 1983; I.H. Marshall, "Palestinian and Hellenistic Christianity: Some critical comments", in *NTS*, 19, 1973, 271-287.

[7]Following the punctuation of R.E. Brown, *The Gospel According to John* I, Anchor/Doubleday, New York, 1966, 319 ff.

[8]See C.H. Dodd, *According to the Scriptures*, Collins, London, 1952.

[8a]C.F.D. Moule, *The Birth of the New Testament*, A. & C. Black, London, 1973, 69.

[9]See P.W. Barnett, *Is the New Testament History?* Hodder and Stoughton, Sydney, 1986, 96-98.

[10]Manual Disciplines vi, 13-24 in T.H. Gaster, *The Dead Sea Scriptures*, Doubleday, New York, 1956.

[11]See further, N.S. Fujita, *A Crack in the Jar*, Paulist, New York, 1986, 109-158.

7

Jerusalem to Antioch
(c. AD 34-37)

What next? The New Testament story now passes into a phase where we catch only passing glimpses of people and events. Through the first seven chapters of the Acts of the Apostles we have a reasonable idea of the character of the earliest history of the new movement between Jesus and Paul. Similarly the Acts and letters of Paul combine to give an expansive and detailed account from the late forties into the early sixties. But there is only scanty information about the period between the death of Stephen c. AD 34 and the missionary conference in Jerusalem c. AD 47.

So the courses of those two branches of our New Testament story/river are not, at all points, visible to us. The point at which they fork (the withdrawal of the believing Hellenists after the death of Stephen c. AD 34) is clear enough. Also visible is the critical meeting of the Antioch and Jerusalem delegates fourteen years later. It is in the intervening period that the two branches are not always in full view.

The Acts of the Apostles passes over the thirteen or fourteen years between AD 34/47 in only five chapters, which are for the most part devoted to such major events as the exploits of Philip (Chapter 8) and Peter (Chapters 10-12) and the conversion of Saul (Chapter 9). Apart from information about the attack of King Herod Agrippa on the Jerusalem church — in c. AD 43 — we are given little information about events within Judaea or the passage of time covered by Acts 8-12. Thus the history of the "Hellenist" branch is more accessible to our enquiry than the history of the Hebraic branch.

The letter of Paul to the Galatians, however, does give a precious chronological outline which assists us to create an overall time frame of the period.

In this letter Paul acknowledges his assault on the believers, whose date we have estimated at AD 34, "you have heard of my former life in Judaism how I persecuted the church of God violently and tried to destroy it" (1:13). He then refers to God's "revelation of Jesus Christ" to him which, according to the Acts of the Apostles, occurred near Damascus soon after the death of Stephen and Saul's attack on the church of Jerusalem (i.e. in c. AD 34), "But when [God] who had set me apart. . .and called me was pleased to . . .reveal his Son to me." (1:15-16)

Paul also gives two chronological points after this fateful occurrence c. AD 34, both introduced by "then" (Greek: *epeita*) followed by the number of years which had passed, as I believe, from the time God called him. Paul's calling/conversion was the point from which he measured time. (It should also be noted that biblical writers count inclusively, that is, parts of years are numbered as if full years.)

Paul's first chronological marker after his conversion is, "Then after three years I went up to Jerusalem to visit Cephas. . .I [also] saw. . .James the Lord's brother" (1:18-19). Counting inclusively from his calling/conversion c. AD 34 this would mean that c. AD 36 Paul journeyed from Damascus to Jerusalem. The former persecutor was making his first visit to the city as proclaimer of the Son of God.

A further visit is mentioned immediately, although it occurred many years later, "Then after fourteen years I went up again to Jerusalem with Barnabas, taking Titus with me" (2:1). Counting inclusively from his calling/conversion means that the second visit to Jerusalem occurred in c. AD 47.

It was c. AD 47 that a little noticed but very important private meeting between the delegates from the Jerusalem and Antioch churches occurred. A far-reaching agreement was reached whereby the Jerusalem delegates should take the gospel to Jews and the Antioch delegates should take the gospel to Gentiles (2:7-9). This conference marks one of the great moments in New Testament history. It is quite clear, therefore, that there had been significant developments within the fourteen year period under review. To these developments, three in number, we now turn.

1   The scattering of the Jerusalem church

By his own testimony Saul/Paul launched a significant attack upon the Jerusalem church. He wrote to the Galatians that, "I persecuted the church of God violently and tried to destroy it" (1:13). His means of finding believers was through the synagogues to which as Jews they belonged. In a speech quoted in the Acts of the Apostles Paul said that, "I punished them often in the synagogues and tried to make them blaspheme" (26:11). Moreover, according to the same speech in Acts, many were imprisoned and killed. "I not only shut up many of the saints in prison, by authority from the chief priests, but when they were put to death I cast my vote against them." (26:10 cf. 8:3)

So zealous was Paul against the believers in Jerusalem that he sought to eradicate them in other places as well. The Acts of the Apostles states that,

Saul...went to the high priest and asked him for letters to the synagogues at Damascus so that if he found any belonging to the Way, men or women, he might bring them bound to Jerusalem. (9:12 cf. 26:11)

Duly authorized, Saul/Paul set out for Damascus (c. AD 34) only to be confronted on the way by the glorified crucified One. It is striking that Christianity had spread to Damascus, so soon after the crucifixion/resurrection of Jesus. We do not know how, or by whose influence.

Saul's devastating attack led to the scattering of the members of the Jerusalem church throughout wider Judaea-Samaria and Galilee (Acts 8:1; 9:31). According to the Acts narrative only the apostles remained in Jerusalem, though this may be a mild overstatement. Presumably in time many members of the Jerusalem church returned to the city once the threat posed by Saul/Paul had been removed. The Jerusalem believers who remained in Judaea-Samaria and Galilee probably established churches in these regions.

This is the natural inference from the narrative "Now those who were scattered went about preaching the word." (8:4)

Apparently it was as the Jerusalem church was scattered' and took root wherever the members came to rest that the new churches were established. Paul speaks of "churches of Christ in Judaea" which were in existence by AD 36 when he first visited Jerusalem as a Christian (Galatians 1:22 cf. 1 Thessalonians 2:14). The Acts of the Apostles makes the same observation when, after the cessation of the persecution of Saul, it notes, "So the church [=the Jerusalem church which had been scattered — 8:1] throughout all Judaea and Samaria and Galilee had peace and was built up [and] was multiplied." (9:31)

More details emerge incidentally as the Acts narrative proceeds. There is reference to,

"a city of *Samaria*. . .they. . .believed. . .were baptized" (8:5,12);

"the saints. . .at *Lydda*" (9:32);

"at *Joppa*. . .saints and widows" (9:36, 41);

"at *Caesarea*. . .Cornelius [already] 'knew' [something about] the word" (10:36).

Presumably the churches in Judaea-Samaria and Galilee were Aramaic speaking and established by scattered Hebraic members of the Jerusalem church. But the names of their founders have not come down to us.

The identity of the founder of the churches listed above in Samaria, Lydda, Joppa and Caesarea is, however, known to us. He is Philip, the second listed Hellenist after Stephen, who we are told went to Samaria; Acts narrates the events in detail (8:4-13). (We assume Philip to have gone to Greek-speaking towns in Samaria.) Acts also remarks that Philip evangelized all the towns from Azotus, near the coast opposite Jerusalem, to Caesarea on the coast at the extreme north of Judaea-Samaria. Lydda, Joppa and of course Caesarea would have been among these Greek-speaking coastal towns visited by Philip, who ultimately settled in Caesarea, becoming in time known appropriately as "Philip the evangelist". (Acts 21:8)

Acts also refers incidentally to other coastal towns, not far to the north of Caesarea, where churches were to be found: Tyre (21:3-4); Ptolemais (21:7); Sidon (27:3). These Phoenicean churches, located as they were in Hellenistic cities, and in existence by the late forties (Acts 15:3) had probably also been evangelized by Philip the evangelist since they are just to the north of Caesarea (cf. Acts 11:19).

Thus Acts of the Apostles, when carefully read, gives indication of the spread of Christianity from Jerusalem throughout the Aramaic speaking inland hill country of Judaea-Samaria and Galilee, as well as to the Greek-speaking towns along the southern half of the coastal plain of Palestine, from Azotus opposite Jerusalem, to Sidon opposite Damascus.

In time, however, other and unnamed Hellenists who had been forced out of Jerusalem travelled as far as Phoenicia and Cyprus and Antioch (11:19). Thus the people of the northern seaboard of the eastern Mediterranean also came to hear the Word of God. Only Jews were addressed at first. But when unnamed men from Cyprus and Cyrene came to Antioch, "Greeks" (=Gentiles) were also evangelized and a great many became believers. While it is not possible to establish precise dates for these events, we may reasonably set the conversion of Gentiles in Antioch in the late thirties (but not earlier) or the early forties (but not later).

Over the next decade Antioch, which was after Alexandria the largest Hellenistic city in the world, would witness a significant growth of Christianity. It was in Antioch that believers were first called "Christians" (Acts 11:26). During those years the church of Antioch, which was predominantly but not exclusively Gentile in composition, would begin to rival Jerusalem as the largest Christian church. Its growth was so great that the church in Jerusalem came to hear of it. The Hellenist branch had begun with the expulsion of Philip and others of that group. The formation of churches in Greek-speaking coastal areas culminated in the creation of the church at Antioch. The Hellenist branch was now clearly defined.

The Jerusalem church, however, saw itself having some responsibility for this rapidly growing Hellenist church; so Barnabas was sent to see what was happening. It will be mentioned in the next section that Peter earlier went

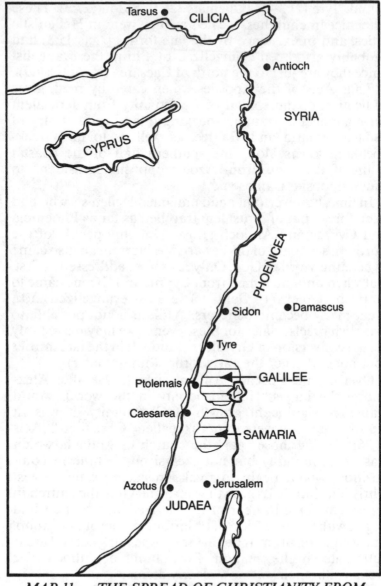

MAP 11 — THE SPREAD OF CHRISTIANITY FROM JERUSALEM TO ANTIOCH

The Hellenists, after their expulsion from Jerusalem, travelled north. Churches were established in Samaria and Galilee and in the Greek cities along the coast.

from Jerusalem to Samaria, Lydda, Joppa and Caesarea to consolidate (and perhaps check up on?) ministry exercised in these places by the Hellenist Philip. Probably the despatch of Barnabas to Antioch should be seen in the same light. The choice of Barnabas was prudent since he was himself a Cypriot-Hellenist, a Christian leader of proven character. He is described as "a good man, full of the Holy Spirit and faith". (Acts 11:24 cf. 4:36-37; 9:27)

Barnabas, however, engaged in significant ministry in Antioch; he was, after all, a pastor, an encourager. Some time after his arrival (in c. AD 44) it became apparent that he could not do the work unaided. So he went to Tarsus, which was quite near Antioch, to seek the assistance of Paul. For a year, that is c. AD 45/46, Barnabas and Saul worked together in Antioch teaching "a large company of people". (Acts 11:26)

2   The Hebraizing of the Jerusalem church (c. AD 34-47)

We turn back now to the now-predominantly Hebraic Jerusalem church. The history and character of the church in Jerusalem throughout this period, and indeed beyond, must be understood in terms of the strongly marked trends within Judaean society.

Broadly speaking the period after the death of the emperor Tiberius in AD 37 witnessed a deterioration in relationships between Palestinian Jews and their Roman masters. This in turn created a volatile atmosphere in Judaea which was marked by the rise of an apocalyptic religious nationalism. The existing antagonism towards the Gentiles and Hellenism increased in this environment. Christianity in Jerusalem became increasingly Hebraic/ Aramaist in character. Christian Hellenists or those in some way sympathetic to their emphases would have found the church in Jerusalem increasingly intolerant of them. Thus, for example, more moderate leaders like Peter and John were not able to remain in Jerusalem after the late forties, leaving the sole leadership of the Jerusalem church to James, the brother of Jesus.

The death of Tiberius in AD 37 brought a significant

change in relationships between Jews and Romans not only in Palestine but throughout the empire. Successive Roman rulers for more than a century had prudently recognised both the size of the Jewish community within the empire (approximately 15% overall) and the peculiar character of Jewish religious nationalism. Accordingly special concessions were made including exemption from military service (Jews would not fight on the Sabbath nor eat Gentile food!) and the right to send a temple tax to Jerusalem, to assemble for worship and to build synagogues. Certainly if they violated Roman law they were subject to punishment, as for example in AD 19 when Tiberius expelled Jews from Rome for fraudulent activities.[1] Nonetheless, the policies of Julius Caesar, Augustus and Tiberius effectively meant that anti-Semitic actions were illegal. This is not to say that such actions did not occur. Large and unintegrated communities of Jews existed in most large Greek cities and there were endless disputes between Jewish and Greek people and between the leaders of the Jewish communities and the civic authorities.

During the early days of Gaius (or Caligula), who was known to dislike the Jews, the Greek population of Alexandria subjected the Jewish community to numerous acts of violence. Property was looted, synagogues desecrated and Jewish leaders publicly flogged. Jews in other places quickly heard and reacted against these events, including at Jamnia in Judaea where in AD 40 they pulled down an altar of victory set up to celebrate Gaius' recent victories in the German campaign. Gaius retaliated by issuing the command that a huge statue of himself be set up in the temple of Jerusalem. In the end the order was not carried out because the local Roman military authorities recognised that war would break out in Judaea and probably spread throughout the whole empire. Not since the outbreak of the Maccabean revolt two centuries earlier over the desecration of the temple had Jewish religious nationalism run so high.

Inevitably the community of believers in Jerusalem would have come under scrutiny at this time. It is not surprising that Stephen, a severe critic of both law and temple, had been killed some years earlier and his Hellenist companions driven out. But what of moderates like Peter and John Zebedee who, however, had recently fraternized with Samaritans? And what of Peter who had gone to the house of a Roman centurion in Caesarea?

It was no surprise, therefore, that the new Jewish king, Herod Agrippa I, should, on his arrival in Jerusalem, attack those members of the Christian community who had been in some way involved with Gentiles.

Born in 10 BC the grandson of Herod the Great, Agrippa had lived in Rome 6 BC–AD23 where he became boyhood friends of both Gaius (Caligula) and Claudius. The middle part of Agrippa's career AD 23–37, which was largely spent in the East, was a tragicomic sequence of misadventures and misdemeanours — suicide contemplated in Idumea, successive dismissals from posts in Galilee and Syria, and flight from creditors back to Italy where he was finally imprisoned for imprudent remarks about Tiberius. The death of Tiberius, however, brought an astonishing reversal of fortunes for Agrippa. Through the patronage of his old friends Gaius and Claudius, who became emperors in 37 and 41 respectively, Agrippa became king of the Jews. Thanks to Gaius he became king successively of Iturea (north-east of Galilee) in 37 and of Galilee in 39. Claudius dramatically enlarged Agrippa's kingdom in 41 to include Judaea and Samaria.

Agrippa shrewdly read the mood of the Jewish people. The feelings which had run so high when Gaius had commanded the desecration of the temple remained high, but now for the positive reason that in Agrippa a Jewish king ruled them. From the beginning of his reign he cast himself in the role of a devout Jew. According to Josephus,

[Agrippa] enjoyed residing at Jerusalem and he did so constantly and he scrupulously observed the traditions of his people. He neglected no rite of purification, and no day passed for him without the prescribed sacrifice.[2]

Agrippa also became an ostentatious champion of the cause of Jewish religious nationalism. This may be seen, for example, in his appeal to Claudius over Jewish rights in Alexandria and in his fortification of the northern city walls

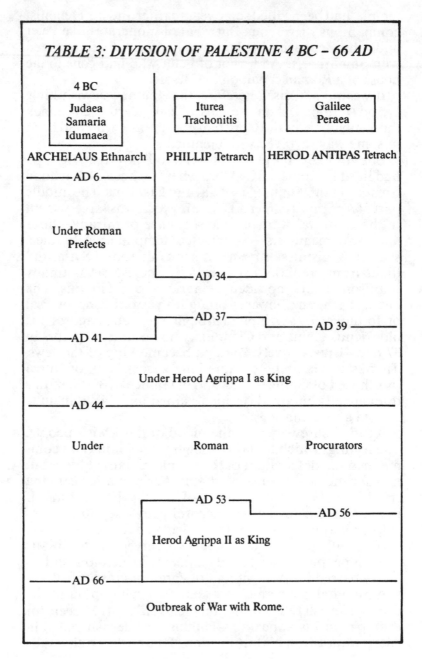

TABLE 3: DIVISION OF PALESTINE 4 BC – 66 AD

4 BC

| Judaea Samaria Idumaea | Iturea Trachonitis | Galilee Peraea |

ARCHELAUS Ethnarch   PHILLIP Tetrarch   HEROD ANTIPAS Tetrach

———AD 6———

Under Roman Prefects

———AD 34———

———AD 37———
———AD 41———   ———AD 39———

Under Herod Agrippa I as King

———AD 44———

Under   Roman   Procurators

———AD 53———
          ———AD 56———

Herod Agrippa II as King

———AD 66———

Outbreak of War with Rome.

in Jerusalem. Agrippa's attack on certain members of the Jerusalem church, therefore, is thoroughly consistent with the new king's deliberately assumed role and policy. It is probably significant that it was James *Zebedee* who was beheaded and Peter imprisoned with a view to execution. Peter had stayed in the Roman Cornelius' house while John *Zebedee*, with Peter, had preached to Samaritans (Acts 10:24-48; 8:14-25). On his escape from prison, Peter withdrew from Jerusalem. He probably did not return until after the death of the king in AD 44.

The end of the reign of Agrippa in AD 44 approximately coincided with the news of the influx of Gentiles into the church of Antioch, leading to the despatch of Barnabas from the Jerusalem church.

The years following the death of Agrippa were full of disappointment to the Jews. It was from that point that we note the unmistakable slide towards the outbreak of war with Rome in AD 66. On the international scene the new Emperor Claudius (AD 41-54) had made some decisions which could not but have upset the Jews. Upon taking office he wrote a severe letter to the people of Alexandria, both Greek and Jewish parties, rebuking them for the recent civic disturbances. The Jews as a group were reckoned as a *politeuma*, a self-contained community with their own constitution and leaders. They had hoped, additionally, to be granted individual citizenship rights of the city. Claudius' letter not only rejected that request but spoke with considerable irritation about the Jews in general. Claudius told them, in the following strong terms:

not to agitate for more privileges than they formerly possessed and not in future to send out a separate embassy as if they lived in a separate city. . .and not to bring in or admit Jews. . .from Syria or Egypt. . .otherwise I will. . .take vengeance on them as fomenters of what is a general plague affecting the whole world.[3]

Equally strong was Claudius' decision in the same year (AD 41) concerning Jews in Rome. Dio Cassius notes that Claudius "did not indeed expel them, but forbade them to meet in their ancestral way".[4] This was a severe restriction on time-honoured Jewish freedom. Then, in AD 49 he expelled the Jews from Rome because they were persistently rioting "at the instigation of Chrestus" [a misspelling of Christus?][5]

Claudius did not distinguish between Jews and Christian Jews. So far as he was concerned they were all Jews. The next Emperor, Nero, however, was quite aware of the difference, as we shall see. For his part, Claudius took a number of actions which Jews throughout the empire would have found extremely offensive.

Closer to home matters were even more discouraging. The death of Agrippa was not followed by the appointment of his son, Agrippa the Younger, in succession. Instead the Romans re-annexed Judaea, and with it Galilee for the first time. Governors, now known as "Procurators", with a tax-gathering rather than a military role, proved to be particularly insensitive and inept. The new arrangements, if possible, made for even more corruption than under the prefects. Moreover, from the mid-forties Judaea underwent a dire famine. This in turn led to wholesale rise in banditry with groups of marauders banding together for armed robbery merely to stay alive. At that time the prophet Theudas arose, taking a multitude with him to the Jordan which, he said, would part when he stood Joshua-like before it.

Clearly the immediate post-Agrippa period was a desperate one for Palestinian Jews both Christian and non-Christian. We sense the rise of religious nationalism within this period. In this context the Jerusalem church appears to have assumed an increasingly Hebraic character, consistent with the context of growing zeal for the nation and her God. Members of the Pharisee party belonged to the Jerusalem church from the middle forties. The pro-circumcision party in the Jerusalem church is probably to be identified with them (Galatians 2:4-5; Acts 15:5). Their attitude to Paul and his ministry among Gentiles would become severe in the following years. For them, who were more Jewish at heart than Christian, circumcision was a critical symbol of loyalty to Israel; Paul's declaration of the "crucified messiah" was a contradiction in terms, especially since this was discerned by him to be the means of a reconciliation with God that extended even to Gentiles.

3 Saul of Tarsus (AD 34–47)

At the time of Stephen's death in c. AD 34 Saul was said to be a "young man" (Greek: *neanias* — Acts 7:58). This is not much help in establishing Saul's age since there is evidence of the word's use for both a youth of seventeen years and a middle-aged man of forty-five.[6] The Mishnah, however, teaches that at thirty "one is fit. . .for authority",[7] which probably indicates that Saul was at least that age when given "letters" by the high priest authorizing him to seize believers in the synagogues of Damascus. (Acts 9:1-2)

That Saul of Tarsus was a Roman citizen by birth (Acts 22:28) indicates that his father had been a Roman citizen, and therefore a man of eminence in the province of Cilicia. (At that time only provincials of wealth and distinction were honoured by Roman citizenship, though in the following centuries all free people were made Roman citizens.)

Nonetheless, it was his Jewishness that Paul chiefly emphasised whenever he recalled his earlier life before becoming a believer. He described himself to the Philippians as, "of the people of Israel, of the tribe of Benjamin, a Hebrew born of Hebrews, as to the law a Pharisee" (3:5 cf. 2 Corinthians 11:22) and to the Galatians as one who, in his "former life in Judaism", had "advanced in Judaism beyond many of my own age and people so extremely zealous was I for the traditions of my fathers". (1:14)

In a speech to the Sanhedrin twenty-five years later he outlined his upbringing. "I am a Jew born at Tarsus in Cilicia but brought up in this city [Jerusalem] and [subsequently] educated at the feet of Gamaliel according to the strict manner of the law." (Acts 22:3)

In time Saul became one of the most prominent and zealous of the younger scholars, the evidence of which was his persecution of the heretical sect of the Nazarenes, as he then regarded them.

All that came to a dramatic end, however, as he approached the end of his journey to Damascus. He was, as he described it, "laid hold of (or seized) by Christ Jesus"

(Philippians 3:12 — my translation). A blinding light flashed, Saul fell to the ground and heard the voice "Saul, Saul, why do you persecute me?" Saul called out, "Who are you, Lord?" and the voice replied "I am Jesus...". (Acts 9:3-6)

Since Jesus addressed him from brightness or glory, that is from God, Saul's only conclusion was that the speaker must be "Lord", even though crucified, and therefore, as Saul had previously thought, under God's curse (Deuteronomy 21:23). At that moment the chief elements of his perception of Jesus, focused as they were on the glorified Lordship of the one who in his death was made a curse for humanity, were established in Saul's mind. Over the next few years he would meet "those who were apostles before [him]" (Galatians 1:17) and receive from them "the traditions" relating to the gospel-outline and the Lord's Supper (1 Corinthians 15:3-5; 11:23-26) but this would only confirm what he now knew from the encounter with the Crucified-Glorified One near Damascus.

Saul was taken, blinded, to the house of Judas who lived in "the street called Straight" where he was visited by Ananias, a Christian believer (Acts 9:10-12; 22:12-13). Saul's sight was restored and he was immediately baptized, calling on the name of the Just One, whose disciples he had come to Damascus to arrest! (Acts 9:18; 22:14-15)

It is usual to refer to Saul's "conversion" on the road near Damascus. It is more accurate, however, to locate his conversion in Damascus at his baptism, prior to which Ananias had promised that he would be "filled with the Holy Spirit" (Acts 9:17). According to Paul what happened on the road to Damascus was that God "was pleased to reveal his Son to me in order that I might preach him among the Gentiles". (Galatians 1:16; Acts 26:16-18)

The Damascus road event, therefore, was God's apostolic commissioning of Paul; his conversion followed soon after.

Paul's career over the next fourteen years falls into three parts: the Damascus period; the Syria-Cilicia period; and the Antioch period. In each of them he proclaimed Jesus. It is important to be reminded of this.

It is sometimes thought that Paul was engaged in meditation or reflection throughout these years, only becoming actively involved in evangelism from the time of the first missionary journey. Paul's own words to Herod Agrippa II a quarter of a century later are clear:

...O King Agrippa, I was not disobedient to the heavenly vision but declared first to those at Damascus, then at Jerusalem and also to the Gentiles that they should repent and turn to God. (Acts 26:19,20)

Clearly Paul was engaged in ministry from the beginning.

a. AD 34-36: the Damascus period

(Galatians 1:17-19; Acts 9:19-30; 22:17-21)
According to Paul after God revealed his Son to him, "...I went away into Arabia; and again I returned to Damascus. Then after three years I went up to Jerusalem..." (Galatians 1:17-18)

The geographical sequence is, Damascus, Arabia, Damascus, Jerusalem. It must not be thought that Arabia was some desert region a great distance from Damascus where, as it were, Saul communed with God about what had happened to him recently. The geographic reality is that "Arabia" (the Nabataean kingdom) came to the very walls of Damascus, and was, like the rest of Syria and Palestine, an urbanized area. (Damascus for the period between AD 34-62 was under Roman control; more typically Damascus was part of "Arabia".) It is clear that, wherever he was, Paul was actively engaged in evangelism.

Initially in Damascus he proclaimed Jesus as the "Son of God" in the synagogues, to which ironically he was to have come seeking to arrest Jesus' followers. Then he must have proclaimed him in "Arabia" since the Damascus-based Ethnarch of the Nabataean King Aretas subsequently sought to capture him in Damascus (2 Corinthians 11:32-33). On his return to Damascus his life was endangered, presumably because of his ongoing involvement in evangelism, and he was ignominiously lowered down the city wall in a basket to escape both Jews and Arabs. (Acts 9:23-25; 2 Corinthians 11:32-33). When he came to Jerusalem he proclaimed the message so effectively that the non-converting Hellenists sought his life, so that once again he was forced to move on. (Acts 9:27-30)

It was evident that the now-commissioned/converted Saul of Tarsus was a storm-centre wherever he was!

b. AD 36-45: the Syria-Cilicia period
(Galatians 1:21; Acts 9:30; 11:25)
While we have little direct information about this decade-long period, it is evident that Paul remained actively involved in Christian ministry. Even the churches in far away Judaea heard the astonishing reports from Syria-Cilicia that the former persecutor now "proclaimed the faith he once tried to destroy" (Galatians 1:23).

Moreover, the punishments meted out by Jews and Romans on account of trouble caused by Paul's ministry probably occurred within this period, since we have no other knowledge of them (apart from the Roman flogging at Philippi; Acts 16:22-23): "Five times I have received at the hands of the Jews the forty lashes less one. Three times I have been beaten with rods." (2 Corinthians 11:24-25)

The one who had inflicted punishment on believers in the synagogues had gone to the synagogue of Syria-Cilicia preaching about Christ and had been the recipient (on five occasions?) of the floggings he had once inflicted (Acts 22:19; 26:10-11). It may have been complaints from the Jews that led to his Roman flogging on two occasions within this period. (Philippi was the third occasion — Acts 16:22.) Clearly Paul's ministry in Syria-Cilicia is presupposed by these punishments. Another hint is given by the Acts reference to churches in Syria and *Cilicia* in the decree of the Jerusalem church (15:41). Evidently Paul's ministry in Cilicia led to the formation of churches there.

It was within this decade in the region of Tarsus that Paul experienced the vision/revelation about which he wrote to the Corinthians in c. AD 56.

I know a man in Christ who fourteen years ago [i.e. in c. AD 43] was caught up to the third heaven/into paradise ...and he heard things that cannot be told, which man may not utter. (2 Corinthians 12:2-4)

That vision/revelation, however, was accompanied by the unidentified "thorn in the flesh to harass me" which, despite his prayer, remained with him permanently (2 Corinthians 12:7). There can be no doubt that Saul/Paul was actively engaged in ministry throughout these years.

Tarsus, the probable base of his activities, was a significant Hellenistic city ("no mean city" Acts 21:39) and well known as a seat of learning. Now freed from his Hebraic shackles Paul may well have expanded his knowledge of Greek language and thought as a result of involvement in ministry to Gentiles. Certainly within a few years he began to write his famous letters which reflect a superior knowledge of Greek and contain a number of quotations from Greek writings.

c. AD 45-47: Paul's Antioch period
(Acts 11:25-26; Galatians 2:1-10)
As noted earlier, the burgeoning, Gentile-dominated church of Antioch was too much for Barnabas to lead, unaided. Barnabas travelled the relatively short distance (four days by horse?) to Tarsus where he found Saul/Paul and brought him back to assist in the work at Antioch. The two men worked side by side for a year teaching the large community of believers in Antioch.

Then in the fourteenth year after Paul's commission/ conversion, during which he ministered in Damascus, Syria-Cilicia and Antioch, there occurred an event of momentous significance which would change the whole direction of Christianity. This event illuminates both the Aramaic and Hellenist branches of the church.

The Missionary Agreement, Jerusalem c. AD 47
During the year Barnabas and Paul worked together in Antioch (c. AD 46) some prophets from Jerusalem arrived. Agabus, one of their number, prophesied a great world-wide famine, perhaps as a·prelude to the close of the Messianic Age (Acts 11:27-28). The Antioch church decided to send relief to Judaean believers. This was a generous action considering that the Antioch church was founded by Hellenist refugees who had been forced out of Jerusalem partly by Hebrew Christians, for whom the relief would be applied.

The Antiochene Christians were not the only ones to send assistance to Jerusalem. The royal family of Adiabene, a kingdom beyond the Tigris river, who were converts to Judaism, also sent gifts to aid the people of Jerusalem. This famine is mentioned by the historian Josephus as occurring during the procuratorship of Tiberius Alexander[8] (AD 46–48).

Barnabas and Paul were sent to Jerusalem bearing gifts for the elders to distribute to the people (Acts 11:29-30). This was the second visit of Paul the Christian to Jerusalem, according to the Acts of the Apostles (see 9:26-30). It was also the second visit in Paul's own account in Galatians 2:1-10. Although Galatians 2:1-10 does not give famine relief as the purpose for the visit, there can be little doubt that it was the same occasion. AD 47, the fourteenth year after Paul's conversion (Galatians 2:1) coincides closely with the famine Josephus says occurred between AD 46–48. Moreover, the same personnel were involved, Barnabas, and Paul (the same order in both Acts 11:30 and Galatians 2:1). Furthermore Paul's final comment that he was eager to remember the poor, as if in the future, could well be translated as: "...to remember the poor (in the future) which very thing I had been eager to do", that is as referring to the famine relief which had been brought as the occasion for the visit.

According to Paul's account in Galatians 2:7-9 a private meeting occurred at that time in Jerusalem between the "pillars" of the Jerusalem church James, Cephas and John and the delegates of the church of Antioch, Barnabas and Paul.

Important decisions were made at that meeting. First, the Jerusalem "pillars" formally recognised the truth of the gospel message as understood and taught by Saul/Paul (Galatians 2:2,6). They supported Saul/Paul, over against "false-brothers" (Pharisaic Judaizing believers recently incorporated in the Jerusalem church? — Galatians 2:3-5). Paul was assured that the message he had received near Damascus (Galatians 1:12,15-17) was complete and needed nothing added to it. Eight years later Paul outlined the fourfold summary of the gospel to the Corinthians (Christ died for our sins, was buried, was raised the third day, appeared to the twelve/Cephas) adding, "so we [the apostles including James and Cephas *and* Paul] preached and so you believed" (1Corinthians 15:11).

Second, that both parties recognised that there were now two fields of missionary endeavour — one among Jews, the other among Gentiles. James, Cephas and John acknowledged that Paul had been entrusted with the gospel/apostolate to Gentiles. Saul/Paul (and Barnabas) acknowledged that Cephas had been entrusted with the gospel/apostolate to Jews. Each group declared that God was working through the other group.

Third, and most significantly of all, an agreement was struck, sealed by "the right hand of fellowship", that Barnabas and Paul should go to the Gentiles and that James, Cephas and John should go to the Jews. In other words, the momentous decision was reached not just that each group would continue to work among their respective racial groups but that each would also now *go* to them, in a more precise way.

In our next two chapters we will briefly chart the courses of these two apostolates, one to the Jews the other to the Gentiles. The apostolate to the Jews occurred in two missions — one to Aramaic-speaking Jews in Judaea (led by James), the other to Greek-speaking Jews outside Palestine (led by Peter and John). This will cover a period of somewhat less than twenty years, by the end of which James, Cephas and Paul would be dead. James would be executed in Jerusalem in AD 62, Cephas and Paul in Rome in the middle sixties.

The story of the mission to the Gentiles is substantially documented through the letters of Paul, the apostle, to his Gentile churches and by the narratives of Luke, Paul's friend and apologist, recorded in the Acts of the Apostles. The history of the other mission, that to the Jews, in both its parts, can be recovered at very few points, due to the sparseness of surviving literature. To these two stories, respectively, we now turn.

Further reading to Chapter Seven:

F.F. Bruce, *New Testament History*, Anchor, New York, 1972.

M. Hengel, *Acts and the History of Earliest Christianity*, Fortress, Philadelphia, 1980.

I.H. Marshall, *Luke, Historian and Theologian*, Paternoster, Exeter, 1970.

Notes

[1] Josephus *AJ*, xviii, 65-84.

[2] *AJ*, xix, 331.

[3] "Claudius' Letter to the Alexandrians", 90-100 in C.K. Barrett, *New Testament Background: Selected Documents*, Harper and Row, New York, 1961, 46.

[4] Dio Cassius, *Hist.*, 60.6.6.

[5] Suetonius, *Claudius*, 25.4.

[6] cf. Moulton & Milligan, *Vocabulary of the Greek New Testament*, Eerdmans, Grand Rapids, 1974, 423 and *AJ*, xviii, 197.

[7] *Aboth*, 5:21.

[8] *AJ*, xx, 51-53, 101.

8

The Decade of the Two Missions (c. AD 47-57)

The decade following the missionary agreement c. AD 47 between delegates of the churches of Antioch and Jerusalem was one of high drama.

During this period, representatives of the church of Antioch began to take the Christian message in a westerly direction to Gentile peoples. First these emissaries from Antioch established assemblies of believers in the inland province of Galatia. Next, they travelled through northern Greece, south to Corinth in Achaia, then back across the Aegean to Ephesus in the southern part of Roman Asia. Many new congregations were formed on the way and their most striking feature was their predominantly Gentile membership.

In spite of the missionary agreement, there was a negative reaction to this missionary expansion among sections of the Jerusalem church. This in turn was partly due to the worsening political situation in Palestine. Affairs in Palestine were bad under the procurator Ventidius Cumanus (AD 49–52), but they deteriorated even further under his successor Antonius Felix.

The famine in Palestine during the time Tiberius Alexander was procurator (AD 46–48) had inevitably stimulated the rise of bands of brigands. James and Simon the sons of Judas the Galilean were captured, tried and crucified, doubtless for brigandage/rebellion.[1] In the early days of the next procurator, Cumanus (AD 49–52), Eleazar son of Deinaeus, a notorious brigand from the mountainous region (of upper Galilee?) became prominent and was followed by large numbers of famine-affected Jews. According to Josephus, "From that time [Cumanus' time] the whole of Judaea was infested with bands of brigands."[2]

Matters were made worse by Cumanus who arrived in the aftermath of the famine. He was so incompetent as to be recalled to Rome in disgrace. During one Passover a Roman soldier desecrated the sanctity both of the temple and the ceremony by exposing his genitals to the crowd. In the riot that followed many pilgrims were killed.[3] Soon afterwards, a Roman soldier publicly tore up a copy of the Torah while uttering blasphemies. The whole nation came to hear about these gravely offensive actions and an atmosphere both of tension and hostility was doubtless created.

So far as I can see it would have been about then that the Hebrew Christians in Jerusalem received the alarming news of the activities of Paul and the church at Antioch.

When the missionary agreement at Jerusalem was completed Barnabas and Saul had returned to Antioch, bringing with them John Mark (Acts 12:25). After fasting and prayer the community recognised that Barnabas and Paul had been called by the Holy Spirit for ministry to Gentiles and released them for that work. (Acts 13:1-3)

Taking John Mark with them they went first to the island of Cyprus, Barnabas' home. From that point the Acts refers to Saul as Paul, possibly to acknowledge how significant it was that the Roman proconsul Sergius Paulus had become a believer (Acts 13:12). The men then sailed to Perga on the coast of Pamphylia where, instead of travelling westwards by sea, they struck out inexplicably for the remote upland plateau regions of Pisidia and Lycaonia (southern Galatia). It has been suggested that Paul was unwell at that time and needed the climatic condition a higher altitude would provide. He reminded the Galatians that,

it was because of a bodily ailment that I preached the gospel to you at first...and...my condition was a trial to you. . .you would have plucked out your eyes and given them to me. (Galatians 4:13-16)

At least four congregations (Antioch of Pisidia, Iconium, Lystra and Derbe) were established, with elders appointed, in these regions of southern Galatia. Paul and Barnabas (note the order, Paul now being the leader) returned to Antioch. John Mark had returned earlier to Jerusalem. Was he unhappy because his uncle Barnabas was no longer the senior missionary? Or was he concerned about Paul's preaching about Christ to the Gentiles, which did not require them to submit to the Jewish law?

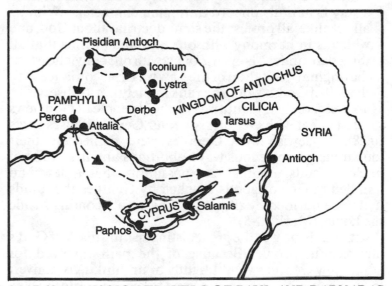

MAP 12 — MISSION TRAVELS OF PAUL AND BARNABAS (AD 47-49)

It may well have been John Mark who was the source of information received c. AD 48/49 about developments in Antioch and Galatia, which sections of the Jerusalem church found so extremely alarming. It should be remembered that they had recently been confronted with insults and abuse of the Jewish law especially during the stormy procuratorship of Ventidius Cumanus.

It should also be remembered that we only ever hear

Paul's side of these disputes. But it is worth reflecting that Jews were horrified and offended by the idolatry and gross immorality practised in the pagan world. The evil picture of Gentile behaviour painted by Paul in Romans 1:18-32 is confirmed at many points by Roman writers like Seneca and Juvenal. Jews regarded their law as God-given, their greatest possession.

Later in the century Josephus would write in praise of the law,

To this cause [=the Law] above all we [Jews] owe our admirable harmony. Unity and identity of religious belief, perfect uniformity in habits and customs, produce a very beautiful concord in human character. . .With us all act alike, all profess the same doctrine about God, one which is in harmony with our Law and affirms that all things are under his eye...For us, with our conviction that the original institution of the Law was in accordance with the will of God, it would be rank impiety not to observe it.[4]

To preserve their identity as the holy people of God, Jews would not eat with Gentiles, or enter Gentile houses (Acts 10:28). To Jewish eyes Gentiles were defiled by their idolatrous, promiscuous ways, abortions and the eating of unclean foods. Against the possibility that a Jew had handled money or goods touched by Gentiles the hands had to be purified by ritual washing before coming inside the home. (Mark 7:1-5)

Circumcision was the great distinguishing mark of God's law-keeping people. Because of the pain involved for adults, few Gentiles would lightly or unthinkingly convert to Judaism; so circumcision served to keep separate the law-keepers from the law-breakers. Izates the king of Adiabene (beyond the Tigris) during the mid first century was keen to become a Jew, but his mother Helena tried to persuade him not to accept circumcision, as did Ananias the Jewish merchant who first told them about Judaism. However, another Jew, the Galilean Eleazar, told him,

in your ignorance, O King, you are guilty of the greatest offence against the Law and thereby against God. For you ought not merely to read the Law but also, and even more, to do what is commanded in it. How long will you continue to be uncircumcised?[5]

The news of non-observance of the law from Antioch and Galatia (as reported by John Mark?) therefore would have caused great consternation among the saints in Jerusalem, especially as there were now members of the Pharisaic brotherhoods among them. They heard that Jewish Christians in Antioch were eating with Gentiles and that Paul had extended the promise of salvation to Gentiles without any requirement to keep the law or to be circumcised.

Clearly the missionary agreement of c. AD 47 whereby Paul should take the gospel to the Gentiles had produced unforeseen and unfortunate consequences at least from the Jewish point of view.

The letter to the Galatians, which is here taken to have been written c. AD 48/49, reflects from Paul's viewpoint, the surfacing of two major and related sets of problems — one in Galatia, the other in Antioch itself.

Serious difficulties in the newly formed Galatian churches had been brought to Paul's attention. The churches were being "troubled" by a group of Jews led by an unidentified individual (Galatians 5:10,12; 3:1; 1:6) who said circumcision was a prerequisite for membership of the "Israel of God" (3:6-14; 6:16). These people were applying pressure to the Jewish believers to compel Gentile Christians to submit to circumcision (6:12). They were claiming that Paul owed his authority to the Jerusalem church leaders (1:18-19) and that he himself believed in circumcision (5:11). It is not clear who these "agitators" were or where they received the impetus for their Judaizing activities. Were they Galatian Jews who decided to bring the churches into line? Or had they come from Jerusalem for that purpose? Lack of information prevents a certain answer.

The other conflict occurred in Antioch and Paul himself was directly involved. The issue was whether Christian Jews and Christian Gentiles should eat together. The practice had apparently arisen in Antioch in which members of the two groups did eat together. Cephas (Peter), who was in

Antioch at the time, was no stranger to eating with Gentiles; he had stayed with the Gentile Cornelius ten years earlier (Acts 10:48). In Antioch Peter openly ate with Gentiles, as did Paul's travelling companion Barnabas. Suddenly, however, Peter and Barnabas discontinued the practice and a great dispute erupted between them and Paul. As Paul darkly puts it, "certain men, came from James. . . the circumcision party" (Galatians 2:12) and Peter and Barnabas, out of fear of these men, stopped eating with Gentiles. Had these men been sent by James or had they come on their own accord? The Acts of the Apostles quotes James as saying, later, at the Jerusalem Council, "Some persons from us have troubled you with words unsettling your minds, although we gave them no instructions." (15:24)

Who were these men who came from the Jerusalem church, but not with James' authority? According to Acts they were "believers who belonged to the party of the Pharisees" (Acts 15:5). It is probable that these Christian Pharisees had connections with other Pharisees who, in the time of Cumanus would have been up in arms about the desecration of temple and Torah by Roman soldiers. The problems in Galatia and Antioch over the Jewish law, eating with Gentiles and circumcision, probably originated among horrified Pharisees in Jerusalem who brought pressure to bear among the "Christian" Pharisees and through them upon churches in Galatia and Antioch.

This visit to Antioch had profound effects. Not only Peter and Barnabas but all those Jewish Christians who had become accustomed to eating with Gentiles stopped doing so. The implications were great. If believing Jews and Gentiles could not eat meals together they could not share in the Lord's Supper together. That meant, effectively, that their unity in Christ was no more. There would be nothing else to do but become two separate churches — one Jewish, the other Gentile.

The other alternative, that Gentiles in deference to the Judaizers should submit to circumcision and observe Jewish dietary laws, was unthinkable to Paul. He was quite prepared, voluntarily, to observe Jewish laws (1

Corinthians 9:19-21) and even to circumcise (Acts 16:3). However once these things became *obligatory* for acceptance with God as members of his true people then it was evident that Christ was inadequate for the task of setting men in a right relationship with God. The moment circumcision or law-keeping became mandatory was the moment "the truth of the gospel", as Paul put it, was destroyed. (Galatians 2:3,5, 14)

Paul responded to the crises in the Galatian churches and in the Antioch church in a twofold manner. His immediate response was to write to the Galatians. He established that while the leaders of the Jerusalem church recognised his gospel message it did not originate with them but with God (2:2,6-9; 1:6-7,11-12,15-24). He reminded them that it was not by "works" but by "hearing with faith" the message focused on Christ-crucified that they had received the twin blessings of the Holy Spirit and justification with God (2:16; 3:1-5). Christ, in fact, so far from being only partially adequate in man's redemption, is thoroughly capable of achieving it (1:3-4,16; 2:20; 3:10-13; 4:4-7; 6:2,14). The whole Christian life, therefore, is Christ-focused, Christ-dependent. This is to walk in the Spirit and produce his fruit (5:16-26).

Paul's other response to the twofold crisis was to go to Jerusalem to resolve these issues once and for all with the church leaders. The missionary agreement two years earlier, as it had applied to the Gentiles, had produced unforeseen consequences which must now be dealt with.

The Jerusalem Council c. AD 49/50

After Barnabas and Paul had been received in Jerusalem by the church, the apostles and elders, a meeting was convened to consider the problem of Gentile converts. At the outset the "Christian Pharisees" insisted that Gentiles must be circumcised and committed to keeping the law of Moses. Peter replied that he had been the first to speak the gospel to the Gentiles, referring to Cornelius and his household. God had given the Spirit to those Gentiles just as he had to the Jews on the day of Pentecost, that is, as accompanied by foreign tongues-speaking (Acts 15:8 cf. 10:46). Cornelius had not been circumcised yet the Spirit came upon him, a sign that God had cleansed his heart. Peter concluded that both Jews and Gentiles would be saved by grace.

Barnabas and Paul then related the signs and wonders God had done at their hands among the Gentiles, both at Antioch and in Galatia.

James concluded the debate by giving a prophetic interpretation of an Old Testament passage. James declared that God's visitation to the Gentiles, as related by Peter, was in agreement with the oracle of the Lord which said, "I will rebuild the dwelling of David, which is fallen...that the rest of men may seek the Lord and all the Gentiles who are called by my name." (Amos 9:11 Septuagint)

According to James, the oracle of Amos was in process of fulfilment. First, God had rebuilt the fallen "dwelling of David" in the creation of the community of believing Jews who are focused on Jesus. Second, God had set it up in order that, through its members, the Gentiles would "seek the Lord". James discerned, specifically, that God was reaching out to the Gentiles through the Jerusalem church and that what was now happening was fulfilment of prophecy.

As a result, it was decided, in relation to the major question, that circumcision must not be required of Gentiles. On the subsidiary question relating to Jews eating with Gentiles there was a more complicated decision. Henceforth Gentile believers must "abstain from the pollution of idols, from unchastity, from what is strangled and from blood." (Acts 15:20)

These four "necessary things" (Acts 15:28) appear to arise out of Leviticus 17-18, a passage which sets out requirements for Israelites and the aliens who live among them (Leviticus 17:8,10,13,15). James seems to have regarded the Israelites and resident aliens for whom these regulations were first formulated as an appropriate anticipatory model for the newly constituted people of God, consisting as they did of Jewish believers and Gentile believers.

It should be noted that Paul (and Barnabas) played a minor role at this council. The decisions were made, not by all present but only by the Jerusalem church, its elders and apostles. It was not a democratic decision. The Jerusalem church, through its spokesman James, delivered a decree which the others were expected to accept.

Doubtless these requirements seemed logical at the time, at least to the members of the Jerusalem church who made them. However, they may not have anticipated the difficulties that would arise in ministry to Gentiles.

The prohibition of unchastity, including sexual relationships with close relatives, was straightforward and not in dispute. Desisting from the "pollution of idols", from "what is strangled" and "from blood", however, would effectively mean that Gentile believers must eat only *kosher* meat or become vegetarians. As Paul became more fully conversant with the Gentile world, for example at Corinth, he was to find it impossible to implement literally the food restrictions laid down at Jerusalem. Paul's ambivalence on the idol-food question would be an ongoing source of misunderstanding and tension between Paul and the Jerusalem church.

A letter was drawn up setting out the decisions of the Jerusalem church which was to be delivered to the Gentile churches thus far established in Syria, Cilicia and Galatia. Two delegates of the Jerusalem church, Silas and Judas, accompanied Paul and Barnabas back to Antioch with the Jerusalem letter. It is assumed that Silas and Judas were chosen because of their competence in the Greek language.

When Paul and Barnabas proposed to revisit the Galatian churches a dispute arose because Barnabas wanted to bring his nephew John Mark. Unable to find agreement with Barnabas, Paul took Silas (=Silvanus) with him; Barnabas and John Mark set out for Cyprus.

From Antioch Paul and Silas set out overland through Cilicia to revisit the cities of southern Galatia, where they strengthened the churches and delivered the decisions which had been reached at Jerusalem by the apostles and elders. At Lystra a well-regarded believer, Timothy, was invited to make up the third member of the group. Timothy was the son of a marriage between a Jewess and a Gentile and Paul judged it expedient for him to be circumcised. On the face of it, this was a strange action so soon after the decision in Jerusalem. Paul's intention, however, was to avoid giving unnecessary offence to Jews by giving a position of leadership to an uncircumcised man.

The trio then set out for Asia but were redirected by supernatural means, first to the north and then to the west arriving ultimately at Troas on the coast of the Aegean. Here Luke, the author of the narrative, himself became part of the story which now is cast into the first person plural "we...us". (Acts 16:10)

After further supernatural guidance the four crossed the sea to the Greek mainland arriving eventually at Philippi, the leading city of one of the four districts of the Roman province of Macedonia. The Acts of the Apostles describes the establishment of churches in Philippi, Thessalonica (capital of the province of Macedonia) and Beroea. After the narrative moves on from Philippi it reverts to the third person, "They. . .them", presumably indicating that the author did not continue beyond that point; Luke appears to have remained at Philippi. (Acts 17:1 cf. 20:6)

Paul left Silas and Timothy in Macedonia and sailed alone to Athens. It seems he was compelled by the city authorities (Greek: *Politarchs*) of Thessalonica to leave the province of Macedonia (Acts 17:9). The Acts of the Apostles records that the courageous apostle alone proclaimed the message of Jesus and the resurrection in the *agora* (market place) of Athens and before the Athenians' *areopagus* (senate). Still on his own Paul proceeded to nearby Corinth, capital of the Roman province of Achaia. He stayed with (fellow-believers?) Aquila and Priscilla who had been forced to leave Italy in accordance with Claudius' decree of AD 49 expelling Jews from Rome (Acts 18:1-3). Soon afterwards Silas and Timothy arrived from Macedonia, bringing news from the churches, in particular from the Thessalonians to whom Paul immediately wrote the first of the two Thessalonian letters. A second letter would be written later from Corinth.

We are able to fix the date of Paul's year-and-a-half long stay in Corinth with some confidence. Some time after

Paul came to Corinth the Acts mentions the appointment of the new Roman proconsul Lucius Junius Gallio. As it happens this Gallio is mentioned in the Emperor Claudius' inscription in nearby Delphi.

Tiberius [Claudius] Caesar Augustus Germanicus...[year 12, acclaimed Emperor for] the 26th time...I have for long been zealous for the city of Delphi...the present stories, and those quarrels of the citizens of which [a report has been made by Lucius] Junius Gallio my friend, and [pro]consul of Achaea.[6]

This inscription at Delphi and the expulsion of the Jews from Rome, as recorded by Suetonius, are of significant assistance in establishing the date of Paul's ministry in Corinth.

Scholars of Roman history have calculated that the 26th acclamation of Claudius as Emperor occurred between January and August AD 52. Since proconsuls were appointed on 1 July for a twelve month term we can take it that Gallio held office from 1 July AD 51 to 30 June AD 52.

Soon after Gallio's arrival, the Jewish leaders in Corinth made the serious charge that Paul was "persuading men to worship God contrary to the law" (Acts 18:13). It was, in all probability, Roman law which Paul was accused of breaking. The Jewish spokesmen knew well that Jews alone enjoyed special religious privileges and protection within the empire and that Paul's activities in promoting Christianity were illegal. In a momentous decision the proconsul-judge declared that Paul's ministry belonged within Judaism and was therefore not illegal so far as Roman law was concerned. "Since it is a matter of questions about ...your own law, see to it yourselves; I refuse to be judge of these things." (Acts 18:14-15)

Had Gallio given the opposite verdict it is probable that Jews in every city would have charged Paul before the Roman judges who would have punished him for breaking the Roman law. An adverse decision in Corinth would have effectively silenced Paul and conceivably brought his ministry to an end.

It is reasonable to suppose Paul left Corinth near the end of Gallio's proconsulship so as to avoid facing renewed accusations before an incoming governor, that is in the middle of AD 52. His arrival in Corinth therefore may be fixed at late 50 or early 51. This dovetails with the coincident recent arrival of Aquila and Priscilla whose expulsion from Rome occurred in AD 49.[7]

Paul must have made a deliberate decision to base his ministry in Corinth. It was a large city of up to a million inhabitants and probably the most strategically located commercial centre of the ancient world. Rebuilt on Roman lines in 46 BC after lying in ruins for a century, new Corinth was situated on a five mile wide isthmus which commanded both the north-south overland traffic and the east-west sea traffic from the Adriatic to the Aegean seas. Paul chose Corinth, a commercial centre with a massive movement of people passing through, in preference to the more sophisticated university city of Athens a short distance to the north. The early spread of the new faith owed much to Paul's sense of geography. Doubtless many traders and other itinerants took the message they heard from Paul to other and more remote parts of the Mediterranean region.

After leaving Corinth, Paul travelled across the Aegean to Ephesus, the major city of the province of Asia, accompanied by Priscilla and Aquila. From Ephesus he sailed to Caesarea and from there "up" to "the church" (at Jerusalem? – Acts 18:22). Again he set out for Antioch and soon afterwards travelled through Galatia and Phrygia back to Ephesus. This astonishing round trip — Corinth, Ephesus, Caesarea, Jerusalem, Antioch, Galatia/Phrygia Ephesus — was made in AD 52/53. Presumably its intention was pastoral and diplomatic — pastoral in the churches sympathetic to or founded by Paul; diplomatic in relation to the Jewish believers in Jerusalem where he was viewed with considerable suspicion, at least by the Pharisaic believers.

Paul's choice of Ephesus as a base for a sustained period of ministry would have been motivated by similar considerations as his choice of Corinth. Ephesus was the leading city in what was the wealthiest, most densely populated province in the Roman east. Although Pergamum appears to have been the capital of the province, there was

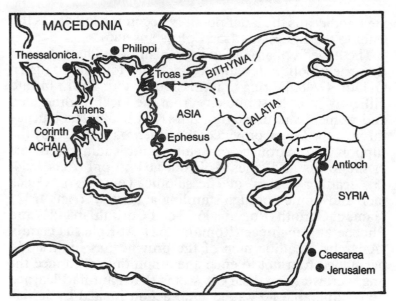

MAP 13 — MISSION TRAVELS OF PAUL
with Silas Silvanus, Timothy and Luke) AD 49-52

no doubt that Ephesus was the largest and most strategically located city in the region.

The harbour for the city was located on the Cayster river six miles from the Aegean coast. The city was the terminus of the great overland road from India, through Mesopotamia, Syria and Phrygia. Ephesus was the through port for goods from all parts of the Mediterranean, Aegean and Black Seas and from the great trade routes of the East. Moreover this city boasted the cult of Artemis whose temple was one of the greatest buildings of the world, to which numerous visitors came.

Paul's tour through the Greek provinces of Macedonia, Achaia and Asia led to the formation of churches in Philippi, Thessalonica, Beroea, Corinth and Ephesus. There is also evidence of churches being established by extension — in Cenchreae near Corinth and in Laodicea, Colossae and Hierapolis in the Lycus Valley to the east of Ephesus.

It was from Ephesus that Paul wrote a number of his famous letters — to the Corinthians, to the Colossians and the Laodiceans the latter possibly becoming known as the letter to the Ephesians. (see Colossians 4:16).

The Aegean phase of Paul's ministry was characterized by a new policy developed since the tour in southern Galatia 47/48. During that missionary tour Paul ran into difficulty in at least one city from the local leading men and women who drove him out (Acts 13:50). His journey through the Greek provinces, however, was marked by the support and patronage of wealthy and leading members of the towns and cities — Lydia at Philippi (Acts 16:14-15), "leading women" at Thessalonica (Acts 17:4), "Greek men and women of high standing at Beroea" (Acts 17:12), Gaius at Corinth (Romans 16:23 cf. 1 Corinthians 1:14) and Phoebe at Cenchreae (Romans 16:1). At Ephesus certain "Asiarchs", leading men of the province, as his friends, persuaded him not to enter the amphitheatre to face the angry crowd (Acts 19:31). It seems that Paul had learned how vulnerable he was to mob action incited by Jewish opponents of his ministry (Acts 13:50; 14:2,5,19; 17:5,13). In seeking to minister to people of wealth and influence during his Greek tour he may also have hoped to secure a measure of protection from mob violence.

Claudius' decision in AD 49 to expel the Jews from Rome meant that Paul was not able to visit that city, something he had wanted to do for some time. He wrote to the Romans, "I have often intended to come to you (but thus far have been prevented)." (1:13)

It was Claudius' policy which apparently prevented the apostle's coming to Rome (but cf. Romans 15:20-22). However, the Emperor Claudius died in AD 54. The incoming emperor, Nero, did not continue this policy and Jews began to settle once more in Rome. It was now possible for Paul to fulfil his long-standing intention and he apparently began to make plans to that effect soon after the news of Claudius' death reached him (cf. Acts 19:21).

Paul's fourth visit to Jerusalem (see above) c. AD 52 (Acts 18:22) would have occurred at or near the beginning of the procuratorship of Antonius Felix, arguably the worst of the Roman governors of Judaea. Felix inherited the social and economic problems created by the famine c. AD 47. Brigandage became rife from that time. His immediate predecessor Ventidius Cumanus had been recalled in disgrace by Claudius. It will be remembered that serious acts of desecration of temple and Torah occurred within Cumanus' procuratorship.

Felix responded to the problems he encountered with extreme ferocity. Josephus commented, "it is impossible to calculate the number of bandits whom he crucified, and of the citizens whom he tracked down as their accomplices".[8]

The Roman historian Tacitus, admittedly no friend of freedmen appointed to high places (as Felix was), said of Felix that, "Practising every kind of cruelty and lust, he wielded royal power with the instincts of a slave".[9]

Inevitably Felix's repressive and violent policies created enormous hostility among the Jews towards Roman rule. It was at that time the Sicarii faction arose, a sect which took its name from the *sica* or dagger used in their assassination of pro-Roman aristocrats. Josephus states that,

> While the country was thus cleared these pests (i.e. the brigands) a new species of bandits was springing up in Jerusalem, the so called Sicarii, who committed murders in broad daylight in the heart of the city. The festivals were their special season...the first to be assassinated was Jonathan the high priest; after his death there were numerous daily murders.[10]

It is probable that the wave of anti-Roman feeling expressed by the Sicarii affected the believers in Jerusalem, particularly those in closest relationship with the Pharisees. This rising nationalism among Palestinian Jews would also have intensified their antagonism to Paul, the apostle to the Gentiles, in far away Greece.

Josephus also speaks of another group which arose in the days of Felix, certain prophet-like leaders who had a powerful influence on the people.

> Under the pretence of divine inspiration [feigning trances?] fostering revolutionary changes [because committed to overthrowing the Romans?] they persuaded the multitude to act like madmen [stirring them to a frenzy?] and

let them out into the desert [the wilderness was important in salvation history] under the belief that there God would give them tokens of deliverance [literally, "signs of freedom". In a new Exodus?].[11]

In Judaea in the time of Felix (AD 52–60), which over-lapped Paul's Aegean ministry (AD 53–57), there appeared several "prophets" whose bizarre, para-normal activities exerted considerable influence upon the people. Once more we refer to Josephus who speaks of the effects of the union of the Sicarii and these prophets.

The imposters [i.e. the prophets who led people to the wilderness] and brigands [i.e. Sicarii] banding together inciting numbers to revolt exhorting them to assert their independence [Greek: *eleutheria* = freedom]...the effects of their frenzy were thus felt throughout all Judaea as every day saw this war being fanned into fierce flames.[12]

Judaea during the fifties was thus gripped by a revo-olutionary and apocalyptic fervour, an extreme Judaic nationalism. It is inconceivable that the Jewish members of the Jerusalem church would not have been significantly influenced by this atmosphere. Can we imagine how the people of Judaea, believers included, would have viewed the Hellenizing activities of the ex-Pharisee Paul in his campaigns among the Gentiles? It was widely believed that he had flouted the decision of the Jerusalem church requiring Gentiles to abstain from idol-sacrificed food and non-*kosher* meat (cf. Acts 21:25). Perhaps even more serious was the belief that Paul had abandoned the law of God and was actively persuading foreign Jews to withhold circumcision from their children (Acts 21:20-24). In the popular understanding Paul was "teaching men every-where against the [Jewish] people and this place [i.e. the temple]". (Acts 21:28)

At this time of extremely high religious zeal Paul was a figure of grave notoriety, a traitor to the national cause and the ancestral religion of the Jewish people.

It is not surprising, therefore, that sometime in the mid-fifties the idea arose in Judaea of a counter-mission to Paul's apostolate in the Aegean region. This counter-mission is known to us chiefly from Paul's second letter to the Corinthians from which we are able to establish an. approximate profile of his newly arrived opponents. Few questions excite as much controversy among students of the New Testament as the question of the identity and mission of the counter-missionaries mentioned in 2 Corinthians.[13]

While conscious of the many views on the subject, I believe it can be plausibly argued that Paul's opponents in Corinth in the mid-fifties came from a Judaean milieu. That they were Hebrew, Israelites, seed of Abraham (11:22) suggests they were Palestinian Jews, and therefore came from the apocalyptic and revolutionary environment of Judaea. Their self-designation as "apostles of Christ" (11:13), as "ministers of Christ" (11:23), their "letters of commendation" (3:1) and their claim to equal status with Paul (11:12) suggests that they have come from the Jerusalem church, or more probably from an extreme sect within it. The genuineness of their adherence to Christ is doubted. Paul's description of them as "ministers of righteousness" (11:15) and his rejection of their message advocating the Mosaic ministry (3:7) is evidence that they sought to bring the Corinthians within the framework of Judaism. It is not at all clear what they proposed. It is possible that they sought to reinforce the Jewish members in a more conservative form of Judaism, countering the Hellenizing influence of Paul. Their mission to the Gentile Corinthians may have been to impose the decree of the Jerusalem council, something Paul had failed to do.

The problem about identifying these "apostles" as Judaizing Jews from Jerusalem is that they themselves display un-Jewish qualities, qualities in fact that seem distinctly Hellenistic. In particular we think of their visions, revelations, ecstasy (12:1,4; 5:13) and their gifts of (Greek) speech and rhetoric (10:10; 11:6). It is pointed out, however, that these apparently un-Jewish qualities could be found in Judaea. The prophetic movement within Judaism, mentioned above, was characterized by "divine inspiration" and people acting "like madmen". Is it possible that these Jewish counter-missionaries to Corinth could have been influenced by these para-normal phenomena as a means of legitimizing their ministry there? What then of their Greek speech and rhetoric? We must not underestimate the competence in Greek of first-century Jews like Silas (=Silvanus) from Jerusalem who wrote the excellent Greek of 1 Peter cf. 1 Peter 5:12). If Paul wrote Greek with some skill even though it was probably his second language what would the capabilities have been of the "Hellenists" whom we referred to earlier? Is it possible that these anti-Pauline emissaries were Hellenist Jews from Judaea whose rhetoric and linguistic skills exceeded Paul's?

There were various ways, therefore, that events of the wider world — Claudius' death in AD 54 and the rise of apocalyptic nationalism in Judaea in Felix's time AD 52-60 — very significantly affected Paul in his ministry in the Aegean region c. AD 53-57.

We have mentioned the success with which Paul acquired the patronage and protection of influential people during his ministry in Macedonia, Achaia and Asia AD 49-52. Careful reading of the Acts and Paul's letters reveals the names of as many as forty people who in some way sponsored Paul's activities. Equally striking was his ability to draw into his circle those whom he called "fellow-workers", "fellow-servants", "partners" or such-like semi-official titles — people like Timothy, Titus, Luke or Aristarchus. As it happens scrutiny of the Acts and the Pauline letters reveals a further forty persons who "constitute his professional following".[14] The existence of eighty or more people, mostly Gentiles, from the Aegean region says something about Paul's capacity as a leader to inspire and secure dedicated support.

Paul's Aegean period was his most prolific. During those five years he wrote two letters to the Thessalonians, four letters to the Corinthians (two of them lost to us), the letter to the Romans and (in the opinion of this writer) the letters from prison to the Ephesians, the Colossians and Philemon.

His visit to Jerusalem in c. AD 52 (Acts 18:22) must have reinforced in Paul the sense of a widening division between

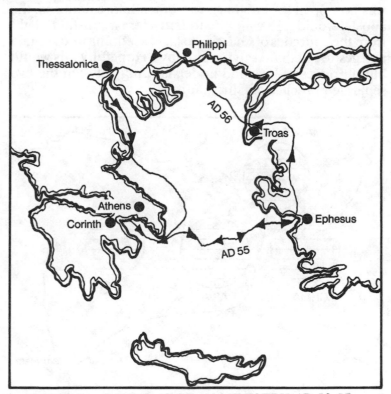

MAP 14 — PAUL'S AEGEAN MINISTRY AD 53-57

the Judaic church there and the Gentile churches established by him. At the meeting in Jerusalem c. 47 he and
Barnabas had agreed to "remember the poor" (Galatians
2:10), that is the famine-affected poor believers in
Jerusalem. That visit to Jerusalem c. AD 52 led, apparently,
to the devising of an ambitious plan whereby the Gentile
churches established by Paul should make a gift to the
Jerusalem church. This "collection", as he called it, was
made not only to help the poor members of the church in
Jerusalem but as an expression of thanksgiving by the
Gentile churches to the Jerusalem church for its gift of the
Gospel to them (Romans 15:25-28). Paul's decision to
implement this "collection" was probably connected with
the news of Claudius' death and the knowledge that the way

was now open for him to go to Rome. Before doing so, the apostle would take with him to Jerusalem a substantial gift from the churches of Galatia, Asia, Macedonia and Achaia as a gesture of thanksgiving and love. Hopefully this would build bridges of love and understanding between the two separate branches of Christianity.

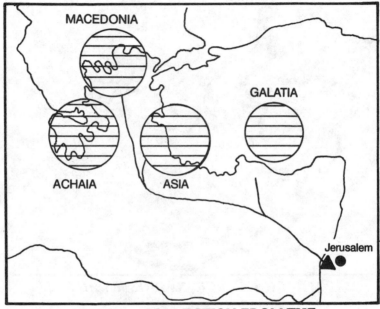

MAP 15 — COLLECTION FROM THE GENTILE CHURCHES FOR THE CHURCH IN JERUSALEM.

This "collection" reveals Paul to have been deeply committed to a world-wide unity between the Jewish and the Gentile churches. It would have been easy for Paul to quit the Aegean region and go direct to Rome and beyond there to Spain for the next phase of his ministry. That he chose to go back to Jerusalem knowing of the animosity directed towards him (Romans 15:31) is evidence both of his love for his fellow-Jews (Romans 9:1-5; 10:1-2) and of his desire for a genuine Christian ecumenicity.

Paul, as the apostle to the Gentiles, as called by God and as recognised at the missionary agreement in Jerusalem c.

AD 47, had by no means turned his back on his fellow-Jews. (see, for example, Romans 11:1-2,11-12,25-27)

Paul's Aegean ministry was dominated by his problems with the Corinthian church and by his awareness of the growing animosity against him from those whose loyalty was more Jewish than Christian. Initially the difficulties in the Corinthian church were characteristically of Gentile orientation — associated with sexual morality, with idolatry, with class stratification at the Lord's Supper, with ecstatic behaviour, with resurrection as opposed to immortality and not least with the Corinthians' sense that Paul did not measure up as a teacher in Greek rhetorical terms. Disciplinary problems associated with these matters caused Paul to write three more letters (two of them lost) and to make a painfully unsuccessful emergency visit.

The arrival of the counter-missionaries from Judaea c. 55/56 marked a major new crisis in Paul's relationships with the Corinthians. There was now the real possibility that the Corinthians would reject Paul altogether and adopt the alternative Moses-centred theology of the new ministers. His second letter to the Corinthians is Paul's powerful if somewhat embittered response to the new situation. A lesser man would have abandoned the Corinthians. Paul, however, after a near scrape with death in Ephesus and an anxious time in Macedonia (2 Corinthians 1:8-10; 7:5-6) made his way once more to Corinth soon after finishing this second letter to them.

Paul spent three months in Greece (Corinth? Acts 20:3) from where it is probable that he wrote the letter to the Romans. This letter, universally regarded as Paul's most careful statement about Christianity, was not written in an emotional or intellectual vacuum. Its patient teaching in the first eight chapters about justification by faith and the gift of the Spirit apart from the works of the Jewish law probably reflects what Paul taught the Corinthians when present with them for the last time. The Judaizing threat in Corinth seems to have passed, judging from the measured tones of this letter written to the Romans from the city which had recently been such a storm-centre.

The later chapters, from 9-16, however may have been

written with the context of Roman believers more clearly in focus. In what was, apparently, a mixed and unintegrated series of Jewish and Gentile sub-churches, news had been spread misrepresenting Paul (3:1,8; 6:1; 9:1; 11:1). The letter to the Romans sought to set the record right about what Paul actually believed and taught, in particular, that he was not against the law of God nor against the Jews. The powerful ethical teachings in chapters 12-15 make clear Paul's deeply moral outlook. The apostle attempted to bring Jewish and Gentile believers into a practical unity (chapters 14-15) and, not least, to dissuade Jewish believers in Rome from adopting the revolutionary anti-Roman attitudes of fellow-Jews in Judaea (13:1-7).

Paul diplomatically disclaims any intention of settling in Rome; he is merely passing through, en route to Spain. In the past he had felt unable to come to Rome because this would be to build on the foundation of "another man" — a probable reference to Peter who may have come to Rome soon after Claudius died (AD 54) when Jews were able once more to live in the city. Clearly a large city like Rome with significant numbers of Gentile and Jewish believers represented major difficulties for the ten-year-old missionary agreement. It is interesting that Paul does not attempt to bridge the gap between the ethnic groups through the collaboration of leaders (i.e. Peter and Paul) but by promoting the members' respect and acceptance of one another.

The letter to the Romans, then, was written mindful of the recent turmoil in Corinth caused by the Judaizers from Judaea while at the same time preparing the way for Paul to go to Rome, a community not as yet united where many erroneous statements about Paul had been circulated.

The story of Paul's journey from Corinth back to Jerusalem is told in the Acts of the Apostles in some detail and with considerable drama. He sailed from Troas on the western Aegean to Caesarea in Judaea, after several changes of ship. It is recorded that he visited believers in Miletus, Tyre and Ptolemais (Acts 20:13-21:8). Despite dire warnings from Agabus the prophet in Caesarea, Paul pressed on to Jerusalem, where he did not stay with James but with Mnason a Cypriot believer from earliest times (Acts 21:10-16).Presumably Paul would cause less trouble in the home of (the "Hellenist"?) Mnason, than with James!

At last Paul came to James, all the elders being present. This was a critical meeting, held ten years after the missionary agreement when the Jerusalem leaders had recognised Paul's apostolate and agreed that he should go to the Gentiles, and they to the Jews. Ten years later reference could be made to significant success in the respective missions.

Although the Acts narrative summarizes Paul's report in one sentence it is clear that the apostle could claim, as he did in writing to the Romans, that he had fully evangelized the region from Jerusalem to Illyricum (Yugoslavia), that is within the provinces of Judaea, Syria-Cilicia, Galatia and Phrygia, Asia, Macedonia and Achaia. The churches he founded were growing in numbers and new ones were being established (see Colossians 1:6; 4:15-17).

According to the Acts of the Apostles James did not speak; those who responded were the elders of the Jerusalem church. They pointed to significant growth in numbers of Jewish believers in Jerusalem (and possibly other places, as well). They told Paul, "You see, brother, how many thousands there are among the Jews of those who have believed; and they are all zealous for the law." (Acts 21:20)

This does not appear to have been a happy meeting. In the narrative, James is not quoted at all. The elders are not reported as making any response of gratitude for the "collection", despite the considerable sacrifice involved for all parties, not least by Paul. They pointedly remarked on the many thousands of Jewish believers there were, who were all zealous for the law, in contrast to Jews whom Paul is reported to have influenced to abandon the circumcising of their children and the keeping of the Law of Moses. Reference to the decree of the Jerusalem church is made, the inference being that Paul's churches have not observed its requirements.

While our immediate reaction is to feel some sympathy

for Paul in this tense situation we should not forget that the Jerusalem elders and James had been through an extremely difficult time, given the severe problems caused by Felix's rule. From their point of view, Paul had caused considerable embarrassment which would not have been easy to explain to ardent Jews, not even to Christian Jews. The agreement about circumcision had been honoured by the Jerusalem church; but Paul appeared to be haphazard in his application of, for example, the ban on Gentile believers eating idol-sacrificed food (1 Corinthians 10:25). It must have been very difficult indeed to defend Paul's actions to people in Jerusalem, especially in times when talk of a war with the Gentile Romans was in the air.

It is possible to detect an element of sadness in the relationship between Paul and James. In the year c. AD 57 Paul had been apostle to the Gentiles for about twenty-three years and James the leader of the Jerusalem church for fourteen years and a member there, in all, for a quarter of a century. Both men were highly dedicated to the apostolate. Each believed he had been called to it by God. Yet the people whom they served, Jews and Gentiles, were so different culturally and linguistically that effective service meant, for each of them, thorough contextual identification. This resulted in an inevitable sense of distance between the two men, who in other circumstances may have enjoyed a close working relationship.

The Letter to the Hebrews

Many opinions have been expressed about this powerful but mysterious "letter" — its self-designation is as "a word of exhortation" (13:22) — whose author nowhere declares the identity either of himself or of those to whom he writes. However, there is a strong argument for placing it in the same decade — AD 47–57 — as that of the two missions.

The "letter" gives a number of clues about when and why it was written. Paul's colleague Timothy is mentioned, indicating that the author and his readers were known outside their community (13:23). Moreover, as mentioned in Chapter Five, there are many references which make best sense if the Jerusalem temple (destroyed AD 70) was still in use (5:1-4; 8:13; 9:6,9; 10:1-3; 11; 13:10-14).

The author and his original community evidently have heard the gospel initially from the apostles and seen signs and wonders (2:3-4). The time of writing, however, is one of great suffering, with much public abuse, loss of property and imprisonment of some members (10:32-39, 6:10). Who were these people? One setting for them that fits the circumstances of the writer and his readers is at the time of Saul's persecution of the Hellenists and other believers c. AD 34 (Acts 22:19; 26:10-11).

Some of their members are still in prison, possibly the same ones (13:3). There is also renewed hostility towards the community (12:3-4), with significant pressure applied to reject Jesus as the Son of God (6:6; 10:29). Exhortations to "hold fast the confession of our hope" and not to "shrink back" (10:23,39), together with teaching that Judaism is now superseded, strongly suggest that the readers were being pressured to turn back to Judaism (e.g. 10:11-14). For his part the anonymous writer calls on the priestly members to turn their back on their temple duties and, indeed, exhorts the general readers to withdraw from Judaism (13:10,13-14).

It is the opinion of this writer that the "letter" was written to Greek-speaking Jewish Christians (composed of some original "Hellenists"?) suffering persecution in Palestine during the fifties or sixties, more probably during the difficult days of Felix in the fifties as previously described. Certainly we know that there were Judaean churches apart from the Jerusalem church. (Galatians 1:22; 1 Thessalonians 2:14)

Who was the author? Many ingenious proposals have been offered down the centuries, including Priscilla wife of Aquila and Mary the mother of Jesus. If, however, the readers were "Hellenist" Christians in Judaea (the "letter" is written in stylish Greek), as this writer believes, then either Barnabas or "Philip the evangelist" qualifies. The strong conviction that temple and high priesthood are now superseded accords well with the Hellenist Stephen's criticisms of these things and may add weight to the suggestion that the author belonged to Stephen's circle, as indeed Philip did.

Whoever he was and whoever his readers were, it is clear that both were at odds with Judaism, though being themselves Jews. In fact the writer (and his readers?) was much more radical in opposition to Judaism than Paul. As such he and they are in strong contrast with James who appears to have desired a close identification with Judaism.

These differences remind us of the complexity of early Christianity. The missionary agreement in Jerusalem c. AD 47 did not lead to clear-cut expressions of ministry in ethnic or cultural terms. Paul, the apostle to the Gentiles, for example, remained profoundly concerned for the salvation of Jews (see Romans 11). This anonymous author, although a Jew, is, in effect,opposed to Judaism. Peter, although having an apostolate to Jews (Galatians 2:7-9), lived like a Gentile (Galatians 2:14), argued against the necessity of Gentile circumcision (Acts 15:7-11) and directed much of his first Letter to Gentile readers (1 Peter 1:14-18; 4:3)

Such complexities serve to remind us of the overarching greatness of the Lord they served — Jesus was too great to be neatly pigeon-holed by some man-made missionary agreement.

Further reading to Chapter Eight:
F.F. Bruce, *New Testament History*, Anchor, New York, 1972.
W.A. Meeks, *The First Urban Christians*, University Press, Yale, 1983.
C.F.D. Moule, *The Birth of the New Testament*, A. & C. Black, London, 1973.
J. Murphy-O'Connor, *St. Paul's Corinth*, Glazier, Wilmington, 1983.

Notes
[1]*AJ*, xx, 102.
[2]*AJ*, xx, 124.
[3]*AJ*, xx, 105-113.

[4]Josephus, *Apion*, ii, 179, 181, 184.

[5]*AJ*, xx, 44.

[6]See C.K. Barrett, *The New Testament Background*, 48-49.

[7]Suetonius, *Claudius*, 25:4.

[8]*BJ*, ii, 253.

[9]*Histories*, V.9, cf. *Annals*, xii, 54.

[10]*BJ*, ii, 254, 256.

[11]*BJ*, ii, 25, 8-9 cf. *AJ*, xx, 167-8.

[12]*BJ*, ii, 265.

[13]See P.W. Barnett, "Opposition in Corinth", *Journal for the Study of the New Testament*, 22, 1984, 3-17.

[14]E.A. Judge, "The Early Christians as a Scholastic Community", *Journal of Religious History* 1/3, 1961, 125-137, cf. E.E. Ellis, "Paul and his Co-workers", *NTS* 17, 1971, 437-452.

9

Jerusalem and Rome:
The Decade of Crisis (AD 60-70)

The fifth book of the New Testament, the Acts of the Apostles, is probably mis-titled. Of the twelve apostles named in Acts 1, only Peter and the Zebedee brothers John and James are again mentioned by name. John Zebedee does not appear after chapter eight nor James his brother after chapter twelve, when he was killed under Agrippa I c. AD 43. Peter is last mentioned in Acts 15 (c. AD 49). There is no reference in Acts to "the apostles" later than chapter fifteen, when they are bracketed with "the elders" of the Jerusalem church (vv. 4, 6, 22, 23). That only "the elders" are mentioned in Acts 21:18 suggests that the apostles were no longer in Jerusalem. Where they went and what they did is a matter for speculation, based on doubtful information from later centuries. Apart from Paul and James the brother of the Lord the Acts of the Apostles makes no reference after AD 50 to any apostolic figure, neither by name nor title. Who, then, were the real leaders of early Christianity?

The private conference recorded in Galatians 2:7-9 suggests that by c. AD 47, when the meeting occurred, the leading figures in Christianity were the three "pillars" of the Jerusalem church, James the brother of the Lord, Cephas and John; and Barnabas and Paul, the two delegates from Antioch. However, there is no later reference to John anywhere in the New Testament. The (later) gospel and letters attributed to John are in fact anonymous. Barnabas is last mentioned in the mid-fifties (1 Corinthians 9:6). However, there is information about the later activities of James, Cephas and Paul.

These three men were significant as leaders of the three branches into which by the sixth decade of the first century the river of New Testament history had flowed. James was the principal figure in Hebraic Christianity, based in Jerusalem. Cephas/Peter had become a travelling pastor and minister to Hellenistic Jews outside Palestine, settling finally in Rome. Paul continued as an itinerant apostle to the Gentiles.

This decade proved to be the most critical period in Christianity's brief history.

By the mid-sixties, all the great leaders with the probable exception of John had gone. James was killed in Jerusalem in c. AD 62. In AD 64/65, shortly after the great fire in Rome, Peter and Paul were also killed.

By the sixties, the movement was sufficiently well established to be known both to the Roman authorities and to the international Jewish community as a separate, rapidly spreading and dangerous sect.

Furthermore, the sixties were dominated by the Parthian threat, the destruction of Rome by fire and the catastrophic war in Palestine between the Jews and the Romans, which culminated in the destruction of the temple in AD 70. To many Christians these horrendous events, together with the passing of the great apostolic leaders, must have seemed like the prelude to the apocalyptic end.

James c. AD 57-62

James was last mentioned in connection with Paul's final visit to Jerusalem c. AD 57. Unfortunately there is no further information about James between that time and his death in AD 62. We are, however, able to comment on the ebb and flow of the political and social life in Palestine between those years.

Josephus describes the further deterioration in the fabric of Jewish society c. AD 57 as the Jews edged closer to war with the Romans.

At this time King Agrippa [the younger Agrippa, now King of Galilee] conferred the high priesthood upon Ishmael, the son of Phabi. There now was enkindled mutual enmity and class warfare between the high priests, on the one hand, and the priests and the leaders of the populace of Jerusalem on the other. Each of the factions...collected for itself a band of the most reckless revolutionaries...they used abusive language and pelted each other with stones. And there was not even one person to rebuke them...the high priests...actually were so brazen as to send slaves to...receive the tithes that were due to the priests, with the result that the poorer priests starved to death.[1]

This was the King Agrippa before whom Paul was soon to appear (Acts 25:13-27). He, as the newly appointed ruler of Galilee, was responsible for the appointment of the high priest, Ishmael, to replace Ananias. (Acts 23:2)

The letter which bears the name of James may have been written at this time. Its strong condemnation of the rich in their oppression of the poor may reflect the evil days of Ishmael the high priest (c. AD 59-61).

Come now, you rich, weep and howl for the miseries that are coming upon you. . . Behold the wages of the labourers who mowed the fields, which you have kept back by fraud. . . You have lived on the earth in luxury and in pleasure. . . (5:1-6 cf. 1:9-11, 2:6)

The letter of James is addressed to Jews who live "in the dispersion" (1:1). This is in keeping with James' involvement with the mission to the Jews (Galatians 2:7-9). It is written in good Greek, possibly but not certainly, by an assistant. While he may have spoken Greek it is difficult to believe that a person of such humble and obscure background as James would have been able to write such sophisticated Greek. Whoever wrote it, the letter indicates that there were Jews in Jerusalem at that time capable of launching the counter-mission against Paul in the Greek world, as reflected in 2 Corinthians, as previously discussed.

As it happens part of the letter sets out to correct what the author appears to identify as Paul's doctrine of justification by faith (see Galatians 2:16: "a man is not justified by works of the law but through faith"). James' letter asks, "What does it profit, my brethren, if a man says he has faith but not works? Can his faith save him?" (2:14-15). Careful reading of Galatians and James shows that the words "faith" and "works", in fact, are used differently by each author and that there may be no doctrinal difference between the two letters over this issue. Nevertheless, there are echoes of a debate between the Jerusalem church and Paul here, ironically marked by misunderstanding and cross-purposes.

We constantly hear echoes of the teachings of Jesus in the letter of James. James' words about,

the Father's generous gifts to his children (1:17 cf. Matthew 7:11);

the need not merely to hear but to do the word (1:22-25 cf. Matthew 7:24);

the unity of the law (2:10-11 cf. Matthew 5:19);

the plight of the hungry and ill-clad (2:15 cf. Matthew 25:3);

the effects of evil speech (3:6 cf. Matthew 12:36; 15:11);

the wrongness of judging a brother (4:11-12 cf. Matthew 7:1);

the ban on oaths (5:12 cf. Matthew 5:34-37);

the nearness of the Lord to the doors (5:8-9 cf. Matthew 24:33);

and the importance of saving a sinner (5:19-20 cf. Matthew 18:11)

bring to mind the teachings of his brother as we find them in the gospels. We find the instruction of Jesus on every page of James' letter.

Who, then, did James think Jesus was?

It comes as no surprise that James writes of "the wisdom from above" (3:17) in a manner suggestive of Jesus as the incarnation of "wisdom". James implies that Jesus was the "Righteous One" who did not resist his oppressors (5:6). Explicitly, he refers to Jesus as "Messiah" (1:1; 2:1) whose return as "Judge" was near (5:8-9). Above all, James uses the same word of Jesus as he does of God, namely "Lord" (1:1 cf. 1:8; 5:7,8,15). This "glorious Lord" (2:1) will "raise up" the sick and, by implication, the dead at the end (5:15).

James' concentration on the wise teachings of Jesus should not lead us to think that he did not regard Jesus as a supernatural, eschatological figure.

In c. AD 59(?) Felix was relieved of office by the Emperor

Nero and succeeded by Porcius Festus, one of the better procurators, who died two years later. In the unexpected interregnum following Festus' death, the high priest Annas (spelt Ananus by Josephus) had James killed. Josephus' description is quite detailed.

> Upon learning of the death of Festus, Caesar [Nero] sent Albinus to Judaea as procurator. The king [Agrippa II] removed Joseph from the high priesthood, and bestowed the succession to this office upon the son of Ananus. . . The younger Ananus. . .was rash in his temper and usually daring. He followed the school of the Sadducees, who are indeed more heartless than any of the other Jews, as I have already explained, when they sit in judgement. Possessed of such a character, Ananus thought that he had a favourable opportunity because Festus was dead and Albinus was still on the way. And so he convened the judges of the Sanhedrin and brought before them a man named James, the brother of Jesus who was called the Christ, and certain others. He accused them of having transgressed the law and delivered them up to be stoned.[2]

But why did Annas the younger take such drastic and illegal actions? (In Roman provinces the governor alone had authority from the emperor to impose capital punishment.) Three reasons, not necessarily exclusive of each other, are suggested. First, James' condemnation of the exploitation of the poor by the wealthy (as expressed in his letter) may have been offensive to the aristocratic Sadducean party. Second, the Sadducean intolerance of the Christian doctrine of resurrection (both Jesus' historic resurrection and the believers' coming resurrection). Third, and most probably, James was killed because of dynastic jealousy. James was leader of a large community of Jerusalem Jews whose loyalty to him would have exceeded by far any loyalty the members of the wider community had towards the high priest. Moreover, from Annas' point of view James was brother of the false-messiah, Jesus the Nazarene whose execution Annas the Elder had secured thirty years earlier. Dynasties were a fact of life in Palestine at that time, as the following tables relating to dynasties of high priests, Jesus, rabbis and revolutionaries indicates.

TABLE 4: DYNASTIES IN FIRST CENTURY PALESTINE

i) A Dynasty of High Priests	(ii) Jesus' Dynasty	(iii) A Dynasty of Rabbis	(iv) A Dynasty of Revolutionaries
			Ezekias d.47 BC
		Hillel the Elder fl.c.20 BC	
Annas HP AD 6-15			Judas son of Ezekias d.AD 6/7
Eleazar, son of Annas HP AD 17			
Caiaphas. son in-law of Annas HP AD 26-37	Jesus d. AD 33		
Jonathan. son of Annas HP AD 37		Gamaliel the Elder fl.c.35	
Theophilus. son of Annas HP AD 37			
Matthias. son of Annas HP AD 41	James brother of Jesus, leader of the Jerusalem church c.AD 43-62		James. son of Judas d. AD 47 Simon. Son of Judas d.AD 47
Annas. Son of Annas HP 62, 66- 68		Simeon son of Gamaliel fl.c. 65	
			Menahem, son of Judas d. AD 66
	Simean cousin of Jesus leader of the Jerusalem church c.AD 70		Eleazar ben Jair relative (?) of Judas d. AD 74

This table of dynasties shows how customary it was for members of the family to continue the teaching and traditions of their relatives. Once Peter was unable to continue as leader of the Jerusalem church the choice would have fallen, fairly naturally, upon Jesus' brother James and then, after his death, on Jesus' next close relative, his cousin Simean. We know of no relatives of Jesus after Simean acting as church leaders in Jerusalem.

Josephus, having narrated the stoning of James, continues,

> Those of the inhabitants of the city who were considered the most fair-minded and who were strict in observance of the law were offended at this. They therefore secretly sent to King Agrippa urging him, for Ananus had not even been correct in his first step, to order him to desist from any further such actions. Certain of them even went to meet Albinus, who was on his way from Alexandria, and informed him that Ananus had no authority to convene the Sanhedrin without his consent. Convinced by these words, Albinus angrily wrote to Ananus threatening to take vengeance upon him. King Agrippa, because of Ananus' action, deposed him from the high priesthood which he had held for three months and replaced him with Jesus the son of Damnaeus.[3]

Something of James' greatness is indicated by Josephus' remarks. He devotes more space to James than to his brother Jesus. King Agrippa II was unlikely to have deposed Annas for stoning someone who was of no importance in society. As it was, protest was made by "the most fair-minded and . . .strict in their observance of the Jewish Law", people who from this description would have been leading Pharisees. James, though a Christian, seems to have been a popular, highly respected member of the wider Jerusalem community, and whose death created a scandal at the time.

Porcius Festus was followed as procurator, first by Lucius Albinus (AD 62–64) and then by Gessius Florus (AD 64–66). According to Josephus these procurators were singularly corrupt, engaging in wholesale extortion and blackmail, and using their troops for what were, in effect criminal actions against the population. Meanwhile the Sicarii and other revolutionary groups expanded both in numbers and in activity. It was now only a matter of time before open conflict between Jews and Romans erupted.

In May AD 66 a series of events took place which led directly to the outbreak of hostilities. Violence broke out in Caesarea Maritima between Jews and Greeks over the vexed question of Jewish citizenship rights. Fighting in Jerusalem began soon afterwards between Florus' legionaries and bands of Jews, forcing the procurator to withdraw from the city. The pleas of King Agrippa II for peace were rejected and the loyal sacrifices for Rome were discontinued in the temple. By October Cestius Gallus, Legate of Syria, arrived in Jerusalem from Antioch with a large army only to withdraw immediately and inexplicably. Jewish revolutionaries destroyed Gallus' retreating troops at Beth Horon a few miles to the north-west of the city. Clearly, a state of war now existed between the Romans and the Jews of Palestine.

Given the apparent nationalism of the Jerusalem church it is a little surprising to discover that its members distanced themselves from the Jewish cause. According to Eusebius the fourth century church historian (relying on sources less than a century after the events),

the people of the church of Jerusalem, in accordance with a certain. . .revelation to approved men there, had been commanded to depart from the city before the war, and to inhabit a certain city of Peraea. They called it Pella.[4]

This is an intriguing development. What was the "revelation" that led them to depart the city? Had some prophets reflected on the words of Jesus that "those who are in Judaea [should] flee" when they see "the desolating sacrilege set up where it ought not to be" (Mark 13:14) and exhorted the people to leave? Whatever the circumstances were, the community somehow withdrew to Pella in the Decapolis where they remained till the end of the war (cf. Revelation 12:13-14).

Their action clearly demonstrates the sense of separation these Christians felt from their fellow-Jews. Moreover, the Jewish community at large would hardly fail to have noted the withdrawal from their midst of this messianic Jewish community. From this point Christian Jews were no longer regarded as an acceptable part of the Jewish community. Henceforth they would be regarded as *minim*, heretics. A decade or so after the war a council of Jewish rabbis meeting at Jammia composed the following Benediction for use in the synagogue: "For the renegades let there be no hope and may the arrogant Kingdom be rooted out in our days and the Nazarenes and *minim* perish as in a moment..."

Clearly Christian Jews were no longer welcome to attend the synagogue. The separation was complete.

Nonetheless the church in Judaea continued to exist after the war of AD 66–70 and its membership continued to be exclusively Jewish. Where possible the leaders were chosen from those who were in some way related to Jesus. In the second century there was a weakening within the Jewish church of belief in the deity and the pre-existence of Jesus with a corresponding strengthening of emphasis on the keeping of the Jewish law. This theology was called "Ebionite" by Gentile Christians, from a Hebrew word meaning "poverty", implying a poverty of faith in Jesus as the Son of God. In AD 132–135 the Romans again invaded Judaea to defeat the forces of the pseudo-messiah Bar Cochba. The Emperor Hadrian determined that Jews must leave their homeland and Jewish Christians along with other Jews were forced to live in the Diaspora. Ebionite Christianity survived in pockets for a period before finally disappearing.

The future of Christianity now lay with the Gentiles.

Paul
(Acts 21-28; Philippians: 1 and 2 Timothy; Titus)
Our last reference to Paul was at the meeting with the elders of the Jerusalem church in AD 57/8 when he presented the "collection" from the Gentile churches.

The very next day, when he was seen for the first time in public in Jerusalem, events took a dramatic turn which changed the course of the apostle's life. When he came to the temple a riot broke out from which he was barely rescued by the Romans, followed by another riot and another rescue. The next day when Paul was placed before

TABLE 5: RULE IN JUDAEA AD 54-62

Emperor	Ruler in Judaea	High Priest
Nero 54-68	Antonius Felix, Procurator, 52-60	Ananias, son of Nebedaeus 48-59
		Ishmael son of Phabi 59-61
	Porcius Festus Procurator, 60-62	

TABLE 6: THE LINE OF THE AGRIPPAS

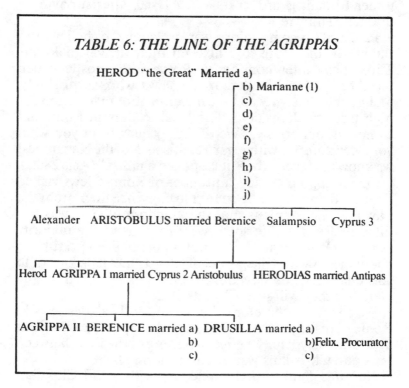

HEROD "the Great" Married a)
b) Marianne (1)
c)
d)
e)
f)
g)
h)
i)
j)

Alexander   ARISTOBULUS married Berenice   Salampsio   Cyprus 3

Herod AGRIPPA I married Cyprus 2 Aristobulus   HERODIAS married Antipas

AGRIPPA II BERENICE married a) DRUSILLA married a)
b)   b)Felix, Procurator
c)   c)

the Sanhedrin for trial there was yet another riot and another rescue! More drama followed on the third day. The Romans got wind of a conspiracy to kill Paul necessitating the removal of this troublesome man to the protection of the military garrison at Caesarea Maritima.

Although the procurator Felix was unconvinced by the high priest's case against Paul the apostle was kept in prison at Caesarea for two years in the hope that a bribe would be paid for his release.

Paul appeared before the newly arrived procurator Porcius Festus where he demanded, as a Roman citizen, to be sent to Rome for trial before the emperor. Ironically, had he not appealed he would have been released since the procurator in consultation with King Agrippa II deemed him to be not guilty of any crime.

Accompanied by Aristarchus and Luke, Paul was brought under Roman guard to Italy c. AD 60, after surviving a dramatic shipwreck.

Paul and his companions were welcomed by believers in Puteoli in the south and also on their arrival in Rome. Three days after coming to Rome, the apostle called together the local leaders of the Jews who, surprisingly, had not received any communication about Paul from the high priest in Jerusalem. The local leaders in Rome did comment, ominously, "We desire to hear from you what your views are; for with regard to this sect [of the Nazarenes] we know that everywhere it is spoken against." (Acts 28:22)

On an appointed day, a number of Roman Jews visited Paul's lodging where he sought to convince them from the Law and the Prophets that the kingdom of God was fulfilled in Jesus. While some were responsive the majority were not. Paul's reaction sounds a note of deep pessimism about the Jews and the gospel of Christ. "Let it be known to you then that this salvation of God has been sent to the Gentiles; they will listen." (Acts 28:28)

We conclude, therefore, that by the early sixties Jews in Rome were fully aware of, but strongly opposed to, the faith proclaimed by Paul. In effect a parting of the ways between Jews and Christians was already taking place.

Nor was Paul entirely welcome within the Christian

community. The letter to the Philippians, apparently written soon afterwards, speaks of "brothers. . .[who] preach Christ from envy and rivalry. . .out of partisanship, not sincerely, but thinking to afflict me in my imprisonment". (1:14,15,17)

Paul does not disclose the identity of these "brothers" but it is reasonable to assume they were believers who were conservatively Jewish and who were deeply unhappy with Paul's failure to press the claims of Judaism on Gentiles.

Paul's appeal to Caesar was successful, as he had expected (Philippians 1:25), leading to further travels and missionary work. According to his letters — First and Second Timothy and Titus — Paul visited Ephesus, Troas, Macedonia and Crete, though we do not know for how long nor in which sequence (1 Timothy 1:3; 2 Timothy 4:13,20; Titus 1:5). The second letter of Timothy depicts Paul again in prison (1:8) and awaiting execution at any moment. "I am already on the point of being sacrificed; the time of my departure has come" (4:6).These are among the last recorded words of Paul the apostle.

A letter written from Rome by Clement, some thirty years later, stated that in the time of Nero "the greatest and most righteous pillars of the church [Peter and Paul] were persecuted and contended unto death".[5] Clement praised Paul as

having preached in the east and west, attained the noble renown won for him by his faith, teaching righteousness to the whole world and reaching the farthest limits of the west [Spain? More probably, Rome].[6]

Clement does not specifically locate the deaths of Peter and Paul in the assault of the Emperor Nero on the Christians in AD 64. They may have met their ends then or, indeed, a year or so later. What is clear from the historian Tacitus' account of these events is that by AD 64 the Roman authorities had recognised that Christians were different from Jews and had no claim to the same protection. Times had changed since c. AD 52 when Gallio the Proconsul of Achaia had declared that Paul's teachings and activities were part of Judaism and therefore subject to Jewish not Roman jurisdiction. (Acts 18:14-15)

By AD 64 the Christians were clearly recognised by

everyone as distinct from Jews, and suitable scapegoats to deflect public animosity from Nero over the devastating fire which had left hundreds of thousands homeless. According to Tacitus,

...all human efforts, all the lavish gifts of the emperor, and the propitiations of the gods did not banish the sinister belief that the conflagration was the result of an order [from Nero]. Consequently, to get rid of the report, Nero fastened the guilt and inflicted the most exquisite tortures on a class called Christians by the populace.[7]

Not only was this attack on Christians awesome in its scale and ferocity, equally seriously, it advertised the hard reality of their separate existence. Clearly the Christian group must have been sufficiently large to be an effective scapegoat. Closely related to this was the awareness of the international community of Jews of the threat to it of the rapid spread of the heretical and schismatic sect of the Nazarenes. Whatever difficulties Christians had encountered in the past, these were relatively minor compared with the informed hostility they would now face wherever they were, from both Jews and Gentiles.

Peter

In the period between AD 34–47 Peter had been involved in frequent travel within Judaea (Samaria, Lydda, Joppa, Caesarea). In the period following the missionary agreement in Jerusalem c. AD 47, however, we see him increasingly outside Judaea.

For the past fifteen years God had both entrusted to Peter leadership in evangelizing Jews and had effectively enabled him to do it. The success in bringing the gospel to Jews in Jerusalem and Judaea had, to a significant degree, been due to him.

The missionary agreement recognised this and also looked to the future. It is clear enough that Barnabas and Paul were to "go" to the Gentiles. What is not so often noticed is that it was agreed also that James, Cephas and John should "go" to the circumcised. It is interesting that while the Greek sentence does not use the verb "go" for either group it is clearly intended to be understood as applying to both.

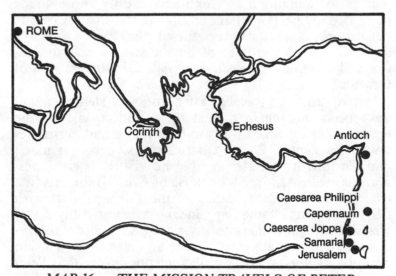

MAP 16 — THE MISSION TRAVELS OF PETER

Peter certainly travelled from Antioch to Corinth. Possibly he travelled through Asia Minor, visiting the churches established by Paul, with special concern for the Jews.

Subsequent to this meeting we hear of Peter in three locations outside Jerusalem/Judaea. In all probability he worked mainly among non-Palestinian, Greek-speaking Jews — Christian and non-Christian. First, "Cephas came to Antioch" (Galatians 2:11) in c. AD 48/49 where initially he shared table-fellowship with Gentiles. This was consistent with the liberty he had entered into after the vision at Joppa of the unclean animals which the Lord instructed him to "kill and eat" (Acts 10:10-16). It will be remembered that this vision cleared the way for Peter to eat with and evangelize the Gentile Cornelius and his family (Acts 10:24ff). Paul quotes the exact words he spoke to Peter in Antioch at that time, "Though a Jew [you] live like a Gentile and not like a Jew." (Galatians 2:14)

In other words Peter had by then been emancipated from Jewish strictures on eating with Gentiles. Paul's complaint was that Peter not only changed his practice when the Judaizers came to Antioch but actually began to "Judaize", that is to demand that Gentiles eat only those foods permitted to Jews (Galatians 2:12-14). In the ensuing debate Peter appears to have recognised the force of Paul's argument. When we hear of him next, at the Jerusalem Council meeting, he rejected the call for circumcision of Gentiles. (Acts 15:7-11)

Where did Peter travel to after Antioch? He appears to have been moving in a westerly direction, visiting the territories evangelized by Paul (just as he had earlier retraced the steps of Philip?). Between his visits to Antioch and Corinth it is quite possible he visited Jewish communities within the great expanse of Asia Minor. His first letter is addressed to "exiles of the Dispersion [Jewish Christians?] in Galatia, Cappadocia, Asia and Bithynia..." His second letter refers to mystical and gnostic aberrations which were, apparently, specially prevalent in Asian cities like Colossae. It is a distinct possibility that Peter passed through Asia Minor as he travelled from Jerusalem to Corinth.

The next sure location where we meet Peter is Corinth, as reflected by several references in First Corinthians. That a faction supporting "Cephas" in Corinth is referred to suggests that "Cephas" had in fact visited the city some time between c. AD 52, when Paul left Corinth, and c. AD 55, when Paul wrote 1 Corinthians (see 1:12; 3:22). Paul's question, "Do we not have the right to be accompanied by a wife, as the other apostles and brothers of the Lord and Cephas?" (1 Corinthians 9:5) hardly makes sense unless the apostle Peter had visited the city and become known to the people.

To whom did Peter minister in Corinth? Our assumption is that he evangelized Greek-speaking Jews in Corinth, in the terms of the missionary agreement c. AD 47. It is also likely that he ministered to believing Greek-speaking Jews within the Corinthian church. Unfortunately there is an almost complete lack of detail upon which to reconstruct the length of his stay or the nature of his work.

Where did Peter go next? The probability is that Peter

journeyed on from Corinth to Rome. It will be remembered that Claudius' death in AD 54 would have made it possible again for Jews to live in Rome. It may well have occurred while Peter was at Corinth. A further detail bearing on this question is found in Paul's letter to the Romans, written c. AD 56/57, in which he makes it clear that he is merely passing through Rome en route to Spain (15:24). Paul's aim is not to "build on another man's foundation" (15:20). "Another man" may well be Peter who, within the years AD 54–56/57, could have laid a "foundation" of ministry in Rome, among Greek-speaking Jews.

Travelling north and westward from Jerusalem after c. AD 49 Peter may well have arrived in Rome by the mid-fifties in the early years of Nero, the emperor under whom he would lose his life a decade later.

Since Claudius had expelled the Jews from Rome in c. AD 49, Christian Jews included, it is reasonable to conclude that Gentile believers predominated in the early years of Claudius' successor. In time, however, we assume Jewish numbers in Rome increased again, and with them Christian Jewish numbers. Obviously we do not know the numbers of Gentile and Jewish Christians. But it does appear from Romans 14-15 that these groups were separate and unintegrated. As already suggested it is very probable that Peter was the "other man" on whose "foundation" Paul did not feel free to build — to do so would have been a breach of the Jerusalem missionary agreement c. AD 47.

It is quite likely that Peter spent the last decade of his life in Rome teaching and consolidating the Jewish believers and evangelizing Jewish unbelievers. Certainly by the time of Paul's arrival in the early sixties the unbelieving Jews were perfectly well aware of Christianity, probably through Peter (Acts 28:22). Moreover, as we have noted there were numbers of believing Jews of the Judaizing kind in Rome by then (Philippians 1:15-17). The closing scene of the Acts of the Apostles, in which Paul declares that the "Gentiles ...will listen" to the Christian message, suggests that at the time, the number of Jewish believers in Rome was neither significant nor expected to increase to any extent.

Some aspects of Peter's ministry in Rome are found in his

first letter. The letter was sent from "She who is at Babylon" (5:13) which is usually taken to mean the church in Rome. ("She" could refer to the church as the bride of Christ while "Babylon" was the code word for Rome in the Book of Revelation — see 14:8; 18:2.) The references in First Peter to the sufferings of believers (e.g. 4:7,12; 5:6-11) may be to what had already occurred or what was about to occur in Rome rather than to Peter's readers in far away Asia Minor. It is tempting to see in his words, "do not be surprised at the fiery ordeal which comes upon you to prove you" (4:12) a reference either to the fire which destroyed ten of Rome's fourteen districts in AD 64 or to the fiery end with which many believers met their deaths on the order of the Emperor Nero. According to Tacitus, some Christians were covered with tar and set alight to illuminate the emperor's gardens and as a public spectacle.[8] The first letter of Peter gives evidence of being sent from Rome in the early to mid-sixties and many scholars take it to have been written then.

The first letter of Peter also indicates that Gentiles were included among its readers, as well as Jews.

Jewish Christians are addressed by the author's opening words, "Peter, an apostle of Jesus Christ to the exiles of the Dispersion [Greek: *diaspora*] in Pontus, Galatia, Cappadocia, Asia and Bithynia." (1:1 cf. 2:12)

There were Jews from Pontus, Cappadocia and Asia present on the day of Pentecost when Peter first gave witness to the risen Lord. It is possible that he had visited those regions at some point to provide pastoral care to Greek-speaking Jewish believers and to evangelize other Jews in the synagogues, in fulfilment of the missionary agreement that he should go to the circumcised (Galatians 2:7-9). As we have already suggested it is possible Peter visited the general area of Asia Minor in the period between his visit to Syria c. 48/49 and his visit to Corinth c. 52-55.

His first letter, however, also has Gentiles in mind when it refers, for example, to "Let the time that is past suffice for doing what the Gentiles like to do, living in licentious-ness, passions, drunkenness, revels, carousing and lawless idolatry." (4:3 cf. 1:14,18)

Since only Gentiles would engage in "lawless idolatry"

they must be among Peter's intended readership. It may be that, just as Paul when writing to the Romans addresses both Jews and Gentiles (e.g. 11:11-14), so Peter addresses both groups. If this is the case it would mean that the lines of demarcation set out in the missionary agreement had by then become somewhat blurred. Possibly, with the passage of time, the agreement had become somewhat irrelevant. Moreover, by then the Jews may have become fully aware of the threat to Judaism posed by this new movement and increasingly resistant to it, so that the number of Jews converting to Christianity had been drastically reduced.

Another detail in First Peter which bears on historical reconstruction are the two persons named as associates of the author — Silvanus and Mark. It is significant that both Silvanus or Silas, as he is called in Acts (18:5;2 Corinthians 1:19) and Mark (Acts 12:25; Colossians 4:10) had also worked as missionary associates of Paul in the apostolate to the Gentiles. That Silvanus and Mark worked alongside both the apostle to the Gentiles and the apostle to the circumcised is further evidence that spheres of ministry clearly separated at the missionary agreement had become far less important. Christ transcended nationality. It may also support the notion that Peter's ministry might to some degree have been redirected to Gentiles because so few Jews were responding to the Christian message.

The Petrine Circle
Peter is associated with the writing of three documents which in time became part of the New Testament — First and Second Peter and the gospel of Mark. But while the fisherman from far away Capernaum may have achieved some competence in Greek speech by the mid sixties it is very unlikely that he would have been capable of writing the fluent Greek of these books. There is good evidence, however, that he had colleagues who could have written this literature in association with him. We may characterize this group as the Petrine Circle.

We consider in turn the first and second letters of Peter and the gospel of Mark.

The first letter identifies Peter's scribe as Silvanus — "By (Greek: *dia*) Silvanus. . .I have written to you" (5:12). It is possible, but less than likely, that *dia* means Silvanus delivered the letter. Many scholars have taken *dia* to mean that Silvanus' role was rather more than a humble clerk who merely wrote at Peter's dictation. If Silvanus had a broader, more interpretative role it would explain, for example, the elegant Greek in a letter bearing the name of a Galilean fisherman! Moreover, since Silvanus' name was bracketed with Paul's in the writing of the first and second letters to the Thessalonians, it would help explain the Pauline format of First Peter. As a prophet and leader in the Jerusalem church (Acts 15:22,32), as trusted emissary of that church to the church of Antioch in troubled times (Acts 15:22), as the chosen companion of Paul into what would be the first major thrust into the Greek world (Acts 15:40) including at Corinth (2 Corinthians 1:19; 1 Thessalonians 1:1; 2 Thessalonians 1:1) and as Peter's "faithful brother" (1 Peter 5:12), Silvanus was by the time of the writing of First Peter, an exceptionally experienced missionary. The Jerusalem church's choice of him to deliver their letter to the Greek-speaking churches of Syria, Cilicia and Galatia probably indicates significant competence in Greek language, as does Paul's choice of him as a co-worker in the second missionary journey.

Light is perhaps thrown on the writing of Peter's first letter by Josephus' references to the means by which he wrote the *Jewish War*. In fact there are a number of interesting parallels between Peter and Josephus. Both were Palestinian Jews who settled in Rome, Peter in the mid fifties (?) Josephus in the early seventies. For both Aramaic was their "first" language but they also had some competence in Greek. Josephus explicitly states this to have been the case; [9] with Peter it is a reasonable inference given his extensive travels in Greek-speaking parts of the Empire.

Josephus originally wrote the *Jewish War* in Aramaic but then immediately translated it into Greek.[10] The Greek styles of the *Jewish War* and First Peter are, in different ways, quite sophisticated, and not at all what we might expect from writers for whom Aramaic was their mother tongue. Josephus claims to have made a study of "Greek prose and poetry"[11] on coming to Rome but this cannot account for the level of Greek used so soon afterwards in the *Jewish War*. The explanation of the puzzle is provided by Josephus himself in one of his last works when he explained how he wrote the *Jewish War*. ". . .in the leisure which Rome afforded me. . .and with the aid of some assistants (Greek: *synergoi*) for the sake of the Greek, at last I committed to writing my narrative of the events."[12]

Since the language of the *Jewish War* shows no sign of Aramaic grammatical style we may take it that Josephus' assistants or co-workers, rather than Josephus, were responsible for the high standard of Greek we find there.

I suggest this represents a method of operation which may well explain how Peter, an Aramaic-speaking fisherman from Galilee, could be identified as the author of so well-written a work as First Peter. Silvanus would then be no mere secretary such as Pliny the Elder had permanently at his side, mechanically copying down the thoughts of the great man.[13] Rather, as an experienced Christian leader in his own right and with skills in Greek, Silvanus would have enjoyed considerable freedom to express things in his own way. Something like this may have occurred, though with different associates, in the writing of Second Peter and Mark.

To return to Peter himself, we are unable to find any explicit data from the New Testament indicating what happened to him. The earliest documentation after the New Testament is found in a letter written by Clement from Rome to Christians in Corinth, about thirty years later than the event.

Through jealousy and envy [of the Jews?] the greatest and most righteous pillars of the church were persecuted and contended unto death. . .Peter, because of wicked jealousy, suffered not one or two but many trials, and having borne witness there went to the place of glory which was his due.[14]

Clement wrote in the nineties only about thirty years after these tragic events which occurred "among ourselves", that is, in Rome. The general context matches Tacitus' description of Nero's assault on the Christians in AD 64.

Clement's account of Peter's martyrdom finds support in the Lord's prophecies about Peter's end as set out in the gospel written by his friend, John, the Beloved Disciple (13:23; 20:2; 21:7). On the night before his crucifixion Jesus told Peter "Where I am going you cannot follow me; but you shall follow me afterwards" (13:36). On the third occasion the risen Jesus appeared to his disciples he told Peter,

Truly, truly, I say to you, when you were young, you girded yourself and walked where you would; but when you are old, you will stretch out your hands, and another will gird you and carry you where you do not wish to go. (This is said to show by what death he was to glorify God.) And after this he said to him, "follow me". (21:18-19,22; see also 2 Peter 1:14)

Jesus knew that Peter would not follow him to death at the time of his own crucifixion; rather Peter would deny him. Jesus foresaw, however, that Peter would do so at some future time. This was to occur not in Jerusalem but in far away Rome, thirty years later.

As we have commented earlier, Peter's is an astonishing story and one which by its very character bears witness to the resurrection of Jesus. How else can we account for the remarkable career change from fisherman to witness/ pastor which took him from Capernaum in Galilee to Jerusalem, to Antioch, to Corinth and ultimately to Rome, the world capital?

Peter's second letter is self-consciously aware of the first letter (3:1) and that it comes from the apostle Peter (1:1). Yet this second letter is so different in style from the first that it is necessary to suggest that it was the work of another hand.

Who that "other" person may be we can only guess. One inspired guess that fits well with certain strands of evidence is that the secretary-writer of 2 Peter is Jude, the brother of James.

We may note, first, that 2 Peter reproduces the greater part of the letter of Jude. On this theory Jude, as Peter's associate and assistant, has expanded and adapted an earlier letter to meet a new set of needs.

Second, in 1 Corinthians 9:5, Paul joins unnamed brothers

of the Lord "and Cephas". Was Jude, the brother of the Lord, a companion of Peter's in Corinth sometime in the early fifties? Had they together travelled through Asian regions like Colossae encountering the mystic and gnostic aberrations which both Second Peter and Jude appear to be addressing?

Third, Second Peter comes from *Simeon* Peter. It should be noted that Paul calls the apostle to the circumcised "Peter" only in the letter to the Galatians and that he never refers to him as Simon, or Simeon. Paul generally called him "Cephas". "Simon Peter", however, is Jesus' preferred mode of address (Mark 3:16; 14:37), and it is a variant of this "Simeon" we find at the beginning of 2 Peter. It is significant that James the brother of both Jesus and Jude refers only to "Simeon" (Acts 15:14). It may be that the name "Simon/ Simeon (Peter)" as preferred by Jesus came to be pre- ferred also by the Lord's brothers James and Jude. It is an interesting possibility, therefore, that this is reflected in 2 Peter which on this theory was the work of Jude, brother of both James and Jesus (cf. Mark 6:3).

What then of the third document often linked with Peter, the gospel of Mark?

In his second letter, Peter, discerning the evil signs of the times under Nero and mindful of the Lord's prophecy referred to above, wrote, "I know that the putting off of my body will be soon, as our Lord Jesus Christ showed me" (1:14). He continued immediately, "I will see to it that after my departure (Greek: *exodus*) you may be able at any time to recall these things." (1:15)

Since he is not referring to the contents of the letter, to what is he referring? Because it was universally agreed by second century Christian writers that the gospel of Mark arose out of Mark's association with Peter, it may well be that 2 Peter 1:15 had the gospel in mind.

Irenaeus who wrote barely a century after Peter's death stated that "after the death (Greek: *exodus*) of these [Peter and Paul] Mark, the disciple and interpreter of Peter, also transmitted to us in writing the things preached by Peter".[15]

Because the use of the Greek *exodus* for death is rare it is probable that, in using it, Irenaeus had 2 Peter 1:15 in mind.

If that were the case, Irenaeus could be explaining that Peter's puzzling words were in reference to a gospel soon to be written, that is, by Mark. Mark, whom Peter affectionately called "my son", was with Peter at the time of the writing of First Peter (5:13) and therefore had the opportunity to do it.

Another writer, Papias, writing only about six decades after Peter's death and quoting "the Elder", a man of apostolic times, stated that:

Mark, having become the interpreter of Peter, wrote down accurately whatever he remembered of the things said and done by the Lord. . .he [did not] hear the Lord, nor follow him. . .but afterward. . .Peter. . .

[Mark] took forethought for one thing, not to omit any of the things that he heard [from Peter], not to state any of them falsely.[16]

The account of the "Elder", as quoted by Papias, tells us that Mark was Peter's "interpreter" which probably means, as it were, Peter's (posthumous) *amanuensis*. Just as Silvanus and Jude (?) interpreted Peter's spoken words in writing First and Second Peter, so too Peter's other colleague, Mark, interpreted what Peter taught in Mark's own words in the written gospel that bears his name. Irenaeus, whom we referred to above, stated that: "Mark ...transmitted to us in writing the things preached by Peter".

Papias, quoted above, wrote something similar: "Mark ...the interpreter of. . .Peter who adapted his teachings to the needs of his hearers."

According to the second century writers the written gospel of Mark arose out of "the things preached by Peter", "Peter's own teachings". Certainly Mark was a wide'ly experienced Christian leader in his own right. The cousin of Barnabas (Colossians 4:10) Mark accompanied Paul and Barnabas on their missionary journeyings to Cyprus, acting as their "catechist" (Acts 13:5) — Greek: *hyperetes,* a word for the synagogue catechist (cf. Luke 4:20). Since he was from a financially secure Jerusalem family (Acts 12:12-13) it is reasonable to suppose that he was educated, as well as being well known to Peter, Barnabas and Paul. There is no good reason to doubt his capacity to write the gospel that bears his name.

During the 1930s a noted British scholar, C.H. Dodd, submitted the preaching of Peter recorded in the Acts of the Apostles to careful analysis. He showed that Peter's preaching about Jesus (e.g. in Acts 10:36-43) set the historic events about him in the same order as followed in the gospel of Mark. Dodd's conclusion, which has extensive acceptance, is that the written gospel of Mark arose out of the verbal gospel attributed by Acts to Peter. Dodd's findings, in effect, go close to confirming the opinion of Irenaeus and Papias that Mark was Peter's "interpreter"

To sum up, it seems that Peter met his death in Rome in the middle sixties, although nothing in the New Testament explicitly says so. A number of important books from the New Testament appear to have been associated with Peter in his last days, though it is unlikely that these were written directly by Peter himself, but by close colleagues who freely adapted his teachings. First Peter was written by Silvanus some time towards the end of Peter's life; Second Peter probably by an unknown amanuensis (Jude?) near the time of Peter's death. The gospel of Mark was written by Mark, a close friend and follower of Peter, soon after his death, and was probably completed in the middle sixties.

We have likened the New Testament story to a river which divided into two streams, one Hebraic, the other Hellenist, with the onslaught of Saul on the Jerusalem church c. AD 34. Saul became the most famous leader of the Hellenist tributary of Christianity, meeting his death in Rome in the mid-sixties. The Hebraic stream divided c. AD 47 at the time of the Jerusalem missionary agreement. One stream, the strictly Hebraic, continued in Jerusalem, being led by James the brother of the Lord. James was killed in AD 62. The other Jewish stream, led by Peter and John, concentrated on Hellenistic Jews outside Palestine. Peter was killed in Rome in the mid-sixties.

During the period AD 57–67 James, Peter and Paul, the greatest leaders of the movement, were removed by violent death. Moreover, events of apocalyptic magnitude had occurred. The city of Rome was virtually destroyed in AD 64 and the war in Judaea commenced in AD 66. Could Christianity survive these crises?

Further reading to Chapter Nine:

F.F. Bruce, *New Testament History*, Anchor, New York, 1972.
Paul, *Apostle of the Free Spirit*, Paternoster, Exeter, 1977.
A.N. Sherwin-White, *Roman Society and Roman Law in the New Testament*, Oxford University Press, Oxford, 1963.
J. Foster, *After the Apostles*, SCM, London, 1961.
O. Cullman, *Peter, Disciple, Apostle, Martyr*, Meridian, New York, 1958.
E.G. Selwyn, *The First Epistle of Peter*, Macmillan, London, 1961, 9-17.
J.A.T. Robinson, *Redating the New Testament*, SCM, London, 1976, 118-199.
R.L. Wilken, *The Christians as the Romans Saw Them*, Yale University Press, New Haven, 1984.

Notes

[1]*AJ*, xx, 179-81.

[2]*AJ*, xx, 197-200.

[3]*AJ*, xx, 201-203.

[4]Eusebius, *H.E.*, III. 5. 3.

[4a]Benediction 12 cf. C.K. Barrett, *Background: Selected Documents* S.P.C.K, London, 1961, 167.

[5]1 Clement 5:1-4, 5.

[6]1Clement 5:7.

[7]Tacitus, *Annals*, xv, 44.

[8]*Annals*, xv, 44.5.

[9]*AJ*, xx, 263.

[10]*BJ*, i, 3.

[11]*AJ*, xx, 263.

[12]*Apion* i, 50.

[13]Pliny, *Epistles* iii, 5.

[14]1 Clement 5:1-4, 5.

[15]Irenaeus, *Against Heresies* III.1.2.

[16]Papias, cited by Eusebius *H.E.* III xxxix.15.

10

The Gospels

Anyone who reads the gospels can see that they relate the story about Jesus, what he did and said, and the things that happened to him. They are the main sources of information about the chief figure of Christianity. When we add to the gospels the Acts of the Apostles we are also able to recapture the history of the early church over the next thirty years after Jesus and in continuation with him. The gospels and the Acts of the Apostles form the historical "core" of the New Testament and the New Testament story; without them it would not be possible.

The gospels and the Acts of the Apostles, however, were not written at the same time as the events they relate. They are not like newspaper reports, written and published within a short period. In fact, and this may come as a surprise, the gospels and the Acts were among the last parts of the New Testament to be written.

It was no small thing to write a gospel. Many months work was involved in gathering the source material, organising it and finally writing or dictating it. The author would need to be provided for financially while he wrote, so that benefaction or patronage may also have been involved. The writer of a gospel needed to have good reasons to go to the trouble to write. One reason, clearly, was to leave behind a secure record about the words and the works of Jesus of Nazareth. Less obviously, but no less true, the writer was probably also concerned about contemporary issues relating to the Christian faith. Thus the written gospel was both an historical record about Jesus and also the writer's attempt to address problems of the moment, which he did through the written page.

Thus the written gospels, composed as they were a generation after Jesus and for the people of that time, are themselves part of the New Testament story. They tell the story as it occurred a generation earlier while at the same time reflecting the circumstances of the church at the time they were written.

So how do we date the gospels and Acts?

Here we face the problem that books published at that time, the gospels/Acts included, often did not state the year of publication. However, we are able to set early and late limits. Since Jesus died c. AD 33, it is obvious the gospels could not have been written earlier than that. On the other hand, they must have been in circulation well before AD 100 because they begin to be quoted in books written late in the first and early in the second century. The gospels must have been written between AD 33 and 100.

By comparing their texts we can also establish that Mark was written prior to Matthew and Luke since these authors clearly incorporate Mark's gospel within their own. Comparison of texts also establishes, to the satisfaction of most scholars, that John did not use Matthew, Mark or Luke when he wrote his gospel. This means either that John wrote earlier than the others or, alternatively, that he wrote in physical isolation from them.

Moreover, we are assisted to some degree in the date of the gospels by examining the flow of the broader historical stream of the period. It is probable that the great crises which occurred in the first century have left their mark in the gospels and Acts, in particular the turbulent sixties.

The major source of instability within the empire in the sixties was the young and eccentric emperor, Nero Caesar. Due to his neglect of the affairs of state a major frontier problem existed along the eastern borders, which were very difficult to defend. The formidable Parthians had, a century earlier, invaded Palestine. Relationships with the large Jewish community within the empire had seriously deteriorated, especially in Palestine. James, brother of Jesus and leader of the Jerusalem church was killed during these troubles. There were major problems between Jews and Gentiles in Caesarea Maritima, capital of Judaea, and these would erupt in AD 66, spread to Jerusalem and lead to the outbreak of the devastating war between Romans and Jews. This would be followed by the Roman invasion of Palestine, the siege of Jerusalem and the destruction of the temple. The Jerusalem church fled from Judaea to the safety of the Decapolis for the duration of the war.

In Rome itself, a great fire wiped out three-quarters of the city in AD 64. Already unpopular in many quarters, Nero was actually blamed for the fire since it was known that he wished to rebuild the city. To deflect attention from himself he accused the Christians of responsibility for the fire. Large numbers were arrested and publicly executed, among them Peter and Paul. Soon afterwards Nero survived a conspiracy of senators against him. His suicide in AD 68 precipitated a series of civil wars within the empire, as four ambitious generals each attempted to gain the supremacy. In AD 69, Vespasian emerged triumphant and established a new dynasty of emperors, known as the Flavians. Titus, son of the new emperor, over-ran Jerusalem in AD 70 after a long siege. The great temple of Herod was devastated, never to be rebuilt.

Christians had been affected by the events of these turbulent years. Three of the greatest leaders were killed and the oldest church community was forced to leave its city, Jerusalem. It is probable that the gospels would bear the imprint of these events and in such a way as to bear on the question of their dating.

Matthew's gospel appears to have been written either during the sixties or very soon afterwards. It refers to certain false prophets (7:15; 24:11-12,26) who, as we know from Josephus, were active before, but not after, AD 70. Moreover, his numerous references to the Sadducees suggest a pre-70 dating since the sect of the Sadducees did not survive the Jewish war and references to them would soon be meaningless to the readers. Further, Jesus' words encouraging the payment of the temple tax (17:24-27) suggest the gospel was written before the temple was destroyed; thereafter the temple tax became unnecessary. For these reasons, and others, it appears that the gospel of Matthew was written before, or perhaps not much later than, AD 70.

But this means the gospel of Mark must have been written some time earlier because, as we have noted, Matthew used Mark as his major source. It is likely that the death of Peter, which occurred during Nero's bloody assault on Christians in Rome, motivated Mark to write his gospel. If Mark was written by the middle sixties it would allow time for Matthew to be written by the late sixties or, perhaps, at the latest, the early seventies.

When was Luke's gospel written? Here too the events of the sixties appear to be relevant. There seems little doubt that the siege of Jerusalem is in view within this gospel, implying a post 67 date. "Your enemies will set up siege works. . .will encircle you. . .will bring you to the ground . . .this people will be carried captive into all countries. . ." (19:41-43; 21:20,24)

It is noteworthy, however, that Luke says nothing about the destruction of the temple.This suggests that Luke, like Matthew, was written in the late sixties or perhaps in the early seventies. Consistent with this is Luke's silence about the deaths of Peter and Paul in the mid-sixties, which he would surely have mentioned if more than a few years had passed since the tragic loss of these famous leaders.

What of the gospel of John? The reference to the death of Peter (21:19) suggests that this gospel was written after AD 64. The absence of any reference to the Jewish War, the siege of Jerusalem or the destruction of the temple, however, probably points to a mid-sixties date. References to the temple and the Pool of Bethzatha/Bethesda (2:20; 5:1) are such as to imply that these buildings were still standing, which they would not have been after AD 70. Indeed the writer's extensive knowledge about the Pool of Siloam (9:7, 11); the Portico of Solomon (10:22); Bethany (11:18); the Kidron Valley (18:1); the house of Caiaphas and the praetorium (18:28); the pavement (19:13) and Golgotha (19:17) are all suggestive of a pre-70 description of the buildings and topography of Jerusalem. After AD 70 the city lay in ruins, never to be rebuilt along the lines of

Herod's Jerusalem. For this reason it became impossible to pinpoint the exact location, for example, of Golgotha. So violent was the Roman assault on the city that its physical appearance was permanently changed.

Other reasons for a pre-70 dating of John include a pre-war political milieu which is evident in the trial of Jesus and the use within the gospel of John of primitive-sounding Aramaic words like *messias* (1:14; 4:25) and *rabbi/rabboni.*

Why did the early Christians feel the need for written gospels?

After all they had managed to propagate their message for thirty years by means of the spoken word. Why did they need to write it down? The clue answering that question is to note when it was the gospels began to appear. So far as we can see no complete written gospel was in existence before the mid-sixties, though it is almost certain that at least one written account of Jesus' final week and several written collections of Jesus' teachings were in circulation before that time. The great catalyst which stimulated the comprehensive writing of gospels as from the mid-sixties was the removal of the great mission leaders James, Peter and Paul. Their deaths made it painfully clear that the Lord was not about to return, that the Christian movement was destined to be around for some time and that the events and teachings associated with Jesus had better be committed to writing in the near future while people able to vouch for what would be written were still alive. The appearance of the gospels within a relatively short space of one another is itself a commentary on that painful realization.

John and Mark, the first gospels to appear, were written for evangelistic purposes.

John explicitly states that he wrote about the signs Jesus performed so that his readers would believe that Jesus was the Christ, the Son of God (20:30-31).

This gospel looks beyond Jerusalem, where much of the story is located, further afield even than Judaea and Galilee. It refers to "the [Jewish] dispersion among the Greeks" (7:35), to "Greeks" who seek Jesus (12:20), to the "world" having gone after Jesus (12:19), to "other sheep" (10:16) and to those not belonging to the original disciples who nonetheless believe their word and who, it is prayed, will be "one" with them (17:18-23).

These also are Jews, but *Greek* Jews, Jews of the dispersion scattered far and wide in racially segregated communities in the great Gentile cities like Alexandria, Antioch, Smyrna, Corinth and Rome. There were as many as seven million Jews within the Roman Empire but perhaps fewer than a million living inside Palestine. John's "book" was written, in all probability, to evangelize and teach the Greek-speaking Jews of the dispersion.

The gospel of Mark does not declare its aim explicitly, in the way John does. Nonetheless it may be inferred that Mark's primary aim is evangelistic. The opening words "The beginning of the gospel of Jesus Christ the Son of God", form the title and set the direction for what will follow. The format of Mark closely follows the outline of the evangelistic preaching of Peter as recorded in the Acts of the Apostles (e.g. 10:34-43). In the dozens of short cameos that compose the gospel the author rivets our attention on Jesus, challenging us repeatedly to ask ourselves "Who is this man?". The climax of the gospel occurs at the crucifixion when the centurion declares "Surely this man was the Son of God" (15:39).

That it was a Roman centurion who answers the question about Jesus' identity is good reason to believe that Mark is addressing a Greek-speaking Roman audience. Jewish practices are explained for Gentile readers (e.g. 7:3 "...the Jews do not eat unless they wash their hands") and a number of Latin words are used within this gospel (e.g. 5:9 "Legion"; 15:39 "centurion"). Since the Roman emperor was regularly referred to as "son of a deified person" and the word "gospel" was used in connection with the blessings brought to mankind by the Emperor Augustus, Mark's opening words about a "gospel" about "Jesus Christ the Son of God" and a climax in which a Roman centurion recognised him as such, especially in the context of crucifixion which Romans regarded as unmentionable in polite company, are evidences of a book pointedly directed to Roman readers.

Matthew's concerns are also discernible within his pages. He saw a need for a more complete statement than Mark's. He supplies a genealogy of Jesus, gives details about the birth of Jesus in Bethlehem and, in particular, provides long passages of Jesus' teachings (e.g. chapters 5-7 — the Sermon on the Mount). Matthew's gospel presents Jesus as a royal person ("the Christ", "the son of David", "the king"), a divine figure ("Emmanuel", "the Son"), an object of worship ("they worshipped him") and a saviour ("he will save his people"), whose teachings, given at such length, form the basis of a life of discipleship for his people.

The centre of Matthew's world is Galilee of the Gentiles. Particular point is made of Jesus' family settling in Galilee (2:22) from which Jesus went to the Jordan for baptism by John (3:13) and to which he returned to commence his ministry (4:12), being specifically located in Capernaum (4:13). It was in Galilee of the Gentiles, in the ministry of Jesus, that God's light has shone (4:13). Galilee, to which Jesus came after his resurrection (26:32; 28:7,10) was to be the launching pad for the spread of discipleship to the Gentile world (28:19).

Since Christians were in Galilee from the mid-thirties (Acts 9:31), if not earlier, there is good reason to believe that the movement continued in that region after the time of Jesus and that the gospel of Matthew was written from Galilee some time in the late sixties. If the readers' region was Galilee of the Gentiles, in which God's great light had shone and from which Jesus had commissioned the preaching of the gospel to all the Gentiles (=nations), perhaps one of the purposes of Matthew's gospel is to promote the preaching of the gospel by Galilean Jews to the nations surrounding them.

Luke's concerns are evident in the opening sentences of his great two-volume work. He saw the need to consolidate various incomplete written accounts which he had received into one comprehensive and chronological narrative beginning with the birth of John the Baptist in Judaea c. AD 7 and concluding with the arrival of Paul in Rome c. AD 62. Theophilus, to whom this work in both its parts is dedicated, was probably a "godfearer", that is, a Gentile who showed interest in converting to Judaism.

One of Luke's concerns was to explain to "godfearers" how it was that God's historic people the Jews rejected the salvation of God which came to them in Jesus and how this salvation was received, instead, by the Gentiles. It is on this tragic note that Luke-Acts concludes. Clearly Luke sets out to demonstrate that the controversial figure Paul was a true apostle. Godfearers, set between Jews and Gentiles as they were, were subject to the strong anti-Paul sentiments expressed by Jews, including Christian Jews. There was particular need to defend Paul to this group, and this Luke does.

From what has been written about the gospels and the Acts of the Apostles, composed as they were three or four decades after Jesus, it must now be clear that they are not "straight" histories of Jesus. Not that there is such a thing as a "straight" history — either then or now. Each evangelist wrote out of the concern he had for ministry to a particular group at a particular time. John and Mark wrote evangelistic works for non-Palestinians, Jews and Gentiles respectively, while Matthew wrote for Galilean Jews and Luke for non-Palestinian "godfearers". These authors each sought to meet unmet needs which confronted them.

Moreover, each writer could not have escaped the impact on him of the events of the wider world, tumultuous as they were during the sixties when one crisis followed another. Traces of these crises within the gospels suggest they were not written prior to the sixties while the absence of reference to the destruction of the temple suggests that we should not locate the gospels after AD 70. We have suggested that the death of the great mission leaders James, Peter and Paul was the particular catalyst which stimulated the production of all four gospels within a brief space of time.

The gospels themselves, by what they betray about the circumstances under which they were written and the ministry concerns their authors reveal, were themselves part of the on-going development of the New Testament story, while at the same time being the chief quarry for information about Jesus and the earliest community of believers who came after him.

Further reading to Chapter Ten:

E.E. Ellis, "Dating the New Testament", *NTS,* 26,1980, 487-502.

J.A.T. Robinson, *Redating the New Testament*, SCM, London, 1975; *The Priority of John*, SCM, London, 1985.

C.F.D. Moule, *The Birth of the New Testament*, A. & C. Black, London, 1966.

11

Patmos

The New Testament story ends at Patmos, a small island in the Aegean Sea, about sixty miles west of Miletus. It was from this lonely, desolate place that a man named "John" wrote the remarkable Book of the Revelation in the last decade of the first century.

John wrote his book to the churches of seven cities scattered through the Roman province of Asia. This area, located as it is at the western side of Asia Minor facing the Aegean, had been subject to Greek influence and culture for hundreds of years before Christian times. In the century and a half prior to Jesus this region had fallen to the Romans as their empire expanded eastwards. Ultimately it was annexed as the Province of Asia. By New Testament times, therefore, these cities had become Graeco-Roman in town planning, architecture, religion and culture. Ephesus, for example, was a city of a quarter of a million inhabitants, with wide streets, reticulated water, underground sewerage services and a Roman-style amphitheatre.

In writing to the churches in these seven widely distributed cities John was, in effect, writing to Christians in the whole province. John's book, then, unusual as it is, should by no means be thought of as of marginal importance. On the contrary, it was a significant statement about Christianity to numerous widely dispersed Christians in one of the major provinces of the Roman empire. It is the only part of the New Testament to be addressed to people in such a large area.

One of the problems facing readers outside the original

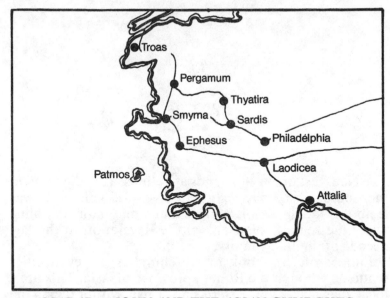

MAP 17 — JOHN AND THE ASIAN CHURCHES

circle to whom John wrote is that the Book of Revelation
uses a secret code. The writer and presumably also his
readers knew what he meant but most others down through
history have found much of it quite baffling. Doubtless
the Roman authorities would have regarded the book as
treasonable, had they understood what the writer meant.

However, not everything is obscure. The "synagogue
of Satan" at Smyrna and Philadelphia (2:9; 3:9) almost
certainly refers to the grave problems now created for
Christians in these cities by the Jewish synagogues.
Although Jews were disliked within the Graeco-Roman
cities of the empire, their communities were, in comparison with the churches, both well established and well
connected. This was particularly the case in proconsular
Asia. Jewish leaders had a good network of communication
within the empire and they had long since come to regard
the rapidly growing Christian movement as a schismatic
and heretical cult. Their opposition could only have been
intensified by the reversals they had suffered at the hands of
the new régime of emperors, Vespasian and his sons Titus

and Domitian. Under these emperors, in contrast with the more sympathetic Julio-Claudians who preceded them, the Jews had suffered to an extreme degree. Jerusalem had been sacked, the temple desecrated and destroyed and now, in a highly symbolic and oppressive gesture, the international Jewish community were compelled to pay a tax formerly given for the upkeep of their temple to the temple of Jupiter in Rome. Their animosity towards Christians in the area, whose sufferings in recent times may have been less than theirs, should not surprise us. Nonetheless the payment of the tax (known as the *fiscus Judaicus*) did secure them immunity from participating in the rituals of the emperor cult, an immunity which the Christians did not enjoy.

While we may with some confidence identify the "synagogue of Satan" we are driven to guesswork and speculation regarding other groups who were a source of difficulty to the Christians. The "Nicolaitans" (2:6,15) do not appear elsewhere in the New Testament; there is no way to identify them with any certainty. The word may be derived from the Greek *nikan* (=to conquer) and *laos* (=the people), perhaps suggestive of some form of religious triumphalism now active in these cities. This, however, is only a guess, illustrating how much in the dark we are in these matters.

John also wrote of the "teachings of Balaam" held by some members of the church in Pergamum (2:14) and also of a self-styled "prophetess" in Thyatira whom he calls "Jezebel" (2:20). The "teachings of Balaam" which "Jezebel" promoted, apparently encouraged the public "eating of food sacrificed to idols" and also (sexual) "immorality" (2:14,20). It is clear that idol-worship and sexual laxity were part of daily life in these elegant Graeco-Roman cities. The "teachings of Balaam" as advocated by "Jezebel" sought to discourage Christians from distancing themselves from these pagan practices.

The major difficulty, however, faced by John's readers in the Asian cities lay neither with Jewish harassment nor with advocates of syncretism within the churches but with Roman civic authorities integrally involved as they were with local religious worship. So pervasive was pagan government/religion in the cities of the Roman Empire, so integrated was it with the whole fabric of domestic, economic and municipal life, that Gentile converts faced grave difficulties from the beginning. The worship of a multitude of gods, the resort to astrology, the practice of magic, impinged on everybody in all aspects of life from the cradle to the grave. Religion played an extraordinary part in Graeco-Roman society at that time.

The emperor Domitian had, by deliberate policy, joined Roman religious practices even more closely to indigenous Asian cultic activities. The local gods of these cities (e.g. Artemis in Ephesus) had for some time been linked in a general way with the Roman gods. Recent archaeological evidence from these cities, however, suggests that under Domitian there had been an even more intensive "marrying" of the Roman and the Graeco-Oriental cults.[1] Certainly, the worship of the emperor as a god first arose in this province and spread from it to other parts of the empire. The Emperor Domitian, in whose principate (AD 81–96) John wrote his book, required that people address him as "Lord and God". It is probable that an escalation of Rome/emperor worship occurred in the 80s and 90s and that Christians were very apprehensive about where it would lead. There were particular problems in Pergamum the provincial capital where a Christian named Antipas had recently been killed and also in Ephesus the largest city, where an eight-metre-high statue of Domitian had been placed in a temple specially constructed for that purpose.

The Roman proconsul had customarily participated in the venerable Asian ceremonies and, naturally enough, in the more recently introduced Roman rites. In the course of a year there were many occasions when the local citizens would have been expected to attend such functions, for example, to celebrate the emperor's birthday or to mark the opening of local athletic competitions.

It is true that evidence is lacking of significant persecution of Christians in Asia under Domitian. Nonetheless it is clear that developments outlined above would have caused considerable anxiety to the churches of Asia, especially in view of the well remembered, bloody assault on believers in Rome under Nero in the mid-sixties.

Domitian is viewed as a kind of second Nero. There is a mood of impending crisis running through John's book.

The time is close. . .(1:3)

. . .the devil is about to throw some of you into prison, that you may be tested (2:10)

. . .the hour of trial is coming on the whole world. (3:10)

. . .woe to you, O earth and sea, for the devil has come down to you in great wrath, because he knows his time is short. . .(12:12)

Using coded language John writes of the menace of Rome to Christians. Rome is portrayed as the instrument of "a great red dragon . . .that ancient serpent who is called the Devil and Satan, the deceiver of the whole world. . .who accuses our brothers. . .day and night". (12:9)

This dragon gave its authority to two beasts, a sea beast and an earth beast, to "make war on the saints and to conquer them" (13:17). The "sea beast" is John's code for the Roman emperor whereas the "earth beast" represents the high priest of Asia, who officiates at the major cultic activities within the province. The "earth beast" engages in magical arts to hoodwink the populace into worshipping the image of the "sea beast" (13:13-15).

Every indication was that the situation was precarious and that circumstances would deteriorate. Already Christians were "marked" men and women, limited in their freedom to "buy or sell", that is, engage in basic trading activities within their communities (13:16-17).

In those grim times John taught these churches the paradoxical truth that Christ, their Lord, was both slain and victorious. Christ is both the "faithful witness" and "ruler of the kings of the earth" (1:5); both the "lion of the tribe of Judah" and the "lamb. . .slain". He is the true ruler who unseals and unrolls the scroll of history (5:9) calling forth from it those who appear to rule on earth (6:1,3,5,7). Despite the awesome menace of evil rulers depicted as fierce beasts, John declares, ". . .the kingdom of the world has become the kingdom of our Lord and of his Christ, and he shall rule forever and ever". (11:15)

Although the dragon appears to be rampant on earth he is, in fact, bound, limited, circumscribed throughout the period between Christ's resurrection and his return — symbolically a thousand years (20:1-3). Those who have lost their lives for Jesus' sake, who have not worshipped the gods of Rome and Asia, reign with him throughout the millennium, sharing his victory over the dragon (20:4).

Finally, Christ, portrayed as "faithful and true", "the Word of God" and "King of Kings and Lord of Lords", wearing a robe dipped in blood and astride the white horse will appear to judge the rulers of the earth and to destroy the sea beast, the false prophet (=the earth beast — 19:19-21) and, last of all, the great red dragon (20:10).

On the farther side of these dramatic acts of God's final judgement John describes a "new heaven and a new earth", that is the New Jerusalem, the bride adorned for her marriage with the Lamb (21:1-2). God and his people will be physically united and tears, mourning and death will be no more (21:3-4). In place of their aweful experience of the dragon, the harlot city (Rome), believers look forward to another city, the City of God, and to another woman, the bride of Christ.

In the face of these present hardships, but in view of what lies in the ultimate future, John powerfully exhorts and encourages his readers. He calls the Christians in these Asian cities to "endurance" (2:2,3,19; 3:10) and to faithful acknowledgement of Jesus in spite of strong pressure to deny him (2:13; 3:8), for the "cowardly and the faithless" will be thrown into the "lake of fire" (21:18). Repeatedly John exhorts them "to conquer", that is, to remain true to Jesus even though they suffer and die (2:7,11,17,26; 3:5,12, 21; 12:11; 13:17). To be slain, as Jesus was slain, as a "true witness" is not to be defeated but "to conquer". John concludes, "He who conquers shall have this heritage [i.e. the new Jerusalem] and I will be his God and he shall be my son." (21:7)

John's book, therefore, was written above all to strengthen and encourage Christians facing harassment and persecution from Roman officials in the cities of the Province of Asia.

John was deeply conscious of the political events in the wider world. He made many references, in particular, to the critical events of the sixties, but in tantalising and elusive ways.

The massing of the dreaded Parthian cavalry near the Euphrates in AD 62 and the barely averted conflict with Rome's eastern legions[2] appears to be in mind on a number of occasions (6:1-8; 9:7-10,14,16-17). John develops horrific images of fiendish galloping cavalry based, apparently, on his knowledge of the Parthians and Euphrates region.

The great fire which devastated the world capital in AD 64 seems to have supplied John with imagery for the coming judgement of the "harlot city". Despite her gaudy opulence and immorality and her immense wealth and power (inspired by memories of Claudius' wife, the notorious Messalina?), God will bring upon her overwhelming destruction in a single day. "She shall be burned with fire" (18:8); and "Shipmasters, seafaring men, sailors and all who trade on the sea stood afar off and cried when they saw the smoke of her burning." (18:18)

Once again John has apparently taken an event in recent history and converted it into powerfully vivid apocalyptic language.

Nero's bloody onslaught on Christians which followed and was a direct result of the fire of Rome also provided much of John's descriptive language. He wrote about "The woman [i.e. the harlot, Rome] drunk with the blood of the saints and the blood of the martyrs of Jesus" (17:6 cf. 6:9-11; 13:7)

Tacitus' account of the fire of Rome and Nero's attack on Christians in Rome vividly corroborates John's lurid picture.[3]

The writer's enigmatic description of the two witnesses/ two prophets who were killed and whose bodies lay in the streets of the "great city" (11:3,7-8) is probably (but not certainly) a reference to the martyr-deaths of the apostles Peter and Paul which occurred in Rome during Nero's persecutions. "When they have finished their testimony the beast...will make war on them and kill them". (11:7)

Nero's own career ended in disaster. He was condemned by the Roman senate in AD 68 whereupon, aged thirty-two, he took his own life.[4] But it was widely believed that this larger-than-life person was not really dead and would return to Rome in triumph. Nero had been specially popular in the east, including the Province of Asia. Several pseudo -Neros arose in the east, one in AD 69, the other in AD 88. Perhaps this widespread belief in *Nero redivivus* lay behind John's description of one of the heads of the sea beast which "...seemed to have a mortal wound...but which was healed". (13:3)

Nero dominated the sixties. To that point in history he had been the greatest enemy of the Christians, satanic in his dimensions of evil. The widely held belief that 666 (13:18) = Neron Caesar, appears to be well founded.

John's reference to five kings (=emperors) who had fallen probably refers to Augustus, Tiberius, Gaius, Claudius and Nero. The one who "is" may be Vespasian (69–79) followed by Titus (79–81) who will "remain only a little time". The eighth king is, in all probability, Domitian (81–96), within whose reign the book was written. Again, it seems likely that John was using the events of the recent past to depict the future as he saw it unfolding.

His description of the nations trampling the "holy city" (11:2) is, almost certainly, in reference to the sacking of Jerusalem in AD 70. This momentous event, prophesied by Jesus and described by Josephus and Tacitus[5], was the climax of that eventful decade. This too, John incorporated within his book to the churches in the cities of Roman Asia.

It is, in my opinion, of great significance that John used these dramatic historical events within his book. In earlier decades Christians had expected Jesus to return at any moment (e.g. 2 Thessalonians 2:1-3; 3:11-12). If one had experienced the fiery destruction of the eternal city in AD 64 and the bloodbath that followed, removing as it did the great apostles Peter and Paul, or the sacking of Mount Zion and desecration of the Holy Place in AD 70 it would easily have seemed that the end would come at any moment. Although John quotes Jesus saying "I am coming soon" (22:7), it is quite evident that the author, by his inclusion of so many things which were yet to take place, in fact saw the return of Jesus as not occurring for some considerable period. John's very incorporation of great historical events within his book, which did not prove to be the occasion of Christ's return, is probably his way of telling the readers not to look for the return of the Lord in the context of unpleasant circumstances such as they were experiencing at that very time.

John is deeply aware of the powerful impact on Christians of the massive strength of the Roman Empire and the loyalty-demands it made on everyone, believers included. He further reveals his knowledge of the empire and its history by the sustained comparison he makes of it with the kingdom of God. There is running through the Revelation what Adolph Deissmann called a "polemical parallelism" by which John mocks and parodies the pretentiousness of Roman imperialism. Against the secular gospel of the new age of Rome and of its emperors, John declares the "eternal gospel" that the kingdoms of the world have become the kingdoms of our Lord and of his Christ. The sovereign Lion who is the Lamb with a death wound is aped by the beast-emperor with an unhealed wound. How pathetic that the Lord God Almighty, whose deeds are just and true, should be imitated by the mere man Domitian who demanded that subjects call him *Dominus* and *Deus*, "Lord and God". Thus the bride of Christ, the "woman" against whom the dragon makes war, will conquer and will remain faithful for her marriage with the Lamb, whereas Rome, the great harlot who is drunk with the blood of the saints will be cast down and destroyed. Babylon (=Rome) the persecutor will fall but the New Jerusalem, immense in its dimensions, will come down from God as the new heavens and the new earth. John is true prophet of the kingdom of God testifying against the false prophet of secular materialism embodied in all-powerful Roman civilization. The secular gospel is: "worship the emperor" but the eternal gospel is: "worship God". It is only in this century that scholars have begun to have an appreciation of John's profound awareness of and audacious attack upon the theological pretentiousness of Roman civilization.

John made extensive use of the Old Testament as a quarry for the ideas which appear in this book. The creation story of Genesis 1 (8:6-13), the picture of paradise in Genesis 2 (22:1-2), the plagues of Egypt in Exodus 7-11 (16:1-21), the destruction of the pursuers in the sea in Exodus 14 (15:2; 19:20; 20:14-15), the song of Moses in Exodus 15 (15:1-2), the fall of proud Babylon in Isaiah 47 (18:1-7), the vision of the New Age in Isaiah 25 and 65 (21:1-4) are only some of the many Old Testament passages on which this writer draws. Clearly he was so steeped in the Old Testament that it is difficult to escape the conclusion he was a Jew. He reflected deeply on these scriptures in light of Jesus' present and future fulfilment of them. Nonetheless it is a curious feature of his book that, although it is filled with Old Testament allusions, he seldom if ever quotes directly from the text of the Old Testament.

John appears to be familiar with a number of New Testament writings, in particular those of Paul, Matthew and the fourth evangelist. The "work. . .and labour" and "the thief" of 1 Thessalonians 1:3 and 5:2, for example, appear to be echoed in Revelation 2:2 and 16:15 respectively. Matthew's "marriage for his son" (22:2) appears to lie behind Revelation's "marriage of the Lamb" (19:7). Most of John's echoing of Paul and Matthew appear to be in eschatological passages which may mean he was using sources which they also used rather than their finished texts. As with the Old Testament, at no point does John quote directly or exactly from a New Testament writing.

There are many points of contact between the book of Revelation and the gospel and letters of John.[6] One is struck by terms like "life", "death", "thirst", "victory" which occur in both sets of writing. Similarly, we find in both references to the "Word", "the Lamb", the "I am" sayings and the single word in the perfect tense declaring "it is finished"/"it is done" (John 19:30/Revelation 21:16). The fact that different Greek words may be used does not detract from the tantalising sense that these two sets of documents are deeply related to each other. The number seven, for example, appears to be structurally important to both the gospel of John and to this book, but to no other part of the

New Testament. Only the gospel of John and Revelation refer to their document as a "book" (biblion). Within the New Testament only these "books" use the rare word "pierced". Of the parts of the New Testament to which he alludes there can be no doubt that the author to whom John is most closely related is the fourth evangelist.

Who is John?

Although this author identifies himself only as "John" (1:1,4 9; 22:8) he does leave behind a number of clues which help us build up a profile of him. Although he uses the word "apostle" he does not indicate whether or not he is one. John writes "prophecy" (1:3; 22:19), presumably indicating he regarded himself as a prophet. Who was this man?

Christian writers of the second century were in no doubt that the "John" who wrote the Revelation was in fact John Zebedee who wrote the fourth gospel. Justin Martyr who wrote barely half a century later and Irenaeus who wrote less than a century later both affirmed this book to be the work of John the Apostle.[7]

This view, however, was challenged as early as the third century by Dionysius the scholarly Bishop of Alexandria who made a close analysis of the vocabulary, style and ideas of the book and pronounced that it was not written by the author of the fourth gospel. A majority of modern scholars endorse Dionysius' weighty verdict.

Nonetheless, while there are good reasons to doubt the common authorship of the gospel/letters of John and the Revelation there are a number of factors which support the more ancient statements of Justin and Irenaeus.

First, the author had extensive knowledge of the cities of Asia to whose churches he wrote. His "salve to anoint your eyes" (3:8), for example, suggests he knew that the Laodiceans produced eye salve. Moreover, these seven widely separated cities were able to be visited by the existing network of roads ·in exactly the order in which John addressed them, presumably by the one courier. This "John" knew his geography of Asia. But so too did John

Zebedee who, according to Irenaeus, lived for many years in Ephesus, the greatest of the Asian cities.

Second, the "John" who wrote Revelation had detailed information about the circumstances of the churches in these seven widely scattered cities. He knew of the "Nicolaitans" at Ephesus and Pergamum, of the "teachings of Balaam" in Pergamum and Thyatira, of the "synagogue of Satan" at Smyrna and Philadelphia and of the lukewarmness of the church at Laodicea. Further, it is apparent that he writes to these churches with immense authority, expecting his words to be heeded and needing no introduction beyond the name "John". All this, however, is exactly what we would expect of an apostolic author, especially one who had lived for many years in that province, as John Zebedee had done.

Third, this writer appears to have been a Jew. His name, his deep grasp of the Old Testament, his abhorrence of idolatry and immorality, his references to the "teaching of Balaam" and the false prophetess "Jezebel" all suggest that John was a Jew. This would be consistent with what we know of John Zebedee as an apostle to Greek-speaking Jews of the dispersion.

Fourth, there are numerous echoes and allusions in this book to the gospel/letters of John, as we have already noted.

For these reasons a good case can be made that some kind of literary relationship exists between this book and the Johannine literature, though it remains a matter of speculation exactly what that relationship may have been.

Several suggestions may be made, both of which depend on the assumption that just as there was a Pauline and a Petrine circle there was also a Johannine circle. Certainly his "I"/"we" references support such a notion (John 21:24-25; 1 John 1:4; 2:1). One possibility is that the apostle John "dictated" his various works in his first language Aramaic to two different amanuenses, one reproducing what had been "dictated" as the gospel/letters of John, the other as the Revelation. Another possibility is that the Revelation was written directly by John Zebedee while the gospel/letters were "dictated" by him and written up by a close colleague. Suggestions like these may explain common authorship while accounting for stylistic differences; however they can only ever be suggestions.

Whatever the explanation is, we may conclude that the author John was indeed a prophet whose grasp of Old Testament text and New Testament thought was matched by his insight into the gaudy pretentiousness of imperial Rome.

This book is frankly realistic about the evil and suffering which continue into history and from which Christians sustain great pain and discouragement. Nonetheless, the evil and suffering, including that which falls to his people, remains within the Lamb's messianic rule. The day will come, however, when not just to the eye of faith but to the naked eye, in fact to every eye, the One whom men "pierced" will return in judgement and salvation. Then the kingdom of the world will become, in human experience, the kingdom of our Lord and of his Messiah. Evil and repressive regimes, which are the visible outcroppings of the invisible and malevolent serpent, will be no more. God and his people will be together and the Lion of Judah, the Lamb slain for their salvation, will be in the midst of them and they will praise his name for evermore.

The New Testament story ends with the exiled prophet John writing to the churches of Roman Asia from lonely Patmos Island. At first sight this appears to be a dis-appointing ending to the New Testament, a sad anti-climax. John's book, written on Patmos, marks the end-point of the apostolic age, the outer historical limit on that body of literature which arose in relationship to Jesus and which the churches came to regard as canonical, as "scripture".

The story of the Christian church, however, continued and indeed is still in progress nineteen centuries later. According to Eusebius, a historian writing in the early fourth century, John was released from exile and returned to Ephesus where he died as a very old man. As it happens, the province of Asia in which John lived and ministered was destined to become a strong centre of Christianity in the next two centuries. It was also destined to become a battleground of bloody confrontation between the Roman state and the church. In what can only be called prophetic, John anticipated what would happen in Roman Asia as he wrote to the mainland churches from Patmos.

Considered in the light of the great struggle between the church and the persecuting state which would follow in the succeeding two centuries, notably in that very region, the Apocalypse of John should not be regarded as an anticlimax to the New Testament, but rather as an inspired scripture, prophetic of the events which would soon take place and which would culminate in the fifth century in the fall of that evil civilization which had assaulted and assailed the bride of the Lamb. From a broader perspective, however, John's Apocalypse speaks to every age where political rulers portray themselves as "messianic", as substitutes for the "King of kings and Lord of lords". The message of John was and remains still: "Worship God ...follow the Lamb wherever he goes".

John's book is a fitting conclusion to the New Testament story. Written to suffering and anxious Christians in Roman Asia at the time of threatened persecution, it holds before readers a majestic picture of Christ. The male child, born of the persecuted woman, was crucified, but has been caught up to God and is alive for evermore. He is the Lion of the tribe of Judah who has conquered, but as the Lamb with the death wound. The kingdom of the world *has* become his kingdom and he will reign forever.

Further reading to Chapter Eleven:
D.E. Aune, "The Influence of Roman Imperial Court Ceremonial on the Apocalypse of John", *Biblical Research* XXVIII, 1983, 5-26.
A.A. Bell, Jr, "The Date of John's Apocalypse, the Evidence of some Roman Historians Reconsidered", *NTS*, 25(19) 93-102.
E.S. Fiorenza, "The Quest for the Johannine School: The Apocalypse and the Fourth Gospel", *NTS*, 23(19) 401-427.

D. Georgi, "Who is the True Prophet?", *HTR* 79, 1986, 100-126.
B.F. Harris, "Domitian, the Emperor Cult and *Revelation*",
Prudentia, xi, 1, 1979, 15-25.
C.J. Hemer, *The Letters to the Seven Churches of Asia in their
Local Setting*, The University of Sheffield, Sheffield, 1986.

Notes
[1]B.F. Harris, op.cit.

[2]Tacitus, *Annals*, xv, 1-15.

[3]Tacitus, *Annals*, xv, 37-44.

[4]Suetonius, *Nero, 49*.

[5]Josephus, *BJ*, vi passim; Tacitus, *Histories*, v, 13.

[6]R.H. Charles, *A Critical and Exegetical Commentary on the Revelation of St
John*, T. & T. Clark, Edinburgh, 1920, The Introduction.

[7]Justin, *Trypho*, 81, 4; Irenaeus, *Against Heresies*, iv, 30, 4, v, 26, 1.